Integrating the Gridiron

Integrating the Gridiron

Black Civil Rights and American College Football

LANE DEMAS

RUTGERS UNIVERSITY PRESS

NEW BRUNSWICK, NEW JERSEY, AND LONDON

First paperback printing, 2011

LIBRARY OF CONGRESS CATALOGING-IN-PUBLICATION DATA

Demas, Lane.

Integrating the gridiron : Black Civil Rights and American college football /
Lane Demas.
   p. cm.
Includes bibliographical references and index.
ISBN 978–0–8135–4741–1 (hardcover : alk. paper)
ISBN 978–0–8135–4997–2 (pbk. : alk. paper)
   1. Football—United States—History.   2. College sports—United States—History.
3. Discrimination in sports—United States.   4. Racism in sports—United States.
5. African American athletes—Social conditions.   6. Civil rights movements—
History.   I. Title.
   GV959.5.U6D46 2010
   796.332′630973—dc22   2009025372

A British Cataloging-in-Publication record for this book is
available from the British Library.

Visit our Web site: http://rutgerspress.rutgers.edu

Manufactured in the United States of America

For Jennifer

CONTENTS

Acknowledgments   ix

Prologue   1

1   Beyond Jackie Robinson: Racial Integration in American
    College Football and New Directions in Sport History   5

2   "On the Threshold of Broad and Rich Football Pastures":
    Integrated College Football at UCLA, 1938–1941   28

3   "A Fist That Was Very Much Intentional": Postwar Football
    in the Midwest and the 1951 Johnny Bright Scandal   49

4   "We Play Anyone": Deciphering the Racial Politics of
    Georgia Football and the 1956 Sugar Bowl Controversy   72

5   "Beat the Devil Out of BYU": Football and Black Power
    in the Mountain West, 1968–1970   102

    Epilogue   134

    Notes   143
    Selected Bibliography   169
    Index   175

ACKNOWLEDGMENTS

Several people have commented on this work and offered valuable input—including Merry Ovnick at California State University, Northridge; Albert Broussard at Texas A&M University; James Vlasich at Southern Utah University; and Mark Dyreson at Pennsylvania State University. I also want to thank the American Heritage Center at the University of Wyoming and the L. Tom Perry Special Collections at Brigham Young University, both of which provided generous financial support, as did the UC-Irvine Humanities Center. Thanks as well to Blackwell Publishing, McFarland Publishing, and the Historical Society of Southern California for permission to reprint previously published material. Finally, my deepest gratitude goes to Dickson Bruce, Jon Wiener, and Mike Davis for their committed guidance and encouragement.

Integrating the Gridiron

Prologue

Floyd Keith, head of an organization called Black Coaches and Administrators (BCA), considers the lack of African American coaches in college football "an outright disgrace." For twenty years, the BCA has advocated for minorities within the NCAA coaching ranks, reminding fans of some startling figures. As of 2009, only 3.4 percent (that is, 4 of 119) of the Football Bowl Subdivision (formerly Division I) schools employ black coaches. BCA has even called on minority candidates to consider pursuing litigation under federal civil rights legislation should the number of black coaches remain so low.[1]

Led by the BCA, along with sportswriters like William Rhoden at the *New York Times,* the debate over black coaches speaks to a remarkable transformation in collegiate athletics. Not only is 3.4 percent lower than the overall proportion of blacks in America (13.5 percent), it is also more than ten times less than the proportion of current college players who are black. In 1990, 37 percent of football players at major NCAA Division I schools were African American, despite constituting only 4 percent of enrolled students.[2] A 2006 NCAA survey found that 19,667 black students competed for 616 football teams (32.7 percent); this figure does not include the hundreds of players who participated at historically black colleges and universities. In 2008, the Institute for Diversity and Ethics in Sport reported that the percentage of African American players on all Division I football teams stood at 45.9 percent.[3]

Fan reaction to minority hiring in the NCAA often invokes a simple question: why are there so few black coaches when so many black students play football? For the many who listen to sports radio, read sports journalism, and follow their favorite teams, debates such as these make college sport a lens for examining complex issues like race, affirmative action, civil rights, and discrimination. Indeed, for some (often younger) fans, college athletics may be the only medium through which they have thought extensively about these important concepts, talked them over with peers, and formed their own opinions.

However, the most important point is usually absent from these discussions: although black athletes seem ubiquitous on today's campuses, they endured more than one hundred years of struggle before they could fully participate in college sport. In terms of black football players at predominately white schools, there were entire decades when participation was zero, and decades more when the 32.7 percent was less than 3 percent.

During the twentieth century, the shifting racial demographics of college football teams reflected broader changes, not only on college campuses but also throughout American society. Unlike the simplified stories of racial progress embraced by many Americans—such as Jackie Robinson's transformation of Major League Baseball (and the country) in 1947—the acceptance and ascendance of black athletes at the nation's universities was a long, painful process. Depending on a given school or athletic conference, predominantly white football teams integrated with black students as early as the 1880s and as late as the 1970s.

Yet college football also offered some of the most dramatic, visual examples of transformation sparked by the modern civil rights movement. The game emerged in the late nineteenth century at the country's most elite institutions; for example, the first intercollegiate contest in 1869 featured Rutgers University and Princeton University. By the turn of the century, an influential group of race scientists, psychologists, and even presidents (notably Theodore Roosevelt) applauded football as a way to prepare Anglo-Saxon youth for their confrontation with the world's inferior races. For the next fifty years, social theorists noted that all-white college teams were evidence of the differences between whiteness and blackness.

But today, a new generation of scholars is drawn to college sport for the opposite reason: the supposed glut of black participants. African American athletes are now more likely to represent their school on radio, television, and in newsprint than any other members of the student body. By the 1970s and 1980s, popular debates centered on the growing number of black athletes, gross recruiting violations at black high schools, and sinking academic standards for black players.

Thus, although the transition from 0 to 32.7 percent required more than a century, it was also sudden and overwhelming. Consider the career of Lou Holtz, legendary coach at Notre Dame University who began his career as a 1960 graduate assistant at the University of Iowa. At that time almost all southern universities, and some northern schools—including schools with the most successful, popular athletic programs—still refused to admit African American students. Holtz's career began two years before the admission of James Meredith sparked riots at the University of Mississippi, and twelve years before the Ole Miss football team admitted its first black player. Before World War II, Notre Dame also refused to admit black students, but, after 1945, the school enrolled its first African Americans. Slowly, their presence increased on its sports teams, beginning on the football squad with Wayne Edmonds and Richard Washington in 1952. By the time Holtz came to Notre Dame as head coach in 1986 the team fielded numerous black athletes. By 2001, African Americans comprised more than half the squad, and after Holtz's tenure the school hired its first black football coach. Surely, the most important and striking transformation in Holtz's long career was the racial makeup of the students he mentored daily.[4]

If such a shift took place during one coach's career outside the South, consider the remarkable speed at which southern schools introduced black athletes. As late as 1966, no African American student participated on any sport team in the Southeastern Conference (SEC), which includes Auburn University, the University of Alabama, the University of Florida, the University of Georgia, Louisiana State University, Mississippi State University, the University of Mississippi, the University of Kentucky, the University of Tennessee, and Vanderbilt University. However, within fifteen years black players were a dominant force in the conference. By 1980, nearly 400 African Americans were on SEC teams—including 33 percent of the conference's football players and 70 percent of its basketball participants. In 1990, 57 percent of SEC football players were black. Moreover, the swift transition was not limited to the South's major conference, as black athletes quickly joined athletic teams across the country, even at schools that saw little increase in overall minority enrollment.[5] The shift was even more pronounced in basketball, where just 10 percent of college teams featured one or more black players in 1948, 45 percent in 1962, and 92 percent by 1975. In 2008, 60.4 percent of all Division I men's basketball players were African American.[6]

Thus, *Integrating the Gridiron* chronicles both a tedious, long struggle and a dramatic transformation. This book also speaks to broader changes in higher education, popular culture, and the role of sport in America. Lou Holtz's coaching career began when televised football was a new and uncertain phenomenon, when universities tended to operate *in loco parentis*, and when society still revered coaches as symbols of paternal leadership. Holtz's coaching career, however, ended amid debates over the growing institutional emphasis on football, the increasing budgets afforded to coaches, stadiums, and athletic departments and between those who argued that "big-time" sport threatened to damage the mission of higher education and the very students it was meant to serve.[7]

Knowing the history of black athletes at predominately white colleges is vital to understanding the issues surrounding minority admissions and the dearth of black coaches. Moreover, a broader examination of sport history can enrich historical analysis of race, media, and popular culture, providing a fresh view that informs the mainstream historiography of modern America. Just like the game Holtz lived and breathed on the sidelines for forty years, history has undergone its own radical transformation; histories have drawn lessons beyond political, social, or economic inquiry and embraced the transformative role of culture in shaping the past. *Integrating the Gridiron* is thus an effort to unite a history of integration in college football with the broader, national civil rights narrative, specifically by investigating case studies that exemplify how reaction to the game altered the discourse of civil rights in America. Making significant contributions to broader scholarship on media, race, and popular culture, this book seeks to explore the largest conflicts over integration in the game. These episodes specifically transcended the realm of sport and entertainment, generating nationwide attention and interregional dialogue in the pivotal years of the modern civil rights movement.

College athletes played a fundamental role in contesting and reshaping the broader social struggle of African Americans in the twentieth century, and their stories were integral parts of the larger civil rights campaign. Because institutions nationwide supported the growth of intercollegiate athletics after World War II, *Integrating the Gridiron* compares examples of football integration from several different regions that historians usually compartmentalize. By examining integrated athletics in the South, West, Midwest, and Northeast, I offer an intriguing, interregional comparison, as opposed to the traditional, postwar civil rights narratives that tend to focus only on states like Mississippi, Alabama, and Georgia. The advent of television spurred institutes of higher education to embrace intersectional contests and a national sporting ethos, most notably in the formation of major athletic conferences, televised "bowl games," and a national ranking system. Yet *Integrating the Gridiron* also provides unparalleled comparisons of popular, local racial discourses, which include the acceptance and treatment of black athletes by peers, coaches, alumni, and local communities.

Understanding the history of college football integration is vital to addressing the current role of athletics and racial diversity at America's universities. Indeed, it should be essential knowledge in contemporary debates over racial tokenism in higher education, campus diversity, and the lack of black faculty, coaches, or administrators. Even today, overall minority admissions are sagging at some of the very schools that recruit large numbers of black football players.

1

Beyond Jackie Robinson

Racial Integration in American College Football and New Directions in Sport History

On 3 December 1898, Harvard's football team held a banquet to celebrate the end of a dramatic year.[1] Having completed an unbeaten season, the squad enjoyed surprise victories over several Ivy League rivals, including the University of Pennsylvania and Yale University. The evening's featured speaker, Theodore Roosevelt, proved to be a boisterous, energetic orator and a huge football fan. Roosevelt, a Harvard alum and newly elected governor of New York, received a warm ovation from an audience of influential administrators, students, and boosters. Yet the evening's largest cheer came with the introduction of Assistant Coach William Henry Lewis. While a student at Amherst, the popular Lewis became one of the first African Americans to integrate the college game when he joined the freshman team in 1888. He was later joined by black teammate W.T.S. Jackson the following year. After graduating from Harvard Law School (where he also played successfully) Lewis was named assistant coach, also a first for a black man.[2]

Lewis's popularity, eloquence, and skill as a jurist helped him join Roosevelt's inner circle—a group of Harvard graduates and future "Rough Riders" in the Spanish-American War, ten of whom listed football as their "occupation" when they enlisted in 1898. According to historian Harold Ward, when Lewis was chosen to deliver Amherst's graduation address in 1892 the event "was publicized as an indication of the black man's 'fitness.'"[3] African Americans from throughout New England came to hear him speak; they included W.E.B. Du Bois, who had delivered his own commencement address at Harvard in 1890. While Lewis himself stayed home during the Spanish-American War and continued to coach, his relationship with Roosevelt persisted until 1907, when the president promoted him to assistant U.S. attorney in Boston. Under the subsequent administration of William Howard Taft, Lewis became assistant attorney general of the United States—at that point the highest federal office ever held by an African American.[4]

William Lewis used the burgeoning game of college football to earn a reputation in the press as a "very strong," "intelligent," and "heady" player.[5] Such an image fit perfectly in Roosevelt's posse of headstrong leaders and administrators. Public discourse of non-whites rarely emphasized rationality or intellect, especially combined with such praise for a black male's physical attributes. In a period of renewed racial animosity, contemporary black leaders had to find some means to forge positive public images if they had any hope of advancement. Within these constraints, Lewis used football to establish himself as an ideal man living the "strenuous life"—an amazing accomplishment considering the strict racial hierarchy that developed and informed Roosevelt's philosophy. The president explicitly saw football as rugged preparation for Anglo-Saxon supremacy and American leadership in the new century.[6]

And yet William Lewis is not thought of as a black sporting hero in the same way as Jackie Robinson or Joe Louis. Unlike boxing and baseball, college football has rarely been the subject of serious study in terms of culture, race, and integration. Rather than examine the nebulous story of integration in collegiate football, scholarly attention and popular memory have both chosen instead to focus on clear and powerful individual stories of integration: the legendary biographies of professional black athletes. This remains the case even for the postwar era, when television exposure continued to popularize the game and made some student athletes household names alongside professional boxers and baseball players.

Since 1985 scholars have explored the process by which black athletes were invoked in a number of debates—including the biological nature of African American physical prowess, dissension over the the black community's perceived emphasis on achievement in sports and entertainment, and the debates surrounding the role of black athletes as community leaders or racial "spokesmen."[7] Yet the issues these studies focus on emerged from a growing African American presence in select professional (not amateur) turn-of-the-twentieth-century athletics, particularly individual sports such as boxing and Negro-league baseball. Many later observers found them particularly difficult to apply to intercollegiate team sports, especially football.

Indeed, neither a single "color line" nor a single integrating figure in college football emerged; instead, a tediously slow and arduous process spanned eighty years and countless players. It is even difficult to identify the first African American participant. While William Lewis played successfully at both Amherst and Harvard in the late 1880s and early 1890s, other black footballers probably participated on club teams before schools officially sanctioned the sport. There is also the problem of distinguishing when exactly football took its "modern" form, as student clubs slowly fashioned the new game from its predecessor, rugby. Historians consider Walter Camp the father of the modern game; after organizing Yale's first team in 1888, Camp radically altered the sport and codified its rules by 1892.

George Jewett, an African American student from Ann Arbor, played football at the University of Michigan in 1890 and 1892, then again while attending medical school at Northwestern University in 1893.[8] From 1891 to 1892, two other black students played on future Big Ten Conference teams—Fred Patterson at Ohio State University and Preston Eagleson at Indiana University.[9] According to historian Albert Broussard, an African American athlete named George A. Flippin played football at the University of Nebraska in 1891, including scheduled games against private athletic clubs and schools outside the state. A team from the University of Missouri even forfeited a game over Flippin's participation. Although the sport—and intercollegiate athletics in general—were still undergoing considerable change, Flippin probably qualifies as the first black student to play organized football outside the Northeast or future Big Ten Conference. His story also earned local media coverage in Lincoln.[10]

Other scholars have recognized the importance of Native American students at the Industrial School at Carlisle, Pennsylvania, where by 1895 successful football teams drew considerable attention and helped popularize the game. Legendary Coach Glen "Pop" Warner joined Carlisle's staff in 1898, and Jim Thorpe—one of the finest athletes of the twentieth century—played football for the school from 1907 to 1912.[11]

Yet in terms of African American involvement, the numbers remained extremely low before World War I. According to one scholar, just thirteen black players participated before 1900 and only twenty-seven more through 1914.[12] Notable participants before 1925 included William Washington (Oberlin College, 1895–1897), Howard J. Lee (Harvard University, 1896–1897), George Chadwell (Williams College, 1897), Alton Washington (Northwestern University, 1898–1901), Matthew Bullock (Dartmouth College, 1902), Arthur Carr (Ohio State University, 1904), Archie Alexander (University of Iowa, 1910–1912), Hugh Shippley (Brown University, 1913), Gideon Smith (Michigan State University, 1913–1916), Joseph Trigg (Syracuse University, 1914–1916), and Edward Morrison (Tufts University, 1914–1916).

In addition, before 1933 several African American players also went on to play professionally, including Jaye Williams (Brown University, 1918–1921), John A. Shelburne (Dartmouth College, 1919–1922), Fred "Duke" Slater (University of Iowa, 1918–1921), James Turner (Northwestern University, 1923), Sol Butler (Dubuque College, 1917–1919), Harold Bradley (University of Iowa, 1927), David Myers (New York University, 1929), Joe Lillard (University of Oregon, 1930–1931), and Ray Kemp (Duquesne University, 1928–1931).[13]

As the modern game formed, black footballers outside the Northeast sparked very different reactions. In 1897, the *New York Times* announced the "first football game ever played by negroes in Tennessee."[14] The result was a fight between the players and a group of "drunken white men," which left one player dead and six seriously injured. While William Lewis helped invent and shape the game at Amherst and Harvard, southern institutions, which became the game's greatest proponents, systematically excluded black participation from the start. Despite the intriguing stories of Lewis, Flippin, and others, football by 1900 was organized enough to distinguish itself as a sport designed for young white males—an activity that perfectly answered Roosevelt's call for a more masculine generation of Anglo-Saxon leaders.

After the modern game emerged on university campuses, only a few dozen African American students played on major college squads for the next thirty years. Those who excelled during World War I—notably All-Americans Fritz Pollard (Brown University, 1915–1916) and Paul Robeson (Rutgers University, 1915–1918)—were extremely rare, making their achievements all the more exceptional. Pollard, the outstanding running back who first integrated the Rose Bowl in 1916 joined Robert Marshall (University of Minnesota, 1904–1906) to become one of the first black players to join the National Football League (NFL) in 1920. Robeson's remarkable life included an outstanding athletic career at Rutgers; as the third black student ever admitted to the school, he was named a first-team All-American in 1917 and 1918. Robeson also played professionally. Despite these notable exceptions, the historian John Watterson is correct when he writes, "Put simply and bluntly, from about 1900 to 1930 few black football players competed for flagship state universities, private colleges, or large private universities. . . . The big-time football of black colleges such as Hampton, Howard, Grambling, and Florida A&M would have seemed far more preferable to black players."[15] At the University of Michigan, only four black lettermen participated in football during the sixty-three years from 1882 to 1945, and zero in basketball.[16] Moreover, no African Americans competed for southern universities before World War II, where state laws prohibited black students from even enrolling in classes, let alone extracurricular activities. Not until 1947, when Harvard University's Chet Pierce played in a game against the University of Virginia in Charlottesville, did a black footballer participate in a game against a white university in the South.[17]

Although it took more than fifty years for a black athlete to appear on a major college field in the former Confederacy, other regions—the West and Midwest—introduced African American athletes much sooner. Of the two black students who played for the University of Southern California during the 1920s, Brice Taylor (1924–1926) was the school's first All-American.[18] Jack Trice, the first African American athlete at Iowa State University, made headlines in 1923 after he died from injuries suffered during his first football game against the University of Minnesota. The national press speculated that Trice's injuries were racially motivated. A note written by him in a segregated Minneapolis hotel room the night before his death indicates the pressure black players faced on the gridiron before World War II:

My thoughts just before the first real college game of my life: The honor of my race, family & self is at stake. Everyone is expecting me to do big things. I will. My whole body and soul are to be thrown recklessly about the field tomorrow. Every time the ball is snapped, I will be trying to do more than my part. On all defensive plays I must break through the opponents' line and stop the play in their territory. Beware of mass interference. Fight low, with your eyes open and toward the play. Watch out for crossbacks and reverse end runs. Be on your toes every minute if you expect to make good. Jack.[19]

In 1997, Iowa State renamed its football field "Jack Trice Stadium" after a twenty-year campaign led by students and alumni.

Along with players like Pollard and Robeson, Trice's dramatic story was one of few exceptions that reinforced the rule: from 1920 to 1945, few black athletes attempted to participate in athletics at major white universities, even as different schools and regions emerged with influential athletic programs. Far fewer blacks participated in football or baseball than in track, yet even in that sport African American students were relatively rare. According to the historian John Behee, only 100 to 200 black students ran track in 1936, the same year Ohio State's Jesse Owens and his amateur teammates excelled at the Berlin Olympics.[20] This small number of black athletes paralleled the lack of African American students overall. From 1924 to 1932, black enrollment at predominately white institutions in the North rose from just 1,400 to 2,538. In 1933, 97 percent of the 38,000 African American college students were attending all-black schools in

Jack Trice with teammates in 1923. Iowa State University Library/Special Collections Department.

the South.[21] Meanwhile, universities in the West began to shape intercollegiate contests; for example, the annual Rose Bowl in Pasadena, California, established itself as the country's preeminent game in the 1920s. Black athletes faced obvious exclusion not only at schools that outright prohibited African American students from enrolling, including southern colleges, but also at celebrated institutions like Notre Dame University.

Even if a university was willing to enroll black students, those who wished to participate in sport were subject to additional discrimination. While the University of Illinois allowed a black athlete to participate in 1937, historians Donald Spivey and Thomas Jones found that the few African American sportsmen at the school prior to 1945 encountered "a pattern of discrimination typical of that to be found in practically every secondary school, college, university, and professional athletic team throughout the United States."[22] In 1922, Dr. Elmer D. Mitchell, former basketball coach and intramural director at the University of Michigan, published an article entitled "Racial Traits in Athletics" in the *American Physical Education Review*. Mitchell articulated both the scientific and popular sentiments, prevalent in the 1920s and 1930s, regarding black student athletes; he asserted that "a colored youth who remains in school until the age of interscholastic competition is usually of the bright industrious type, and the same qualities show when he participates in athletic games."[23] When black students competed on predominately white teams, they were praised only insofar as they followed the directions and leadership of their white teammates. White students were often given free rein over initiating "inferior" players, including lower classmen and blacks. Again, Mitchell praised the black athlete who took such racist criticism from his fellow college students:

> The negro mingles easily with white participants, accepting an inferior status and being content with it. I have often seen a gay-spirited crowd of college players play pranks upon a colored team mate . . . and in all cases the spirit of reception was a good-humored one. The negro, as a fellow player with white men, is quiet and unassertive; even though he may be the star of the team he does not assume openly to lead.[24]

Like the press surrounding William Lewis in the late nineteenth century, Mitchell offered a conflicting portrait of black athletes—one that emphasized subservience yet acknowledged black students as "bright" and "industrious." Nevertheless, while athletics may have provided room for more nuanced portraits of African Americans, Mitchell's study ultimately fit the period's dominant pattern of racialization—defining non-whites by their physical bodies, sexuality, and uncontrolled emotions. Northern teams with one or two black players in the 1920s and 1930s drew praise for "mingling" the races, all within a racial hierarchy completely separate from skill, experience, or the game itself. ˙t Mitchell ominously noted the danger of teams featuring more than one black student: "I have seen cases though where such a star player, if allowed authority, quickly assumed an air of bravado . . . when the negro plays on a team composed of members of his own race . . . he is an inferior athlete, because many things crop out to handicap his natural skill. One of these is the tendency to be theatrical or to play to the grandstand."[25]

In terms of popular "black teams," Mitchell could only refer to the barnstorming, amusement-oriented baseball teams made popular by the Negro leagues. By 1939, one black newspaper counted only thirty-eight black footballers on major white teams throughout the country.[26] That number certainly exceeded that of 1923, the year Jack Trice died on the field, yet more schools were offering football to their students. As a ratio of the total number of participants, black players at white universities remained relatively steady before 1945; most teams featured zero African American players, and very few fielded more than one.

Most important, black footballers were lone individuals who rarely saw playing time and received very little press coverage. Because they were not integral to their team's success, coaches and administrators could bench them for games against segregated schools without creating a stir—the so-called "gentlemen's agreement." By the late 1930s, football fans faced the prospect of major college teams featuring large numbers of black students, but before that northern schools with black players expected them to function under the very racial hierarchy articulated in the *American Physical Education Review*.

From William Lewis, who integrated Amherst football in 1888, to the integration of the University of Mississippi, Louisiana State University, and University of Georgia football programs in 1972, the students who integrated college football were a collective force made up of countless integrating moments. This kind of desegregation more closely resembled the reality of the postwar struggle for civil rights: grass-roots, populist agitation at the local level, particularly in the public sphere. Nevertheless, while the geopolitical ebb and flow of college integration offers a better parallel to this more expansive conflict, sports history still emphasizes the larger than life persona of the professional "race hero." Scholars have focused on a myriad of athletes, from Paul Robeson and Jesse Owens to Fritz Pollard and Jackie Robinson. Despite their value and power, the popularity of these individual stories points to a fundamental undercurrent that continues to influence our understanding of the civil rights movement. Namely, it is a desire to simplify a history that revolves around individual heroes breaking binary racial "lines" or "barriers."

Furthermore, this attempt to ingrain such a formula in popular memory is ongoing even in the twenty-first century. For example, in his study of golfer Tiger Woods, the historian Henry Yu examines how Woods's popularity exemplifies important changes in American notions of race. In particular, Yu focuses on the obsession to define Woods's racial background—a mixture of Caucasian, African American, American Indian, and Southeast Asian ancestry that the star himself has dubbed "Cablinasian." Yu argues that "contemporary descriptions of cultural difference retain many of the problems of older languages of race."[27] Accordingly, soon after his arrival in the professional ranks the popular press began to classify Woods only as "black" or "African American." In reality, Woods's life and racial attributes characterize the shifting migrations of the twentieth century and the complex displacement of race and culture from specific geographic locales. His father was an African American GI who served in the Pacific, his mother a woman of mixed Southeast Asian lineage. However, Yu aptly states that Tiger's image is best marketed toward a global audience that still imagines "the end of race-based conflict in the United States as an act of individual redemption, blinding Americans to the structural bases of racial hierarchy."[28] Thus, Woods's "Cablinasian" heritage has been "blackened" by the mainstream press, which places the golfing star comfortably within the pantheon of twentieth-century African American race heroes.

Thus, biographical portraits of "individual redemption" and the breaking of binary racial barriers have dominated scholarly attention devoted to the sporting world. As a result, historians have focused much more on professional and individualized athletics instead of amateur, team-oriented sports. This line of analysis yields a canon of "race hero" biographies—Jack Johnson, Joe Louis, Jackie Robinson, Muhammad Ali; even John L. Sullivan and Rocky Marciano have been treated largely as race (or ethnic) figures.[29] These scholarly treatments have provided an invaluable foundation, yet they can also obscure the more complex history of racial integration in all facets of American society, not just entertainment or leisure.

Athletes such as William Lewis are largely unknown in popular memory, but professional personalities remain fully ingrained. Central to historians, four black athletes in particular—Jack Johnson, Joe Louis, Jackie Robinson, and Muhammad Ali—have provided the bulk of scholarship intent on probing athleticism and race. It is important to take a brief look at the historiography surrounding these four; each reveals how scholars have laid a foundation for sport history and initially interpreted the use of sport and leisure to examine race in the twentieth century.

Jack Johnson

In 1906, while Lewis prepared to accept his groundbreaking appointment in the U.S. attorney's office, Jack Johnson started to pursue heavyweight champion Tommy Burns with the goal of cajoling him into a fight. Johnson followed the champ everywhere—from the United States to England, to France, and finally to Sydney, Australia—where he made headlines around the world in 1908, knocking out Burns to become the first black heavyweight champion. Undoubtedly, Johnson's biography is a key starting point for examining race and sport in the twentieth century, and historian Randy Roberts has illuminated his story. White America was not ready for a black champion in 1908, and many blacks were not prepared for Jack Johnson. Johnson lived a lavish, sometimes violent life that directly challenged white social norms. He publicly courted white prostitutes, married two white women, and spent exorbitant amounts of money despite massive opposition and pressure from the state. Eventually, prosecutors indicted Johnson under the Mann Act, the Progressive bill that made it a crime to transport young females across state boundaries for "immoral" purposes. The move sent Johnson into European exile in 1913, whereupon an invitational tournament of white boxers crowned a new champion.[30]

Yet Johnson's story did not end when he left the ring. Reduced to managing a saloon in Tijuana, Mexico, Johnson returned to the States in 1920 to serve his prison sentence. Through his savvy manipulation of the press, Johnson was the first professional black athlete to consistently transcend his sport and influence the larger discourse of race in America. Reaction to Johnson from both the boxing world and the American public revealed that influential athletes would be subject to the same scrutiny as African American community leaders. However, critics by and large reserved such judgments for Johnson's behavior outside, not inside, the ring. Although historian Gail Bederman has emphasized Johnson's public persona in the ring (and the stories are many, such as the fighter's penchant for wrapping his penis in gauze to make it appear larger to audiences), in reality, Johnson was discredited as a racial spokesman because of perceptions surrounding his "private" life.[31] Here, then, was a major difference in the way black athletes would be accepted as race heroes. Whereas African American social and political leaders were scrutinized by their public or professional endeavors— the educational philosophy of Booker T. Washington, the public speeches of Marcus Garvey, or the writings of W.E.B. Du Bois—if black athletes were to become serious spokesmen for African American advancement, they would need to make their most significant statements outside their profession.

It is clear Johnson understood the reasoning behind this scrutiny of his private life, yet what remains unclear is just how conscious he was in embracing his role as a race hero. According to Bederman, Victorian "manliness"—a discourse of sexual restraint, genteel behavior, and Social Darwinism that constructed white males as paradigms of civilization—offered the opportunity for the challenges of a Jack Johnson or Ida B. Wells.[32] Yet Bederman characterizes Johnson and others, including Ida B.Wells as "intentional" in their desire to disentangle racism from notions of manliness and civilization, a contention not necessarily supported in the case of Johnson's public life. Most notably, his bitter and outspoken opposition to other black boxers (including Joe Louis) took place exactly along the lines of race and manliness. Linking the work of Wells and Johnson as two similar "campaigns" against middle-class, white masculinity belittles Wells's enormous contribution and incorrectly characterizes Johnson's motivations.

Regardless of his intention, Jack Johnson's fall proved that black athletes would not win broad acceptance without advancing public images that revealed positive aspects of their private lives and moral characters. Johnson had no interest in drafting such images, and indeed he seemed to revel in the fact that his larger-than-life public career was infused with anxious murmurings surrounding his private life. In the end, Johnson played right into these fears by helping the white media thrust his private life into the public arena, with the deliberate intent to shock and surprise. Not only would the legacy of Johnson's story in the ring influence black athletes throughout the twentieth century, but later in life Johnson himself made sure he was not forgotten when another talented boxer began to draw attention in 1935.

Joe Louis

Twenty years after Jack Johnson's exile, critics began to notice the phenomenal potential of a young boxer named Joe Louis. Sportswriters in large northern cities served as a conduit for popular sports in their effort to reach the most profitable audience, and most found many reasons to support Louis's rise; his greatest asset was his marketable image as an anti–Jack Johnson. Unlike Johnson, it was widely accepted that Louis was soft-spoken and well-behaved, "a credit to his race."[33] Common images of Louis in American newspapers throughout the 1930s included pictures of his private world: relaxing around the dinner table, reading the Bible, even helping his mother in the kitchen while clad in an apron.[34] While Jack Johnson had shocked the American public with outrageous behavior and flashy wardrobes, many perceived Louis as a less threatening, more "domesticated" African American athlete. Like Johnson, Louis was also discrediting these powerful linked ideologies of rugged masculinity, race, and civilization that scholars of "whiteness" have outlined. Yet his methods and motive were quite different, as were the results.

Scholars have used Louis's career to analyze America's racial climate during the late 1930s and World War II. Most interpretations focus on his ability to garner immense popularity by playing off these stereotyped images of the moral, quiet, and childlike black man. Historians also point to the series of bouts Louis fought with Italian heavyweight Primo Carnera and the German boxer Max Schmeling; these fights took on more significance in light of European fascism and gave Louis a boost of patriotic support, which solidified his popular celebrity status during the 1940s. Dominic Capeci and Martha Wilkerson have aptly described Louis as a "multifarious hero of a society at war," a sports hero who personified for many African Americans the Double V campaign of "channeling black frustrations into positive, patriotic actions."[35] Meanwhile, Jeffrey Sammons has argued that Louis's career had the unique affect of uniting many southern white boxing fans with African Americans under a patriotic banner that only the war could offer.[36] A similar line of analysis appears in both Chris Mead's and Andrew Edmonds's excellent biographies, which focus predominately on the solidification of Louis's image as "hero" and "champion" through the successful bouts of 1938 through 1940 and the popularity of his wartime public service campaigns.[37] In addition, the last chapter of Lawrence Levine's seminal *Black Culture, Black Consciousness* placed Louis within the pantheon of African American "folk heroes" and outlined the many Louis references that appeared in popular black songs during the 1930s.[38] Louis's significance to cultural historians cannot be denied: his popularity with some white Americans strengthened the resolve of others in search of a "white hope," while his triumphs embodied the African American dream of empowerment and basic civil rights. Although debates may persist about Louis's overall magnitude, there is no doubt that he had become a race hero more than a decade before Jackie Robinson integrated professional baseball.

Joe Louis became the most popular black athlete the nation had ever seen, and unlike Jack Johnson his image appealed to white America. In this way, Louis and his handlers recognized that the general public would either accept or reject professional black athletes on the basis of private innuendo and not athletic achievement. Thus, to construct and maintain his popularity Louis and his entourage put in as much effort outside the ring as they did in physical training for his bouts. Specifically, his small team of black managers helped cultivate his demeanor, emphasized his commitment to domesticity, and carefully scrutinized his public remarks. The mainstream press recognized managers John Roxborough and Julian Black as "college-trained Negro businessmen."[39] Along with black trainer Jack Blackburn, the three were dubbed "the all-Negro Louis ménage" and "the Bomber's board of strategy."[40] Louis's team recognized the importance of emphasizing their fighter's private virtues, especially his devout Christianity and close relationship with family. The Louis camp also celebrated their fighter's strong morals and hard work ethic and helped him enforce a ban on alcohol while training for fights.

For African Americans, it was hard to overstate the significance of Joe Louis's early success in the 1930s. His fights received as much attention from the black press as any other issue, and not just on the days following major bouts. In the many weeks preceding and following a Louis fight, the Brown Bomber commanded as many headlines as hard news stories—the Scottsboro boys, Ethiopia, or the Depression. Joe Louis's early career, particularly his embarrassing defeat by Max Schmeling in 1936, also introduced for the first time the centrality of the African American press in creating athletic celebrities who transcended sport. Louis's image in the press as the anti–Jack Johnson and the harsh debates surrounding his early career reveal black writers who were coming to grips with the risky nature of hero construction—a tenuous process by which the hopes, aspirations, and dreams of the entire community were embodied in one man and a simple sporting event.

Jackie Robinson

For most Americans, Jackie Robinson's integration of major league baseball in 1947 is the definitive proof that sport was important to social integration. Indeed, an overall examination of integrated baseball in the twentieth century is useful for historians looking at race in general. The sport was central to the development of urban life, and as black migration to America's industrial centers increased rapidly after World War I, baseball came to embody the city's multiethnic, multiracial landscape. Moreover, by integrating baseball directly after World War II, Robinson's difficult path to stardom echoed African American's broader call for increased access and opportunity in postwar northern cities. Yet Robinson's oft-told story has always resonated because of its flare for the dramatic: a clear color barrier, a public confrontation, and a single moment of integration. Scholars have correctly moved past this thinking by contextualizing Robinson's fame and his triumph in breaking baseball's color line. Jules Tygiel's influential "biography" of the baseball star was really intended to enrich, complicate, and place the legend within the larger contexts of black ballplayers, the Negro leagues, Jim Crow, and the burgeoning civil rights movement.[41] Like Jack Johnson and Joe Louis, Robinson was not a plastic hero. He overcame incredible odds with diligence and courage, taking on what Tygiel called the "experiment" of integrating the major leagues. Robinson's relationship with Dodger owner Branch Rickey was complicated, and Rickey was certainly not a white patron who simply manipulated an acquiescent, passive Robinson. Instead, Robinson began to shun the image he and Rickey had constructed together (based in large part on Joe Louis) and became more vocal on and off the field. In addition, New York's leftist community—most notably sportswriters at the *Daily Worker*—also shaped how whites would ultimately accept Robinson, as did fans in Montreal, Canada, where Rickey initially assigned him in 1945.[42] The story of Robinson's triumphant "moment" of integration is far more complicated than his legacy in popular memory. Although he was the central figure who "shattered" the color barrier, most major league baseball teams continued to shun integration for the next ten years, while segregated housing and dining facilities remained the norm for players into the 1960s.

At the center remains Robinson's individual story of reform. By refusing to simply be a "credit to his race" and maintaining a tenuous relationship with Rickey, Robinson stepped onto Ebbets Field and presented himself squarely in the public sphere, forcing Americans to reexamine the fundamental tenants of both Jim Crow and northern race relations. With Robinson, integrated major league baseball swept from city to city throughout the North and Midwest, and

along the way it opened doors to a broader and more comprehensive understanding of racism in the pivotal moments preceding the civil rights movement.
Thus, Robinson's story has been central to historians who wish to use sports as
a serious lens for scholarly analysis.

Muhammad Ali

Recent scholars have also explored the life of Muhammad Ali, building on author
Thomas Hauser's authorized biography of the man *Sports Illustrated* named
"Sportsman of the Century" in 1999.[43] If Louis and Robinson symbolized the black
struggle to integrate society on whites' terms, Ali embodied the subsequent
black athletic revolt. Instead of an attempt to mythologize, Hauser intended his
biography to present the fighter as "a superb human being with good qualities
and flaws." By joining the Nation of Islam (NOI), embracing elements of black
nationalism and the counterculture, and refusing to be drafted into the Vietnam
War, Ali both reflected and shaped popular discourse during the pivotal 1960s.
Despite his willingness to use the media spotlight as a platform to speak out on
broad issues of justice and equality, he was able to craft multiple public images
and maintain a sense of anonymity. Hauser attempted to profile the "real" Ali,
insisting that (surprisingly) the man remained largely unknown. Leon Gast's
When We Were Kings, the Academy Award–winning documentary on Ali's famous
1974 bout with George Foreman in Zaire, draws a similar conclusion. Rather than
let his race hinder him, Ali toyed with his own identity and even used notions of
blackness and whiteness as weapons against his opponents: "out-blacking" the
much darker Foreman in front of African audiences one moment and calling Joe
Frazier an uneducated, black "gorilla" the next.[44]

Historian Jeffrey Sammons has also linked Ali's career to the black power
movement by probing the fighter's relationship with Malcolm X and the NOI.
According to Sammons, the Muslim leader tried to influence the sport of boxing and manipulate the heavyweight division, knowing that black fighters
wielded power in the media and were among the nation's most visible symbols.[45] Contrary to the idea that black athletes were meant to be humble and
apolitical, Ali and the NOI's celebration of channeling political/religious dissent through athletics (stamped with Ali's unique brand of humor and cocki-
ness) was threatening to both liberals and conservatives, integrationists and
segregationists. Ali also transformed the very meaning of sport and its impact
on American politics and culture by offering black athletes an alternate vision
of what their role in society could be.

In a different vein, Mike Marqusee has focused on both Ali's early hesitancy
to address larger political and social concerns, and the extent to which his multiple profiles were thrust upon him by both critics and fans. "No other sports figure . . . was so enmeshed in the political events of his time," writes Marqusee,

emphasizing the extent to which Ali himself was shaped by the 1960s: "[W]e cannot allow ourselves to be so seduced by its hero that we forget the confusing conditions in which his story unfolded. It could have turned out otherwise. Doubt and contradiction, misjudgment and compromise contribute as much to the making of a hero."[46] Marqusee also explores Ali's African American fan base and emphasizes the ways in which blacks embraced him as a martyr who willingly took on criticism from mainstream white Americans. Rather than be beholden to white fans, Ali endeared himself to blacks by accepting white critiques of black power (and, indirectly, blackness itself) and celebrating his own demonization.

Finally, the more recent, dramatic turn in public opinion toward Ali has drawn considerable attention; his appearance at the 1996 Olympic Games in Atlanta and subsequent praise in the mainstream media have triggered what *USA Today* dubbed "a renaissance for the greatest." Marqusee writes that Ali "had his political teeth extracted" after the 1970s, while Sammons insists that "the radical who had abandoned Christianity to become a Black Muslim . . . was never really a radical—society merely perceived him as one because he did not follow the guidelines that had been set."[47]

These valuable efforts to illustrate America's ultimate embrace of Muhammad Ali enrich his life story, contextualize his passion, personality, and ideology, and complicate the notion of "athletic heroes." And yet Ali remains a unique, transformative public figure with a powerful voice. Even after stripping away the mythology, his biography is still the greatest testament to the impact an individual professional black athlete can have on American history.

New Directions—College Football

In many ways, these historical-biographical approaches to sport history and race mimic the mainstream historiography of the civil rights movement. In his multivolume biography of Martin Luther King Jr., Taylor Branch grapples with these very issues. Rather than examining socioeconomic conditions or grassroots populism, Branch focuses on King's leadership and individual will as the human agency responsible for the course of the movement; he claims that "King's life is the best and most important metaphor for American history in the watershed postwar years."[48] However, Branch is also adamant that a biography of King as individual hero is not enough to capture the movement's progress or appeal. "But to focus upon the historical King," writes Branch, "as generally established by his impact on white society . . . makes for unstable history and collapsible myth."[49] Historians Michael Dyson and Aldon Morris have made similar points in relation to the movement's leadership.[50] To determine the extent to which King shaped the movement—or the movement shaped King—is difficult, and Branch has devoted three volumes to its consideration. Even the very layout of the National Civil Rights Museum in Memphis, Tennessee, hints at this tension in civil rights historiography. While presenting a series of exhibits on the courage of countless people, the final display is a shrine to King located in the very motel bedroom where he was assassinated in 1968.

Perhaps King's story is not even the best parallel to the biographical portraits of individual athletes. Rosa Parks invariably comes to mind when defining this question of a single, progressive figure or lone integrating moment as defining the movement. Here, too, the parallels are striking; Branch reveals the NAACP's painstaking effort to employ Parks as a symbol. Local activists picked up on the case precisely because her image seemed impeccable. Like Robinson's stint as a Dodger, the commitment to Parks was an experiment that hinged on her ability to fulfill her role and "make a good impression on white judges."[51] According to Jo Ann Robinson, Parks was "respected in all black circles ... a medium-sized, cultured mulatto woman; a civic and religious worker; quiet, unassuming, and pleasant in manner and appearance; dignified and reserved; of high morals and a strong character."[52] Although scholars have emphasized the movement's populism, many still find that the personality-driven characterizations of the "King years" or the "Parks episode" are too powerful to leave behind.

How can a study of integrated athletics inform these analyses of the civil rights movement? If it remains committed to the study of transcendent professional athletes, who merely symbolized broader shifts in America's racial landscape, sport history will fail. There is little benefit to thinking of the 1960s as the "era of Muhammad Ali" instead of the "King years." Instead, sport history needs the kind of enrichment that scholars have brought to the study of other aspects of American culture. Brian Ward's examination of postwar music is an excellent example. In *Just My Soul Responding*, Ward outlines the stark difference between the black music of the 1960s and the "sweet, biracial pop" of the late 1950s. Ward argues that neither one nor the other genre was a more "authentic" expression of popular black consciousness, even though whites were much more likely to embrace the likes of Sam Cooke while soul artists employed rhetoric emphasizing black separatism. Rather than a question of authenticity, Ward sees the era of biracial music as emblematic of a positive hope for social integration, a moment of optimism in music that paralleled public sentiment in the aftermath of the *Brown v. Board of Education* decision. According to Ward, the failure of this broader hope allowed for an era of interracial pop music to fade with it.[53] Instead of focusing on the individual authenticity of a black artist or athlete, other scholars continue to emphasize how black athletes reflected the specific communities from which they emerged. While Ward grapples with biracial pop, Montye Fuse and Keith Miller have argued that Jackie Robinson's success was based on jazz aesthetic—an "improvisational" style of play he learned while living in Kansas City and playing for the Monarchs.[54]

Scholars should continue to apply these same questions to the realm of sport. Is there such a thing as a more "authentic" black athlete? Historians Randy Roberts, Geoffrey Ward, and Gail Bederman may point to Jack Johnson.[55] However, that rubric would posit Joe Louis's success in constructing a more passive image as a kind of inauthenticity, and certainly no one is prepared to criticize Louis for his demeanor or question his "authenticity" as an African American. After all, Johnson, too, was self-consciously constructing an image for the public, just as Louis and his managers did. Perhaps the success of Louis represents a similar moment of biracial hope fueled by patriotic sentiment. The problem with applying these (and other) questions to the sporting world is not that sports have lagged in popularity to other cultural expressions. Nor is it true that sporting fans have historically enjoyed their hobby in a vacuum devoid of meaning. The problem instead is our own knowledge of sport—namely, its lack of depth and limited scope.

Thus, an understanding of athletes like William Henry Lewis and the integration of collegiate athletics represents an important departure from the history that has only celebrated men like Johnson, Louis, Robinson, and Ali. In theory, college football was an amateur sport—one that featured athletes as young as eighteen, participating in a sport that lacked the kind of imaging necessary in constructing "race heroes." Even as its popularity soared with the advent of television, victory on the gridiron most often brought prestige to institutions and mascots, not individual athletes. Despite the exceptional tales of Red Grange, George Gipp, Harry Kipke, Tom Hamilton, or Notre Dame's Four Horsemen—football giants who were among the greatest celebrities of their time—the majority of players were anonymous students, and most athletes, especially blacks, never received recognition outside their campus newspaper. Many Americans know that Jackie Robinson broke major league baseball's racial barrier in 1947. Few realize, however, that Robinson earlier appeared in college football games at the University of California, Los Angeles, and played in front of biracial crowds that exceeded 100,000—twice as many spectators as in contemporary baseball stadiums.[56] In addition, Robinson's collegiate games drew large support from African Americans in Los Angeles, a community that otherwise had little to do with UCLA.

Black college football players helped their schools make headlines throughout the twentieth century, especially after World War II. A few were well known around the country, but most were not. Some spoke out against racism—from the team, on campus, or in the broader community. Many were praised in the black press as symbols of positive change, while others were chastised for not adequately representing their community. Yet, when it comes to athletes as popular racial spokesmen, scholars still insist "there was no Jackie Robinson" in collegiate football.[57] Perhaps that is true, but nevertheless a number of intriguing case studies exemplify how public reaction to intercollegiate integration affected the discourse of race.

As a unique form of cultural expression, football offers rich historical insight. Although football has a fictional component—like the novel or a movie—as a presentation offered to a consuming audience and designed with prescribed messages or meanings, a sporting event is no movie, and its participants transcend more than mere characters. At the same time a quite human, uncertain aspect of sport separates it from other forms of entertainment. This opportunity for impromptu, or even unintended, individual expression distinguishes sport from movies, books, or plays.

The following chapters are framed around four specific case studies of African American football players at predominately white institutions: UCLA (1938–1941), Drake University (1948–1952), Georgia Tech University (1954–1956), and the University of Wyoming (1967–1970). Although examples are numerous, the interaction of black athletes with these particular schools and their surrounding communities sparked the most significant, national dialogues over integration in college football—for very different reasons. UCLA threatened the "gentlemen's agreement" because a group of African American players, not just one student, drove its success in the late 1930s; this was the first major football team to rely on such extensive participation by black athletes. Oklahoma A&M College drew national criticism in 1951 after its football players assaulted Drake University's black running back on the field during a game in Stillwater, Oklahoma. At Georgia Tech University, the controversy centered on Georgia Governor Marvin Griffin's attempt to ban the team from participating in the integrated 1956 Sugar Bowl, which prompted white students around the state (and nationwide) to protest. And at the rural, isolated campus of the University of Wyoming, black footballers in 1969 drew national attention by fueling the largest collective protest by African American athletes in collegiate history.

Often, the discourse surrounding such events circulated via the coverage of influential sportswriters, including some African Americans. According to Michael Oriard, an expert on the game's history and a former professional player, the unique historical role of the sportswriter provides scholars an advantage when pouring over countless sports pages from around the country: "The sports journalism that has always accompanied organized sport virtually from the beginning, offers, not direct access to the minds and hearts of its readers, but at least closer access to them than is usually possible."[58] Nevertheless, these four examples are also important because they reveal how reaction to black athletes elicited response from outside the realm of sport and entertainment, particularly from those not traditionally associated with sport. Although the focus is on football, they offer a surprisingly diverse range of voices: from housewives and professors to politicians and state supreme court justices. In essence, these case studies illuminate how black participation enabled the game to both transcend the discourse of sport journalism and generate front-page headlines and editorials that used collegiate athletics to make significant statements about race in America.

Thus, the stories that follow are drawn from not only historical sports pages but also university archives (including administrative and athletic department files, student publications, and oral histories), author interviews, judicial archives, and individual correspondences. Using these examples, the history of college football reveals complex undercurrents regarding America's commitment to racial equality in the twentieth century—a dramatic departure from the traditional image of popular individual athletes who broke down specific barriers of racism at the professional level. An examination of the diverse public reactions to integrated football reveals how African Americans, sportswriters, institutions, peers, coaches, alumni, fans, and television audiences all symbolically appropriated these players in vastly different ways by attempting to comprehend the geopolitics of college athletics (and amateur student athletes) within the traditional binary frameworks of "race figures," "color lines," and Jim Crow segregation.

Integrated Football at UCLA, 1938–1941

Jackie Robinson's team is a logical place to start. From 1938 to 1941, a group of black students made UCLA's football squad the most racially integrated college team Americans had ever seen. Five black students played for the Bruins, and their collective impact led to disparate reactions on the campus itself, among mainstream media outlets and African American sportswriters, and within the Jim Crow South. UCLA's on-field success garnered high national rankings and publicity, while their popularity with black fans made them the most celebrated team in the African American community.[59]

Critics and fans both struggled to fit the Bruin team within the prevailing "race hero" framework popularized by athletes like Joe Louis and Jack Johnson. UCLA's success came at the height of Louis's prime, and many blacks were hesitant about having young college footballers act as spokesmen for the broader community. In addition, before 1940 integrated teams honored the "gentlemen's agreement"—that is, black players sat out when playing segregated opponents. The Bruin's "black team" forced college football to rethink this method, which had previously allowed segregated teams to play integrated schools throughout the country, especially in the South. Juxtaposed with the rise of Joe Louis in the late 1930s, the story of the Bruins helps delineate the broader context of integration directly before World War II. Some Americans had already begun comparing racial politics at home with perceived injustice abroad, and many blacks considered the war an opportunity for a "double victory" over totalitarian aggression in foreign lands and racism in American society. For the black community, the strategy helped solidify Joe Louis's popularity, yet it also created a milieu of criticism and tension surrounding the expectations placed on black college athletes. By the 1940s, black sportswriters began to realize that student athletes who were integrating important football programs would have to face the same scrutiny as professionals like Louis. Indeed, the trials of individual black football players sometimes met with outright criticism from the black press.

The Johnny Bright Scandal, 1951

After World War II, another example of integration in college football made headlines beyond the nation's sports pages. In 1951, Oklahoma A&M College sought membership in the Big Seven Conference, one of the most prominent and successful conferences in college football. Students and administrators at several Big Seven schools, including the University of Kansas and the University of Nebraska, resisted because of A&M's segregationist policies. The war had severely disrupted America's social fabric, and in certain regions of the country African Americans had taken advantage to advance the cause of civil rights. Jackie Robinson's integration of the Dodgers in 1947 exemplified the transformations beginning to take place in the urban North. Yet the South remained largely immune to these changes, and many southern states used the war to reinforce racial dominance. In cities like Birmingham and Atlanta, segregated public facilities and intensified efforts to maintain racial hierarchies in the midst of heightened criticism from the North greeted black troops returning from abroad. While programs like the University of Alabama and the University of Georgia tightened the bonds of segregation and continued to field all-white football teams, virtually every northern institution had some experience with black student athletes by the mid-1950s. Teams were usually able to stay in their respective regions and refuse to play opponents from across the country, but conferences like the Big Seven and the Missouri Valley Conference (MVC) were hotspots for disagreements over integration. Since the Civil War era in "Bleeding Kansas," the Midwest and Upper South had acted as battlegrounds in the partisan war to define race in America. As the popularity of football progressed in the 1950s, these regions became more influential to the game; schools from Kansas, Oklahoma, and Nebraska began to draw as much attention as powerhouse teams in the Deep South.[60]

Oklahoma A&M's decision to build a major athletic program backfired in 1951, when a nationwide scandal erupted over a split-second play on the football field. Johnny Bright, a star African American halfback at Drake University and arguably the nation's best player, was severely injured on the first play of the game when an A&M opponent viciously attacked him. With a shattered jaw and multiple facial injuries, Bright's college career ended with this wanton act of violence. Administrators at Drake and other schools around the country called on the Missouri Valley Conference to punish A&M and its coaches for encouraging the deliberate injury of its star player. Immediately the issue of race was embedded in the controversy. In the national press players, coaches, and fans accused Oklahoma A&M of deliberately trying to intimidate black athletes in the MVC, and perhaps the larger Big Seven. Drake threatened to leave the conference if sanctions were not imposed on A&M, and students at schools throughout the Midwest debated the role of race in the attack. In the black press, anger that had circulated over the refusal to recognize Bright's accomplishments now turned to outrage over the failure to punish what many concluded was a deliberate act of violence, thinly veiled under the auspices of the game. Eventually, both Drake and Bradley universities severed ties with A&M and the Missouri Valley Conference, and Bright left the country to play in the Canadian Football League.

The debate over the physicality of football—which had circulated in the sport since Theodore Roosevelt and Congress first acted to limit its brutality—now tangled with the debate over racial integration. As the mainstream press ran pictures of the attack on Johnny Bright, some fans in Oklahoma invoked race immediately, yet others refused to acknowledge the role of racial tension. While the Bright attack may have fallen in line with certain rules and racial policies prevalent in the South, it was a blatant affront to the rules of the game. The diversity of responses to the incident illuminates how many football fans in the Midwest and around the country transformed their views of race through the lens of a college game, instead of in response to the carefully groomed persona of professional athletes like Joe Louis or Jackie Robinson.

The Sugar Bowl Controversy, 1956

In 1954, the issue of integrating America's public schools finally reached the Supreme Court. While the landmark *Brown* decision codified integrated education in American law, it also sparked a legislative backlash in a number of southern states. In the world of college football, integration had moved beyond the period of uncertainty characterized by the reaction to black players at UCLA. Joe Louis had ended his career as perhaps the biggest star in the sporting world (white or black) while Jackie Robinson had emerged a national hero seven years earlier. On the gridiron, the National Football League and most northern schools had already opened their athletic facilities to blacks.[61] However, at Georgia Tech University, the school's desire to reap the benefits of national success in football—television dollars, recognition, and so on—clashed with the state legislature's reaction to *Brown* and the specter of forced integration. The issue came to a head in 1955, when a successful Tech football team was invited to New Orleans to participate in the prestigious Sugar Bowl. Football fans, including Georgia Governor Marvin Griffin, were ecstatic until it became apparent that Tech would face the University of Pittsburgh, a team "integrated" with one African American player. The governor and state legislature held eleventh-hour negotiations and forbade the team from playing, whereupon thousands of white students on the

Georgia Tech campus burned the governor in effigy and protested the potential forfeiture.

For such a passionate controversy to explode over the participation of a lone black player in the 1956 Sugar Bowl reveals how strict segregationist ideology still permeated certain regions of the country. It also enriches our understanding of the legislative backlash to *Brown* and the way that reaction trickled into the realm of popular culture in the South. At the same time, the reaction of Tech's administrators and student body shows how the greater rewards awaiting successful college football programs could generate a willingness to fight segregation in exchange for winning football teams. The stark reaction of some Tech football fans is a striking juxtaposition to the 1962 riot over James Meredith's admission to the University of Mississippi. While southern schools largely enjoyed the support of white citizens and students, the importance of participating in a prestigious bowl game seemed to trump, if only briefly, the clear code of segregation at Georgia Tech, seven years before the violence in Oxford, Mississippi.[62]

The "Black 14," 1969

Other examples of integration in college football reveal insights into the heightened period of radicalism emerging out of the civil rights movement in the mid-1960s. While riots, marches, and public confrontations over race merged with growing disillusionment over American foreign policy, college campuses became seedbeds for the black power movement and increasingly militant black nationalist organizations. Many Americans bore witness to this period of heightened black protest through the lens of athletics, most notably the Black Panther protest at the 1968 Olympics.[63] At San Jose State University, radical sociologist Harry Edwards specifically encouraged black collegiate athletes to use their platform in the popular press for the purpose of protest.[64] In the world of football, however, the concept of protest was virtually nonexistent and vehemently punished. With the exception of the occasional lengthy beard or "Afro" haircut worn in defiance of team rules, most major football programs in the late 1960s successfully clamped down on athletes' self-expression.

This makes the controversy over the University of Wyoming's "Black 14" even more intriguing. By 1969, most major college teams (with the exception of a few holdouts, like the University of Mississippi) had integrated their football programs. Indeed, college football was quickly becoming a sport that predominantly featured black players. On the University of Wyoming campus in Laramie, the racial makeup of the football squad paralleled most teams across the country, but the fourteen African American players were nearly the only black students enrolled in the entire school. Like historian Beth Bailey's discussion of the role of "revolution" in transforming rural campuses during this period, the "protest" conceived by the fourteen students seems anything but

revolutionary when juxtaposed with the concept of black radicalism that domi-
nates popular memory and scholarly histories.[65] The black players sought to
wear armbands during a game against Brigham Young University, a rather conservative protest against the Mormon Church's policy of excluding blacks from
the priesthood. Yet the reaction of the coach and Wyoming administrators—to
expel the athletes from the team arbitrarily, without recourse to appeal—reveals
just how large the specter of black protest loomed in Wyoming.[66]

As national media outlets converged on Laramie to cover the story and its
conclusion, counterprotests in support of the head coach and governor continued to increase the tension. The players were accused of organizing at the
request of a new Black Student Alliance (BSA) chapter on campus, and local
papers propagated the myth that caravans of Black Panthers and other protesters were on the way from California to protest at upcoming games. Last-minute
meetings between state lawmakers, the players, head coach, and governor failed
to reach a conclusion. As the black athletes were forced to watch their team
from the grandstands for the remainder of the season, National Guard troops
were stationed below the stands and the town largely rallied in support of the
coach's decision.

This story of football protest in the heartland is valuable in helping understand the evolution of resistance to civil rights and the perception of "black
radicalism" in rural America. Such a mild protest on the part of the athletes,
juxtaposed with the reaction of fans and Wyoming administrators, illuminates
how racial integration on a college team could still reinforce many barriers it
sought to dissolve. As the racial majority on the school's nationally ranked football squad, Wyoming's black students helped generate the school's successful
image and achieve financial success. Yet in the same year that Laramie was voting to expand the football stadium so it could fit nearly 80 percent of the town's
inhabitants, residents were not willing to accept even a hint of militancy on
behalf of racial equity. Local fans and media overwhelmingly supported the decision to expel the students, even as the once unbeaten football team was soon
decimated.[67]

Beyond Jackie Robinson

While popular history yields no lone integrating moment or figure in college
football, it is nevertheless true that African American students led the country's
most popular teams by 1980—in every region. Thus, the story of integrated football represents a logical point of departure from the older scholarship of individual professional heroes. In some cases, these same student athletes emerged
from the amateur ranks of college athletics and joined the pantheon of figures
credited with breaking racial barriers at the professional level. More often, however, they retreated from the limelight altogether. During the course of eighty

years, this group of largely unknown, underappreciated student athletes used college football to both change the racial landscape at America's universities and reconfigure the role of African Americans in the public sphere. Such pressure fell on the shoulders of young black college students, who struggled to keep up with their coursework and fit into campus social life; they were not professional athletes, properly groomed race heroes, or eloquent cultural critics. While the story of Jackie Robinson's first season as a Dodger or Joe Louis's triumphant knockouts appeal to a particular historicization—namely, our desire to create stark racial barriers in order to see them broken down—history yields a more complex story. The integration of college football was a movement of peoples and ideas that better exemplifies the true struggle behind the story of African American civil rights in the twentieth century.

2

"On the Threshold of Broad and Rich Football Pastures"

Integrated College Football at UCLA, 1938–1941

> . . . California of the south
> Accept this pledge of faith to thee!
>
> –Alma Mater, University of California, Los Angeles[1]

> We have yet to find another single coach in the history of football that has had the guts to play three of our race at one time and have five on the squad . . . even against southern teams.
>
> –Fay Young, *Chicago Defender*, 16 December 1939

On the morning of 9 December 1939, the UCLA football team prepared for the most important game of the year. That day's contest versus crosstown rival USC marked the end of a tumultuous regular season, the pinnacle college football match-up of 1939, and a game that drew more than 100,000 spectators to the Los Angeles Memorial Coliseum (at that point the largest audience ever to watch a football game). Yet some who felt the excitement, anticipation, and fear did so for very different, more important reasons. Five African American student athletes stood among the sixty UCLA Bruins warming up on the field. For these five, the exhausting 1939 season represented a turning point in collegiate racial integration, and the significance of the impending contest with USC weighed heavily on the shoulders of the black Bruins.

From 1938 to 1941, the UCLA football team served as an important exception to the "gentlemen's agreement"—the standard, unwritten rule that allowed coaches to bench black athletes during intercollegiate contests with segregated colleges and universities. Three UCLA players—Kenneth Washington, Woodrow Strode, and Jackie Robinson—held prominent starting positions; each played on both offense and defense. Washington, who graduated in 1940, was the most celebrated college football player on the West Coast, and many consider him the

28

best football player in UCLA's history. A Los Angeles native, Washington played tailback for the Bruins from 1937 to 1939 and rushed for 1,914 yards. In 1939, he led the team to its best season ever and a top-ten national ranking. Jackie Robinson, a transfer student in 1939 from Pasadena City College, played two seasons at UCLA and excelled in four sports: football, basketball, baseball, and track. Although he left in 1941 without graduating, Robinson's short career at UCLA is perhaps the most impressive in collegiate athletic history. Woody Strode was a powerful starting end for the Bruin squad and also earned considerable success throwing the shot put.[2]

Washington, Robinson, and Strode—often nicknamed the "Sepia Trio" by the Los Angeles media—formed the core of the team. Washington and Strode also went on to become the first African Americans to reintegrate the National Football League (NFL) in 1946, while Robinson's first season as a Brooklyn Dodger has joined the Montgomery bus boycott, *Brown v. Board of Education*, and the March on Washington as seminal events in the history of American civil rights. Although not a consistent starter, African American end Ray Bartlett also made significant contributions to the UCLA squad, while black teammate Johnny Wynne played sparingly as a lineman. These athletes garnered support not so much as individual race heroes (as Robinson did in 1947) but rather as a "black team," a group of young men who endured derogatory references, taunts, and police brutality. The Bruins reached the height of their success during the 1939 season, when all five African American teammates helped lead the squad to an unbeaten 6–0–3 record and a final game versus USC, with the winner going to the Rose Bowl in Pasadena, California, to face the University of Tennessee.

"Sideline-Stepping Sepias"

Although UCLA was not the first major college team to allow African American participants, it was the first to feature a group of black players in starting positions. Notable black players excelled during the Great Depression. For example, at the University of Iowa, Ozzie Simmons (nicknamed the "Ebony Eel") was an All-American in 1934 and 1935. Former Iowa radio sportscaster (and future president) Ronald Reagan recalled how other teams targeted Simmons because of his race: "The problems were when you played another team that did not have a black. For some reason or another, then they would pick on this one man."[3] Rarely was a prominent team with a national following even willing to accept a lone black player. The 1930s most celebrated squads were fielded by segregated institutions in the South, including the University of Tennessee, the University of Alabama, and Duke University. Yet even prominent northern teams, such as Notre Dame, remained all white. On the west coast, the University of Southern California boasted the most successful football program, a team that had not featured a black player since the 1920s. Woody Strode recalled that USC

Jackie Robinson. Courtesy Associated Students, UCLA.

was a "machine." Along with Notre Dame, the school consistently fielded the country's best teams. "But USC and Notre Dame didn't give the black athletes a chance to play," Strode wrote.[4] Actually, during the 1920s two African American students, including All-American Brice Taylor, had joined the Trojan squad. It was rumored that a "scandal involving a white woman" had led to hardening Coach Howard Jones's prejudice and the end of black football at USC.[5] Strode and his teammates thus chose to attend a smaller school, one with a burgeoning new campus (about five buildings) west of its prominent commuter campus in downtown Los Angeles. "I ended up at UCLA," he wrote, ". . . which I barely knew existed." By 1936, the school was "looking to compete in athletics on a national level" and willing to give African American athletes its full support.[6] Within four years, the Bruins' black athletes were not only national contenders on the field but also central figures in a public dialogue about the role of race in American sport and society.

The players enjoyed widespread acceptance on campus. According to one student sportswriter, most of the UCLA student body agreed that the Bruin football team and its black athletes "oozed class from the moment they trotted on the greensward."[7] Student publications—most notably the *Daily Bruin*—celebrated the success of Kenny Washington and helped make him one of the most popular students on campus. After his final game versus USC in 1939, Washington received an extended standing ovation from his fellow students. The 1938 Bruin yearbook hailed him as "our hero," while student sportswriters concurred with opposing coaches that he was the best athlete in UCLA's history; his abilities surpassed even the mythical talent of Red Grange.[8] When Jackie Robinson joined the club in 1939, the only debate among student sportswriters was whether Robinson and Washington would be awarded the All-American honors they deserved.[9]

The 1939 squad opened with a difficult game against Texas Christian University, the highest-ranked team in the country the previous year. As heavy underdogs, the Bruins shocked the all-white Horned Frogs 6–2 at Memorial Coliseum. The following week, Robinson helped spark his new team in a 14–7 upset over the University of Washington in Seattle. "Our Bruins have just finished astounding the football world for the second week in a row," exclaimed one student sportswriter who traveled with the team.[10] Under first-year Coach Edwin "Babe" Horrell, the squad dubbed "black America's football team" started the 1939 season in surprising fashion by overcoming two difficult opponents. Yet the Bruin footballers garnered the support of UCLA's student body in both success and defeat. Student publications reported with pride when Washington or Robinson appeared in national publications or on the radio, a rarity for black athletes, especially collegians.[11] In addition, students cheered the team en masse at the Memorial Coliseum and gathered to watch film footage from road games.[12]

The success of the 1939 Bruins and their promotion as a "black team" came during a period in which American society was wrought with mixed messages about the role of black citizens. Many African Americans had reshaped the political landscape by abandoning the Republican Party over the previous decade. However, President Franklin Roosevelt proved willing to bypass civil rights to solidify the New Deal's tenuous alliance. The courting of southern democrats was pivotal for Roosevelt, who agreed to segregate the Civilian Conservation Corps (CCC) and Works Progress Administration (WPA) at the urging of southern governors. While the need to mobilize a wartime economy spurred Roosevelt in 1941 to issue Executive Order 8802—prohibiting the federal government from discriminatory hiring practices and creating the Fair Employment Practices Committee (FEPC)—throughout the 1930s he refused to support antilynching legislation urged by Walter White and the NAACP. Coupled with the power of southern Democrats, Roosevelt's sporadic support of civil rights contrasted with the institutionalized white supremacy still championed by many in his own party. Dominated by Jim Crow segregation, white citizens in the South boasted that theirs was the only region to have "clarity" on the issue. Meanwhile, a growing number of blacks were attracted to the Communist Party (CP), which launched an aggressive campaign aimed at solidifying the African American vote. Through the International Labor Defense (ILD), the party's representation of nine Alabama blacks accused of rape in 1932 became an international incident for the remaining decade and sparked continued fear from whites that blacks would seek to reshape American society through radical means.[13]

Such confusion frequently trickled into the realm of popular culture. The growing acceptance of Joe Louis and Jesse Owens as antifascist heroes seemed to belie the reality of prejudice in the late 1930s, especially in the South, where both Louis and Owens earned widespread praise. At the local level, cultural practices simply reinforced regional variation. With the exception of sporadic examples—like a protest of the nationally broadcast *Amos 'n' Andy* program led by the *Pittsburgh Courier* in 1931—local radio generally reflected regional culture and social practice. As major universities sought to establish national recognition in athletics, intersectional sporting contests became an important means by which schools and teams earned rankings, reputations, and popularity.

The rise of the "bowl game" came to epitomize this process of nationalizing college football. Before 1930, the only annual bowl game was the Rose Bowl, but by 1940 there were five such season-ending contests. Along with the growing number of bowls came renewed interest in a stable national ranking system to distinguish between teams from a variety of conferences and regions. Meanwhile, in the 1930s the future Ivy League schools—including Harvard, Yale, and Princeton, where modern football was invented—continued to deemphasize student sports. Nevertheless, administrators and fans at many schools outside the Northeast began to hail the arrival of major college athletics, funding everything from larger stadiums to crosscountry transportation for teams to play against distant opponents. Even before the age of television, by 1939 an invitation to play in any of the five bowls guaranteed the institutions significant income, press coverage, and prestige.[14]

Historians emphasize the 1930s as a period in which Americans sought to renew and preserve local cultures. This included the preservation of folk music and rural literary tradition—such as the formation of the Federal Writers' Project (FWP), the government program designed to catalog folktales, music, and imagery. Although much historiography makes reference to the 1950s, especially the postwar advent of television, as the watershed decade in which popular culture was increasingly nationalized, intersectional play and the establishment of college football as a national pastime were pivotal transitions that preceded World War II. Such development was rife with the prospect of social conflict. Instead of reinforcing local cultural values and homogeneity, the sport grew instead to address the vast discrepancies between institutes of higher education in different regions of the country.

"We Thought We Were White"

Some UCLA students were vigilant about how their school's black athletes would be received in other regions of the country, and many also recognized the simmering tensions over domestic civil rights and the impending international conflict with fascism. In 1935, just four years earlier, A. Philip Randolph and the Brotherhood of Sleeping Car Porters emerged as the most prominent African American union in the country, and opponents specifically linked civil rights agitation to accusations of radical politics. In Los Angeles, the entertainment industry was increasingly tied to communism on a platform designed to confront European fascism. According to Michael Denning, this forging of a cultural component to the political "popular front" allowed for a greater visibility of communism in mainstream progressive circles. Los Angeles was the center of this "cultural front," and Woody Strode recalled how the city's Communist Party routinely courted UCLA's black footballers—just as it did movie stars, professional athletes, and entertainers. The CP invited the black players to "mixed dances . . . with white girls," yet Strode and his teammates were fearful of the repercussions, not only in the national press but also from Los Angelinos.[15] By the late 1930s, UCLA's most famous African American alumnus, Ralph Bunche, emerged as a prominent spokesman on race, civil rights, and black education. Bunche's national success after graduating in 1927 signaled the extent to which the city's black community was central to the national dialogue surrounding race. Like many western cities and institutions, UCLA prided its reputation as a relatively progressive school that stood as a beacon of civil rights in a divided nation.[16]

Poised within this context, student sportswriters at UCLA who recognized the broader significance of their team's African American players were the first to decry any prejudice toward the Bruins. Although the *Daily Bruin* sports department did not appear to have any black students on staff, its editor and columnists were among the more progressive students on campus, especially when it came to issues of racial prejudice. When many writers around the country left Washington off their All-American lists, *Daily Bruin* columnist Milt Cohen responded with a plea to "pick again, boys" and correct the slight against UCLA. "It's with a distinct sour taste in our mouth that we read the lists of All-American selections that are now pouring out of all sections of the country," wrote Cohen. "We don't care what they do with any other ball player in the nation—but we don't like the way they're treating our Kenny Washington."[17] In an even greater slight, Robinson was later left off the first team of the All-Division basketball selections in 1941 despite the fact he had led the conference in scoring. Bruin sportswriters pinned the act on the prejudice of UC-Berkeley Coach Clarence "Nibs" Price, who neglected to list Robinson on any team. "This obviously prejudiced attitude of Price led to the placing of the entire Stanford team in the honored positions, moving Robinson down to the second team," lamented one student. "This in itself is no cause for protest, but the fact that Price didn't even mention Jack on three teams strikes a new low in sportsmanship."[18]

Such student support for UCLA's black athletes helped reinforce the institution's reputation as a racially open campus. "Whatever racial pressure was coming down in the City of Los Angeles, the pressure was not on me in Westwood," wrote Strode. "We had the whole melting pot . . . and I worked hard because there was always the overriding feeling that UCLA really wanted me."[19] The Associated Students of UCLA (ASUCLA), precursor to the athletic department, routinely offered players financial loans. Years later, Strode told *Ebony* magazine that he received $100 per month, "plus $20 a week under the table."[20]

Yet the greatest example of institutional support came in the wake of Jackie Robinson's arrest in October 1938. While cruising with teammate Ray Bartlett after a softball game in Brookside Park, Robinson became involved in an altercation after a white motorist "said something about niggers" at an intersection.[21] Bartlett initially confronted the man, and soon police arrived to find "between 40 and 50 members of the Negro race," all of whom quickly dispersed with the exception of Robinson.[22] Charged with hindering traffic and resisting arrest, Robinson immediately received quick help from powerful Bruin loyalists and Head Coach Babe Horrell. The university refunded Robinson his court costs and fines, hired a "prominent sports attorney," and requested to the judge that "the Negro football player be not disturbed during the football season."[23]

While reaction to Robinson's arrest exemplified UCLA's commitment to an integrated campus and support for African American athletes, it also revealed the nebulous status of its black students, one that called into question whether racial acceptance depended on a certain level of athletic achievement. White teammate Don McPherson recalled that "sometimes Jackie had a little bit of a chip on his shoulder."[24] Robinson ultimately never felt accepted at UCLA, although he wrote a series of personal letters upon his graduation that expressed some positive sentiments: "It really is something to know you have friends like the ones I made while attending UCLA."[25] Nevertheless, Robinson was absent from his senior football banquet, left the university without graduating, and wrote back mainly to request help in obtaining employment.[26] Despite such institutional support, the players were also among the few African American students at the institution, a school that drew its student body from around the country. Even as most on campus seemed to embrace the team, Strode recalled that his first introduction to the "Southern mentality" occurred while on the freshman squad in 1936. He and Washington heard of "some players on the varsity saying they don't want to play with any niggers."[27] After one particularly brutal confrontation on the scrimmage field, a lineman nicknamed "Slats"—a "blond-haired, blue-eyed farm boy from Oklahoma"—called Strode a "black son of a bitch." Recalled Strode, "The bulldog came out of me. I climbed on top of Slats and started punching. The coaches stood around and watched for a little while. Finally they said, 'That's enough, Woody!' and they came and pulled me off."[28]

Even as the black Bruins enjoyed the support of the student body and a progressive institution, they functioned within a community that was still struggling with issues of racial prejudice. Tom Bradley, president of the University Negro Club and future mayor of Los Angeles, joined the University Religious Conference in addressing issues of discrimination on campus.[29] "We had no minorities in our fraternity at that time," recalled William Forbes, a prominent white undergraduate. "I think the main reason would be that there were not that many minorities in Los Angeles at that time."[30] Yet by 1940 there were already 63,744 African Americans in the city, many of whom came to Bruin football games to cheer on the black athletes.[31] The few minority students on campus were expected to steer away from social events, and the African American footballers recognized the unwritten boundaries that existed. Even as the ASUCLA Board of Control lavished praise on the football team and took pride in arranging games with segregated schools, it still found itself at the center of racial controversy involving other minority groups. Japanese American students often complained of being excluded from the ASUCLA. In 1941, the Board, toughening its stance against a student organization called the Japanese American Committee, denied the group use of campus facilities. Blacks embraced Franklin Roosevelt and the prospect of increased socioeconomic opportunity in war, yet the reality of Japanese internment served as a reminder that civil rights would not come easily—even in the North and West.[32]

Student support for the Bruin team also betrayed the hidden structures that permeated racial prejudice throughout the period. When lauding the African American athletes, sportswriters usually praised the black players with racially tinged terminology that emphasized the difference between them and their peers. Along with nicknames like "Kingfish Kenny" and "Jackrabbit Jackie," students routinely invoked allusions like "sideline-stepping sepia" and "dusky flash."[33] The 1941 yearbook featured Kenny Washington in a section entitled "Outstanding Men," placing his face alongside prominent white students like Bob Park, the sweater-toting head of the Rally Committee and "A Man's Man." Yet the publication described Washington as "a boy"—albeit one with "ability, personality, and gameness."[34] Such terminology was hardly unique to the *Daily Bruin*, as many of the most progressive sportswriters and publications nationwide continued characterizing black athletes with racial nicknames and descriptions. Biased language was not reserved for African Americans either, as any contest involving the Stanford Indians inevitably found someone getting "scalped" or "massacred."[35] Perhaps the biggest slight came from the black players' own teammates: mysteriously, Robinson, Washington, and Strode were never named as team captains, a distinction voted on by the entire squad.

Despite these shortcomings, African American players at UCLA enjoyed an unprecedented college experience that was simply unavailable at other white universities. "We were out there knocking down people like we thought we were white," wrote Strode.[36] And in 1939, the Bruins knocked down opponents as well as any team in the country. After its impressive 2–0 start, the squad continued its unexpected success, forging a 14–14 tie with Stanford before rattling off three straight wins over the University of Montana, the University of Oregon, and the University of California, Berkeley. With an unbeaten record of 5–0–1, the Bruins were ranked nineteenth nationally and serious contenders for their first Pacific Coast Conference championship. In addition, the team began to draw attention from America's prominent sportswriters.

"Suppose UCLA Wins"

While the Bruins enjoyed the support of UCLA's 9,600 students, they also became a hot topic of discussion throughout southern California, as local sportswriters welcomed the addition of a second powerful team to the Southland. "Football is the great equalizer," wrote Paul Zimmerman of the *Los Angeles Times*. "You have to throw racial prejudice out the window when a couple of gentlemen like Jackie Robinson and Kenny Washington do the things they do."[37] The annual crosstown meeting with powerhouse USC was shaping up to be a classic, while the most coveted football game—the Rose Bowl—awaited the PCC champion. "The Bruins are capable of giving any team in the United States up to and including Tennessee a very busy afternoon," exclaimed Charles Paddock in the *Pasadena Star-News*.[38] Unbeaten, untied, and unscored-upon in two years, the University of Tennessee's football squad was the most dominant team in the country, which most likely meant a trip to Pasadena if the Volunteers defeated Auburn University in their final regular-season game.

Meanwhile, the city of Los Angeles continued to laud the resurgent Bruins and the "presence of the Chocolate Bombers."[39] Like UCLA's student writers, Los Angeles sportswriters recognized the significance of the Bruin's black players and came to their defense on the national stage. When it was revealed that Kenny Washington was leading the nation in rushing yards, the *Los Angeles Times* proclaimed that Washington had "put to shame those All-America pickers who inexplicably failed to include the great Negro halfback on their 'must' list."[40] Paddock agreed, writing in the *Star-News*, "Anyone who picks an All-America team and leaves [Washington] off needs to have his head examined."[41]

While the local media in Los Angeles echoed the support of the Bruin students, it also grappled with the image of UCLA's African American players in light of the city's racial tension. The *Los Angeles Times* reported that Robinson was arrested in Brookside Park after he "assertedly resisted the officer's attempts to disperse a group of Negroes threatening a white man"; later the paper ran a report that the "negro grid star" failed to appear in court.[42] Los Angeles did not pretend to be the idyllic melting pot that UCLA's campus made claims to, nor were the surrounding Pasadena and Westwood communities free of racial animosity. While Paddock, Zimmerman, and other sportswriters crusaded for UCLA's black athletes on the national stage, Pasadena was locked in a legal battle with the NAACP over the integration of Brookside Park's public swimming pool.[43] And earlier in the year, the black community expressed outrage over an alleged beating of Robinson's younger brother Edgar by Pasadena police, an incident one black newspaper called "the latest instance of flagrant discrimination and brutal treatment of colored citizens in Pasadena."[44] Los Angeles sport fans were called to rally behind their "negro backfield aces" even as the city still grappled with issues of blatant discrimination.[45]

The Bruin football team also received marked attention throughout the nation. As a sophomore in 1937, Washington launched what was then considered the longest forward pass in the game's history, a sixty-two-yard heave against USC; the *New York Times* called it "the longest authentic completed touchdown aerials executed in college football."[46] Washington's epic pass represented an ongoing evolution in football tactics, especially a shift from running- to passing-oriented offenses. The transition created a further demand for black athletes from other sports, notably track and field.

As the 1939 season continued, the nation's sportswriters realized that the Bruin team was contending on the national stage. After starting 5–0–1, UCLA forged another tie against nonconference Santa Clara University. The following week, the Bruins were losing 13–7 against Oregon State University before Washington set off a thrilling last-second touchdown that tied the game. The Bruin's weakest link, their kicking game, failed to convert the winning point. Nevertheless, a sound victory over Washington State University the next week earned UCLA a ninth-placed ranking in the country with only one game remaining. As the team's record improved to 6–0–3, the *New York Times* announced that "the undefeated Uclans remain on the edge of the Rose Bowl picture."[47] UCLA was not only an exciting team for national fans to watch, but it also developed a penchant for big plays and last-second heroics. As one of only two unbeaten teams in the West, the Bruins had found an opportunity to play for the prestigious Rose Bowl against Coach Howard Jones and USC.

As UCLA continued their surprising season on the field, mainstream sportswriters began to foresee the potential for a troubling off-field confrontation regarding race. "If the Bruins should receive the Pacific Coast Conference invitation, the boys who invite the visiting team from another section might find themselves in a very embarrassing position," wrote Paddock in the *Pasadena*

Star-News, "for to date the outstanding eleven in the Nation is Tennessee."[48] The prospect of a match-up between the Bruins and the Volunteers on the game's most important stage, the Rose Bowl, meant that Tennessee's strict policies regarding segregation would be put to the test before a national audience. As Tennessee prepared to ensure its nomination by defeating Auburn, Allison Danzig of the *New York Times* traveled with the team and pondered such prospects. "There is an angle to the situation . . . that seems to have escaped general attention or which is being ignored," Danzig wrote, alluding to the fact that many sportswriters chose to turn a deaf ear to issues of race and segregation on the football field: "There is a possibility that Kenny Washington, Jack Robinson, Woodrow Strode, and associates will . . . win the Rose Bowl assignment from the Trojans. . . . The statement was made here definitely tonight by parties in a position to know that Tennessee will not play in the Rose Bowl if UCLA, with its three colored stars, is the host team."[49] In California, *Oakland Tribune* sports editor Art Cohn was among the most outspoken critics of racism in sport. He called the potential game "an embarrassing situation" for Tennessee but insisted that UCLA would refuse to sideline its star African American players. Nevertheless, "below the Mason and Dixon, men feel strongly," wrote Cohn. "In their blind devotion to a prejudice that makes a mockery of tolerance and justice, they gladly sacrifice everything . . . even $100,000 gravy-bowl games."[50]

The prospect of an integrated Rose Bowl forced sportswriters to grapple with the standard methods by which intercollegiate athletics had dealt with regional prejudice and Jim Crow. Some, such as Bob Foote of the *Pasadena Star-News*, felt that a Rose Bowl involving UCLA's black athletes would pose no threat to the convoluted system meant to pacify schools from around the country. "There is at present a very satisfactory custom in effect between Northern and Southern schools which have conflicting ideas on who should play on college football teams," wrote Foote. "It is just 'When in Rome do as the Romans do.'"[51] While Foote proclaimed that the so-called "gentlemen's agreement" would convince Tennessee officials to allow their team to face black athletes for a game in southern California, other sportswriters, including Allison Danzig, were less sure.[52] Danzig wrote from Knoxville that Duke University or Clemson University would be less likely to "raise the Negro question" if they were to face UCLA; Danzig contended that Tennessee officials found themselves in a tight spot because of a pending lawsuit against the state that threatened to force the university to "admit a number of Negro applicants for matriculation."[53] Curiously, no one questioned how Tennessee residents and the school's rabid fans would react if administrators barred UT's football team from playing in the nation's most prestigious game. Danzig, Foote, and others assumed that southern citizens would accept whatever decision Coach Bob "Major" Neyland and school officials came to, even if the symbolic gesture in support of Jim Crow threatened to ruin the Volunteer's football season.

Only with the looming implications of the USC-UCLA showdown did the mainstream press begin to realize the significance of the Bruins as a "black team." Simply placing its African American players on the bench to avoid controversy was out of the question, for a black student touched the ball on nearly every play UCLA ran. "Coach Babe Horrell most of the time has had a 4-man instead of an 11-man team," Paddock wrote in the *Star-News*, and those four players were each African American.[54] As the USC-UCLA game inched its way closer, Paddock asserted that it was "very doubtful if the authorities at Tennessee would allow the team to play against UCLA . . . unless it was definitely understood that the opponent in question would only use white players."[55] African American fans had long recognized that such a proposition was out of the question when it came to UCLA. Only now, as the Bruins reached the height of their national prominence, did the mainstream media begin to realize what black sportswriters and the African American community had long found so appealing: UCLA was a black team. "Take away the Negro stars from the UCLA team," wrote Paddock, "and you would not have a team."[56]

"We Will Do the Rest"

African American sportswriters had varying reactions to integrated college football and its meanings for the advancement of basic civil rights. In Los Angeles, black newspapers were the first to foresee the importance of football integration at UCLA beyond the region. In particular, J. Cullen Fentress of the *California Eagle* emphasized coverage of black collegians, clearly supporting the Bruins throughout the period. During the 1939 Rose Bowl campaign, Fentress wrote, "If they [UCLA] do get into the Rose Bowl, it will be one of the best things that ever happened to Pacific Coast Conference Football. And that goes for the Nation as well for we have long had the opinion that sports . . . is the most logical medium through which to affect world peace and all it implies."[57] In light of the perceived threat from global fascism that penetrated newspapers throughout the period, many African American sportswriters juxtaposed the plight of black athletes with the supposed American political ideals of democracy and equality. Fentress was no different. He exclaimed that "if for no other reason, we should like to see UCLA . . . get the Bowl bid, and prove to this nation that its peoples can play together in the most approved manner as sportsmen, upholding as they do so the democratic principles as outlined by the signers of the Declaration of Independence."[58]

By 1939, such assertions were helpful in garnering support for Joe Louis and America's black Olympians. Citizens were forced to make symbolic decisions when Louis faced the German Max Schmeling or the Italian Primo Carnera and likewise when Jesse Owens raced under the eye of Hitler at the Berlin Olympics in 1936. However, even as collegiate football was a uniquely American spectacle,

African American sportswriters found it more difficult appealing to patriotic sentiment for black students integrating mainstream teams. Nevertheless, according to the *Eagle* the African American collegian found himself "on the threshold of broad and rich football pastures," and the newspaper's sports pages overflowed with the anticipation and optimism brought by UCLA's black athletes, "the largest number ever to play on a major university team."[59]

Unlike the *Eagle*, other African American newspapers did not have the benefit of a "black team" close to home. Prominent black newspapers like the *Chicago Defender* and the *New York Amsterdam News* focused their attention primarily on recognizing the lone individuals who had managed to infiltrate teams in the North. The *Amsterdam News* lauded the "astounding" thirty-eight African American football players who were listed on northern line-ups in 1939.[60] With a sense of optimism, sportswriters celebrated when Northwestern University's black reserve Jimmy Smith quietly entered a home game against the University of Oklahoma and was promptly booed by the visiting Sooner contingency. Charles Thomas at Boston University and Charlie Anderson at Ohio State University also received attention for their roles on predominately all-white teams. However, while other black athletes had infiltrated white squads, they routinely succumbed to the "gentlemen's agreement," the policy barring them from participating in games against southern Jim Crow teams. As members of large and powerful college squads, the few black students who played football felt pressure to remain on the sidelines rather than stir up controversy. "I didn't really mind not playing," recalled Lou Montgomery, a Boston College running back who was asked to sit out 1939 *home* games against the University of Florida and Auburn as well as the 1940 Cotton Bowl versus Clemson University and the 1941 Sugar Bowl versus the University of Tennessee. After the Florida game, Montgomery explained to the *Amsterdam News* that his coach was "in a difficult spot" and had decided that "it was best not to sacrifice his valuable player to the mercies of the Florida boys."[61] While the threat of violence kept Montgomery out of the South's largest bowl games—the Sugar Bowl took place in New Orleans, the Cotton Bowl in Dallas—the situation surrounding black participants in the Rose Bowl was murkier. No major intersectional bowl game, meant to decide the best teams in the country, could survive without the participation of southern teams.

Unlike the positive relationship between UCLA's athletes and the Los Angeles African American press, black college athletes elsewhere sometimes faced skeptics in the black community. "Do Colored Athletes Help Cause of Jim Crow at Big White Universities?" asked one *Amsterdam News* headline.[62] According to sportswriter Neil Dodson, the answer was clear. "White coaches have a subtle form of convincing colored players to stay on the bench," Dodson wrote. "Negro athletes, caught between their desire to play and the knowledge that they are being discriminated against, usually succumb to the first." Dodson went on to criticize "the average young athlete" who "brushes aside or refuses to

face the fact that accepting discrimination is putting it a step ahead, entrench-
ing it deeper." [63] Rather than fault the extreme power schools gave to coaches
and athletic administrators, including the permission to bench players because
of their race, some in the black community chose to unleash their frustration on
the young student-athletes themselves.

Considering the black press had its share of prominent race heroes to support, sportswriters in the 1930s and 1940s had difficulty in appropriating anonymous "average young athletes" as symbols for broader statements regarding
civil rights. Joe Louis was ubiquitous throughout both the white and black press,
a rehearsed spokesman for his race who had managed to construct a powerful
yet unassuming image and a celebrity who tended to pacify white anxieties.
Obviously, Louis was neither benched, nor did he ever have to share the spotlight with white teammates or participate within the structure of a team sport.
In contrast stood the image of black college football players, a picture that could
generate the very fear and anxiety that Louis sought to avoid. In the mind of Jim
Crow, African American football players presented a group of powerful and
unruly black men, instilling the same fears as the specter of grassroots political activism and black "mob rule" in the South. Therefore, the emergence of
UCLA in 1938 at once gave black sportswriters their wish while simultaneously
confronting them with serious questions about the hagiographic "Joe Louis"
approach to sports integration and the pursuit of civil rights. African American
sports editors thus recognized the significance of college athletes, especially
those at UCLA. "We have yet to find another single coach in the history of football that has had the guts to play three of our race at one time and have five on
the squad," wrote Fay Young in the *Chicago Defender*.[64]

While celebrating UCLA's remarkable success, the black press attempted to
alleviate these underlying tensions by cultivating a positive, unassuming team
image and emphasizing Kenny Washington as spokesman for the black athletes.
As a senior in 1939, Washington was the focus of an unsuccessful campaign
by African American sportswriters to secure recognition as a first-team All-
American. He was lauded for his "level-headedness," and readers were reassured
that "no amount of favorable publicity, however great, would affect the demeanor
of this young man."[65] Despite leading the nation in total yards that season, he was
also left out of the interregional East-West Shrine game. Many decried these
slights as evidence of continued racism on the part of sportswriters throughout
the country, especially in the South. In addition, the NFL, which had been segregated since 1933, declined to draft Washington after he graduated in 1940. Only the
Daily Worker recorded ill feelings from the usually quiet and reserved Washington:
"It's unfair. It's because I am a Negro that they don't want me to play."[66]

The black press also played a significant part in convincing UCLA to hire
Washington as coach of the freshman team upon his graduation, an unprecedented decision. "We believe that Kenny is an inspiration to all youth. . . . He

Kenny Washington. Courtesy Associated Students, UCLA.

knows the game at which he is so adept," an *Eagle* editorial explained. "We take this opportunity to suggest that it would be entirely fitting and proper that he become a member of the coaching staff at the Westwood institution."[67] UCLA's subsequent decision to hire Washington reverberated across the country the following year, when in New York the *Amsterdam News* gave the former Bruin its highest support—not because Washington played for the Rose Bowl, but (forgetting Harvard's William Henry Lewis) because he was "the first Negro in history to coach a major white eleven."[68]

Thus, while the excitement and appeal of the Bruins came from their status as a "black team," African American sportswriters who were used to trumpeting the charisma of Joe Louis and Jesse Owens portrayed the Bruin five no differently than professional celebrities or political leaders. When UCLA's six most prominent black students—the five footballers and Tom Bradley—attended a banquet with local business leaders in Los Angeles, Washington took the podium and "spoke for his mates"; he told the crowd, "we certainly appreciate this manifestation of interest in us. We want action and the opportunity to put our foot in the door. We will do the rest."[69]

While Washington appeared for a time to be spokesman for the black Bruins, it was impossible to construct any one player as "the image" of black athletics at

UCLA, especially after Washington's graduation in 1940. Black college athletes were unique individuals, amateurs with only a fraction of the recognition professional figures received, including entertainers and politicians. It was impossible to characterize the numerous stories of African American student athletes in the same way as celebrities like Joe Louis or Paul Robeson, public personas who were able to triumph across "color lines." The black press and the African American community thus celebrated the emergence of a team, for no longer were black football players lone individuals to be rejected, cut, or conveniently benched in accordance with essentialist logic. "If we drew 100,000 people to the Coliseum," recalled Strode, "40,000 of them would be black; that was just about every black person in the city of Los Angeles."[70] Black individualism struck at the very heart of Jim Crow. Instead of avoiding controversy on the bench, America's black team was introduced directly to college football's heartland: the Deep South.

"Empty Stockings"

The Bruins had run up against three segregated teams during the season by arranging games in Los Angeles versus Texas Christian University, Texas A&M University, and Southern Methodist University. Records indicate that ASUCLA spoke with at least one team regarding a possible potential game in Texas, but the possibility of the black Bruins participating in a game played on Jim Crow turf remained slim.[71] "We couldn't play in Texas because we had black guys on our team," Don McPherson recalled of his African American teammates. "They couldn't stay in the hotels or eat in the restaurants, so we didn't travel there."[72] Yet even black sportswriters praised the southern schools for making the trek west and not calling for the Bruins to change their lineup. When defending national champion Texas Christian was stunned by the 1939 Bruins on opening night in the Coliseum, Fay Young of the *Chicago Defender* lauded TCU Coach Leo "Dutch" Meyer for not asking "any coach to place a team on the field in his home city minus one or more stars because those stars were not white." As a result, Young proclaimed that Meyer and the Horned Frogs had "lost, but lost fairly."[73]

However, even though schools like Texas Christian agreed to play the Bruins in Los Angeles, tension still surfaced beneath institutional rhetoric. One example in particular typified the irony behind TCU's "progressiveness." Coach Meyer, his players, and TCU students had nothing but praise for the Bruin team, dishing out numerous accolades to "UCLA's colored twins."[74] Yet after being humbled on the field, one student reporter recorded the following events on the train ride home:

> Poss Clark [lineman] and Red Palmer [student manager] . . . conspired to scare the negro porter. Poss told the porter Red had running fits and bit people and in the meantime Red had filled his mouth with Alka Seltzer,

which produced a plentiful supply of froth, and started after the Negro. The porter was scared so bad that the boys had to get a new man to make up their beds. Afterwards Dutch [Head Coach Dutch Meyer] tried to sign him up to play football, because anyone who could run that fast would never be touched.[75]

The story speaks volumes about the role of public "color lines" and their nebulous meanings behind the scenes. By agreeing to a game versus the African American Bruins earlier in the day, Meyer participated in making a significant social statement that many, including the *Chicago Defender*, cited as a barometer for civil rights in California and Texas. Yet the coach and his players still operated within a social structure that positioned African Americans as expendable rail porters—a system that could only entertain the prospect of signing a black football player within a context of mockery and facetiousness. Nevertheless, Texas Christian players and student sportswriters were willing to face UCLA's black squad in Los Angeles and offer uncompromising coverage of their defeat at the hands of African American players. Many were left wondering if the Tennessee Volunteers would be willing to do the same.

On December 9, 1939, more than half the seats at Knoxville's Shields-Watkins Stadium remained empty as UT defeated Auburn University. Apparently, nearly 20,000 students and fans were so sure of a Tennessee win that they decided to stay home and save their money to help pay for a trip to Pasadena.[76] Bob Wilson of the *Knoxville News-Sentinel* wrote that it was a "foregone conclusion" the Volunteers would be offered a place in the Rose Bowl. "Tennessee athletic officials have a 'definite understanding' with both Southern Cal and UCLA officials," Wilson wrote. The only suspense now was to sit back and watch for the results of the UCLA-USC game.[77]

As an institution, the University of Tennessee was unabashedly committed to segregation at all levels, from the coaching staff and athletic department to the university administration and state legislature. Some sportswriters as well as school officials, coaches, and players were not convinced that UT would be willing to participate in an integrated Rose Bowl. When Allison Danzig of the *New York Times* asked Coach "Major" Neyland what stand the Volunteers would take if UCLA were the host team, the coach "side-stepped the issue by turning aside to speak to friends."[78]

That whole week, the *Knoxville News-Sentinel* had actually been concerned with two football games. While Tennessee faced off against Auburn, the opposite sports page devoted itself to coverage of the annual "Empty Stocking Bowl." That year, the Knoxville Black Vols and the Brushy Mountain Prison Negro Footballers were set to participate in an exhibition game, with proceeds to "bring joy and happiness to the unfortunate at Christmas time."[79] Local African American players who had been stars in high school made up the Black Vols, while black inmates played for the Brushy Mountain team. "Next to Rose Bowl Its Empty Stocking Bowl in Importance," announced the *News-Sentinel*, the game promised fans a very entertaining afternoon with plenty of "trick plays" and "doped out" formations. "We've got a 'scat' back who can run with the best of them," proclaimed Brushy Prison Coach Pinkie Walden. "All the fingers are off one of his hands, but that doesn't seem to bother him except that he fumbles occasionally. Most of the time he carries the ball in his good hand, though."[80]

Juxtaposed with Tennessee's wait for a Rose Bowl invitation, the Empty Stocking Bowl exemplified the ways in which segregation played out on southern football fields. The very layout of the *News-Sentinel* sports pages testified to Jim Crow, and it was clear that black football players were only acceptable under the rubrics of passive comedy, sambo-esque entertainment, and general buffoonery. In Knoxville, a group of African Americans could not engage in meaningful combat or competition on the gridiron. Playing on an equal footing

Woody Strode. Courtesy Associated Students, UCLA.

simply for competition or victory was out of the question; a "black team" had to be involved in a game that had some sort of positive social impact, like a charity exhibition.

In December 1939, through this lens Tennessee fans sat down to view the results from the USC-UCLA game and the status of the West Coast's "black team." Observers around the nation anxiously tuned in—a UCLA victory all but assuring UT a spot in the Rose Bowl. According to Allison Danzig, as Coach Neyland gathered with a host of other writers and administrators at the Farragut Hotel in Knoxville, "shouts went up" whenever news came that the USC Trojans were moving the ball against the Bruin defense. "It was evident that everybody in the room was pulling for Southern Cal to win or get a tie," wrote Bob Wilson in the *News-Sentinel*.[81] The overtly racist reaction to black players from southern coaches and institutions—the eerie silence of UT's Neyland, the TCU incident on the train home from Los Angeles, or the outright refusal of most coaches to participate in a game against black athletes—indicated that the African American Bruins were poised to create a national controversy over race should they be invited to face Tennessee in Pasadena.

"Two Yards from Heaven"

By all accounts, the 1939 UCLA-USC game was a classic. More than 103,000 fans jammed the Coliseum and watched as both teams battled for "60 sensational minutes."[82] USC nearly scored early in the game, but when quarterback Grenville Lansdell fumbled on the one-yard line Woody Strode dived on the ball in the end zone to avert a Trojan touchdown. For the next three quarters, "the two undefeated teams tore into each other like unacquainted wildcats," yet no one could muster a score.[83] Locked in a scoreless tie, the Bruins launched one last drive in the game's waning minutes. The crowd erupted as Washington, Robinson, Strode, and Bartlett each led UCLA down the field. Fatigue began to set in for both squads, and for a moment it looked as if "the tired Trojans couldn't stop the Bruins."[84] With first down and goal on the Trojan's two-yard line, the Bruins ran three straight unsuccessful plays. Facing fourth down and goal, the players huddled and decided to take a vote. Some wanted to have Robinson attempt a game-winning field goal, others wanted one last chance for a touchdown. In democratic fashion, each player raised his hand to vote. The result was 6–5 in favor of running one last play. The crowd stood as Washington dropped back to pass and heaved the ball over the goal line. Before his ball reached its intended target, a Trojan defender leaped into its path and swatted it to the ground. The game was over, and the USC Trojans had managed to forge a 0–0 tie, thereby assuring a spot in the Rose Bowl.

The next morning, Coach Neyland at the University of Tennessee accepted "with pleasure" an invitation from USC to play in the Rose Bowl.[85] Meanwhile, the *New York Amsterdam News* announced what black Americans around the country already knew. "Rose Bowl Remains White as a New Lily" read the headline, and dreams of what one black sportswriter called a "1939 'Civil War'" were shattered.[86] Although the tie meant that the Bruin season was finished and "plenty of folk both in the North and South could sleep without nightmares," the fact remained that the UCLA team had accomplished an incredible feat while making a symbolic social statement, and America had noticed. More than 400,000 spectators watched the 1939 UCLA Bruins, the largest number of fans for any team in the nation, and millions had followed UCLA's story on radio and in newsprint.[87] Today the 1939 UCLA-USC game remains one of the most celebrated contests in the rivalry's long history.

While the team's Senior Banquet program announced that the Bruins fell "two yards from heaven," UCLA's African American players nearly forced Tennessee's hand. By refusing the Rose Bowl bid, the Volunteers would have sparked a national debate rivaling Robinson's Major League Baseball debut eight years later in 1947. After all, the following season Boston College agreed to leave Lou Montgomery at home before facing Tennessee in the 1941 Sugar Bowl.[88] Certainly Coach Neyland, UT administrators, and fans throughout the state would have expected UCLA to do the same. It was a confrontation that many would have feared and others cherished. Either way, in both cheering and jeering the Bruins from 1938 through 1941, Americans were participating in a meaningful cultural spectacle.

Because a group of African American student athletes built a winning team at a predominately white university, black Americans from around the country adopted the UCLA Bruins as "their team." Similar to the growing consensus that African American civil rights would only be forged via collective action, fans celebrated the team because of its direct threat to the "gentlemen's agreement," which had managed for years to exclude lone black players from participating against segregated squads no matter how talented they were. Echoing A. Philip Randolph's call for collective action in the public square, UCLA helped sporting fans recognize that the depth of athletic talent in the black community meant that there was strength in numbers: if black athletes could participate fully on major white teams and maintain a biracial fan base, then African Americans would occupy an important place in America's most cherished institutions. Black athletes at UCLA had done just that; they provided the nation with a microcosm of equality (albeit imperfect) and a direct encounter with the logic of Jim Crow. Such were the "broad and rich football pastures" black journalists wrote of, for optimism surrounding the coming army of black athletes had begun to grow by 1941, just as Randolph's plans for the nation's first March on Washington forced Roosevelt's hand.

The continued popularity of UCLA's black athletes during and after World War II exemplified their significance to many fans. Kenny Washington starred in

1940's *While Thousands Cheer*, a small film that was well received in the black community. He continued playing football in minor leagues on the West Coast, including stints with the Hollywood Bears of the Pacific Coast Pro Football League from 1940 to 1941 and 1945 and the San Francisco Clippers of the American Football League in 1944. In between, Washington also toured with the United Service Organizations entertaining American troops overseas.

After World War II, the revamped NFL sought to establish a franchise in Los Angeles. Under pressure from the county commission and threats to bar the team from the city's Coliseum, the new Los Angeles Rams signed Washington and Strode in 1946. The two UCLA teammates became the first African Americans to play in the NFL's postwar, modern era; however, by 1946 injuries had begun to plague Washington, and he had little success as a professional. He played just three seasons before retiring in 1948 and working as a police officer in Los Angeles. He was inducted into the College Football Hall of Fame in 1956, and his number thirteen jersey was the first to be retired by UCLA. As for Strode, his athletic frame and good looks helped land him movie roles throughout the 1960s and 1970s.[89] Meanwhile, Jackie Robinson emerged from the world of amateur, team sports to become a civil rights icon. His integration of major league baseball in 1947 represents the moment at which fan optimism about the role of sport and racial integration peaked. Yet for thousands of black student athletes nationwide, the struggle was just beginning.

USC's victory delayed the impending crisis of an integrated Rose Bowl, but only until lucrative television contracts after the war again forced segregated schools to consider accepting prestigious bowl bids without regards to the opponent. While the popularity of college football soon took a back seat to the war, it emerged again in the 1950s stronger than ever. Within ten years, the very questions and debates raised by the groundbreaking UCLA squad would merge with a renewed postwar movement to change the role of race in American society. Yet before attention shifted to school integration in the Deep South, controversy erupted in the Midwest and Upper South—important regions where postwar migration, rapidly growing universities, and the advent of television introduced a new core audience to both intercollegiate football and "the Negro question."

3

"A Fist That Was Very Much Intentional"

Postwar Football in the Midwest and the 1951 Johnny Bright Scandal

... Proud and immortal

Bright shines your name

Oklahoma State, we herald your fame.

—Alma Mater, Oklahoma State University

Seldom has a football incident taken on such widespread proportions

—*New York Times*, 26 October 1951

After earning National League MVP honors in 1949, Jackie Robinson sent a letter of congratulations to Harold Robinson, a young athlete of no relation who had just made the football team at Kansas State University. "He didn't know my address," recalled the younger Robinson, "so he just sent it to K-State Athletics."[1] Ten years after almost reaching the Rose Bowl, Jackie Robinson congratulated the young man for becoming the first African American scholarship athlete in the Big Seven Conference. The letter was more than just a thrill for Harold and his family; it also revealed the importance Robinson placed on his collegiate experience. Even while a celebrated, international figure preparing to star in 1950s blockbuster *The Jackie Robinson Story*, Robinson recognized the importance of black athletes participating in new midwestern intercollegiate conferences, like the Big Seven. Two years later, black baseball players also integrated the conference when Earl Woods, father of golfer Tiger Woods, made Kansas State's baseball team. Jackie Robinson joined many blacks in celebrating the integration of collegiate sport in a region where football was experiencing a growth in popularity.

By 1950, Robinson's success in major league baseball echoed several important advancements in African American civil rights. World War II had disrupted America's traditional social fabric, opening doors for many women and minorities seeking equal opportunity in education, employment, and the armed services. Prominent African American leaders, like A. Philip Randolph, continued campaigns for organizing black labor while simultaneously stressing the importance of integrating America's troops.[2] Although resistance to segregation remained strong, patriotic fervor and organized protest helped achieve a number of real and symbolic victories. One year after America celebrated Joe Louis's knockout of Max Schmeling, Eleanor Roosevelt resigned from the Daughters of the American Revolution because the organization refused to lease their hall for a concert presented by celebrated singer Marian Anderson. Instead, Anderson sang on the steps of the Lincoln Memorial before an integrated crowd of 75,000 and a national radio audience. Two years later, Randolph's threat of an organized march in Washington prompted Franklin Roosevelt to bar discrimination in the defense industry.[3]

During the war, many white intellectuals for the first time began to address the centrality of racial tension in shaping history and identity. In 1944, strong academic reception to Gunnar Myrdal's *An American Dilemma* signaled the widespread emergence of employing social scientific research to study racism in America. Although W.E.B. Du Bois had written of "double consciousness" in the African American experience, Myrdal argued that racism stemmed from a "moral struggle" within white Americans, one in which "conflicting valuations [are] held by the same person." "The Negro problem," wrote Myrdal, "is an integral part of, or a special phase of, the whole complex of problems in the larger American civilization. It cannot be treated in isolation."[4] As some white intellectuals began to acknowledge the basic role of racism in shaping the United States, most citizens continued to experience ideological transformations through the discourse of popular culture. By the late 1930s, Paul Robeson had emerged from his gridiron success at Rutgers University to become a prominent singer and actor, beginning a career that included an influential role in the 1936 film *Show Boat*. Mainstream reviewers called the movie "opulent, spectacular, and generally enchanting." Yet Robeson biographer Martin Duberman notes how "segments of the black press . . . continued to berate Robeson for portraying yet another 'shiftless moron.'"[5] By 1943, Robeson had achieved the lead in a respected Broadway production of *Othello*, "a triumph that would mark the apogee of his career" and a role no U.S. company had heretofore been willing to offer him.[6] His professional transformation echoed the progress of integration in the armed forces during the war, when almost 500,000 African Americans served overseas. Although discrimination remained a daily part of life, black citizens found avenues to serve their country even as barriers persisted well into the 1950s.[7] During the Korean War, Douglas MacArthur's chief of staff announced that blacks were unfit for combat. Nevertheless, according to historian Gerald Astor the valiant sacrifice of black troops in World War II and Korea helped vanquish segregation in the armed forces "years before African Americans achieved full statutory rights in civilian society."[8]

War helped advance the course of civil rights, but postwar America also saddled blacks with new restrictions and barriers to social progress. As historian Lizabeth Cohen explains, the country's embrace of mass consumption and suburbanization "had a paradoxical effect on African Americans."[9] In the ten years following World War II, blacks challenged segregation in a number of public arenas—notably consumption, transportation, and leisure—with protests that garnered greater organization in the mid-1950s. Yet America's postwar economic explosion was built with tools that could just as often reinforce African American inequality. According to Cohen, the GI Bill discriminated against African Americans "insidiously" by barring most from key loans and placing home ownership out of reach for many black veterans.[10]

In terms of higher education, those who were able to gain eligibility for federal benefits still had the added barrier of finding an institution willing to accept them. From 1945 to 1955, historically black colleges reported turning away thousands of veterans for lack of space. Although many schools in the North had opened their doors to minority students, blacks who remained in the South had few options to pursue higher education. Meanwhile, as Americans celebrated victory over fascist tyranny, opponents to integration questioned the integrity of black servicemen. In 1945, Mississippi Senator James Eastland announced on the Senate floor that "the Negro soldier was an utter and dismal failure in combat in Europe . . . they were lazy . . . and disgraced the flag of their country." In the same speech, Eastland assailed "a black Communist in New York named Robeson, an actor or a singer, who holds forth at great length about colored culture."[11] Eastland's comments foreshadowed how some segregationists in the 1950s combined burgeoning Cold War political anxiety with negative reaction to civil rights agitation and black celebrities in sport and entertainment.

Like Robeson, successful black athletes were also not immune to the persistence of racism at the highest levels of American government. During the same summer that he congratulated Harold Robinson for joining Kansas State's football team, Jackie Robinson was called to testify before the House Un-American Activities Committee in regards to Robeson's political comments. Even after cooperating fully with HUAC, successfully releasing *The Jackie Robinson Story*, and negotiating a $50,000 contract with the Brooklyn Dodgers, Robinson's achievements never resonated with some Americans.[12] The black press lamented how whites in cities like Richmond, Virginia, praised the lesson of "democracy" in *The Jackie Robinson Story* even as the movie was screened before segregated audiences.[13]

Postwar society offered blacks a complex mixture of new opportunities and new barriers, but certain issues dominated civil rights discourse. National attention was drawn to public education in the South, where states like Georgia, Mississippi, and Alabama continued to aggressively pursue segregation. However, institutions of higher education in the Midwest—such as Kansas State University,

University of Oklahoma, or Oklahoma A&M College—also found themselves in the midst of racial controversy. With the notable exception of the Big Nine Conference—formed some fifty years earlier to represent the Great Lakes—the rest of the Midwest lacked an athletic conference that could solidify the game's reputation in the region.

Just as UCLA's football team made headlines over the prospect of integrating the Rose Bowl in 1939, the continued growth of athletic conferences after the war introduced racial discord in the Midwest to many observers for the first time. Large universities in the South fielded some of the most committed, successful athletic programs in the country, all of them staunchly segregated. Meanwhile, midwestern universities that had participated only nominally in sport were now seeking to capitalize on everything athletic prestige had to offer, and they sought to fill a growing void left by Ivy League schools that had already begun to scale down their athletic departments. Some observers (including Jackie Robinson) recognized the growing popularity of football in states like Kansas, Nebraska, Missouri, and Oklahoma—and the greater potential for black athletes to draw national attention. While Robinson and his UCLA teammates never had the chance to face the Tennessee Volunteers before thousands of fans, perhaps a new age of television would allow black athletes, like Harold Robinson at Kansas State, the opportunity to play southern teams before millions of viewers.

Harold Robinson's role in integrating the Big Seven was unfortunately barely noticed. The nation's attention was not drawn to midwestern athletics because of a successfully integrated Big Seven team. Instead, the country witnessed what the *New York Times* later called "one of the ugliest racial incidents in college sports history," an episode that took place in the smaller Missouri Valley Conference, specifically at Oklahoma A&M College.[14] National attention was drawn to Stillwater, Oklahoma, in late 1951 over the treatment of a single African American player on an opposing team, yet reaction to the incident can help scholars understand how the dynamics of race in an isolated region outside the Deep South influenced national debate on the cusp of the postwar civil rights movement.

Race and Higher Education in Postwar Oklahoma

Oklahoma hardly plays a role in the historiography of civil rights. The region is usually relegated to studies of either nineteenth-century Native American displacement or Depression-era Anglo migrants escaping the ravages of the Dust Bowl. After World War II, social politics in the state liberalized faster than in the Deep South. Nevertheless, a majority of representatives remained committed to fighting legislative attacks against segregation. In 1950, Johnston Murray assumed the governor's post, the same position his father had held during the Great Depression. William "Alfalfa Bill" Murray was elected in 1930 after denouncing what he dubbed "The Three C's—Corporations, Carpetbaggers, and Coons."

According to Dust Bowl chronicler Timothy Egan, Murray "gave people hope, but he also tried to get them to hate."[15] The son of an Anglo settler who migrated to the territory in the 1889 Sooner rush, Murray made headlines with his searing rhetoric, domineering personality, and constant cigar chomping. Egan describes how Murray believed Oklahoma "could be a great state only if blacks were separated from whites and kept in the proper jobs," and the governor looked to local segregation laws in Texas as a model for state policy.[16]

While the younger Murray sought to distance himself from his father's harsh stance on race and federal interference, he remained as fiscally conservative as "Alfalfa Bill" had been during the 1930s. Blacks in Oklahoma assailed the new governor for flirting with prosegregation Democrats throughout his early tenure in office. The "first evidence that Governor Johnston Murray might be inclined fundamentally to the thinking of his father," read an editorial in the Oklahoma City *Black Dispatch*, came when the governor announced he would "listen to arguments for and against a Dixiecrat movement now developing in the South."[17]

Oklahoma's blacks followed the fracturing of the New Deal Coalition and probed where the state's Democrats would stand on race. They also celebrated important victories that helped spark the NAACP's national campaign to outlaw school segregation. In 1946, Thurgood Marshall achieved partial victory in *Sipuel v. Oklahoma State Regents*, in which Ada Sipuel sued to attend the University of Oklahoma's law school. Although she was subsequently admitted, the university essentially tried to create a separate, one-woman school for her by scheduling classes in which she alone was enrolled. Three years later she was finally granted full admission.[18] The NAACP won a larger victory two years later in 1950, when the Supreme Court ruled in favor of George McLaurin, a schoolteacher in his sixties who sought admission to OU's education school. Like Sipuel, administrators admitted McLaurin but worked tirelessly to provide a Jim Crow atmosphere in the classroom. According to the school's president, George Lynn Cross, the staff attempted to "devise some plan whereby he could attend classes with white students, but be sufficiently 'segregated' to avoid penalty under state laws." The result was one of the more vivid displays of apartheid in the history of American higher education.

> [McLaurin's classroom] consisted of a main section and a little anteroom on its north side. The anteroom was separated, in a sense, from the rest of the room by columns, through which an occupant could have a clear view of the blackboard on the west side of the room, though at an angle of about forty-five degrees. With some misgivings whether the arrangement would meet the test of the state segregation laws, it was decided that all McLaurin's classes would be held in this room, that he would have his seat in the anteroom, and that the anteroom would not be considered a part of the classroom—it would be considered a separate, though adjoining, area.

Although President Cross wrote that McLaurin "seemed satisfied with the arrangements," McLaurin himself lamented the difficulty of trying to learn from the anteroom.[19]

McLaurin's saga drew national attention, and the sheer lunacy of the situation was not lost on Supreme Court Chief Justice Fred Vinson. Vinson's opinion in *McLaurin v. Oklahoma State Regents* not only ruled that McLaurin's treatment at OU was unequal but went even further in arguing that the state's arrangements had "handicapped" his pursuit of graduate instruction.[20] The decision was a clear victory for the NAACP, which chose Oklahoma as one of the first states to challenge segregated education at the graduate level. *McLaurin* and *Sipuel* (along with *Sweatt v. Painter*, which successfully desegregated the University of Texas law school in 1950) were important precursors to the subsequent decision in *Brown v. Board of Education* four years later, which bolstered the NAACP's notion that states in the southern Midwest were important battlegrounds for challenging Jim Crow. According to historian Robert Burk, the *McLaurin* case represented one of the first instances where the NAACP "encouraged the high court to find racial segregation an inherent cause of unequal education, irregardless of the quality of separate facilities."[21]

From the moment the NAACP announced that it had chosen OU to challenge segregation laws, letters surrounding the case poured in from around the state. According to Cross, most supported the integration of Oklahoma's universities, while those in opposition "were from people obviously only semiliterate."[22] Cross even claimed that desegregation at OU was not a particularly contentious process for either Oklahoma students or faculty. He later wrote, "I have never doubted that Negroes could have been admitted to the institution at the time without serious protest." Some white students had even tried to remove the barricades and cut the ropes used to segregate McLaurin's classroom in order to keep them as souvenirs.[23]

Like the *McLaurin* case, antisegregation campaigns in Oklahoma challenged citizens' beliefs that their state was immune to the kind of racial tension permeating the Deep South. Oklahomans had long grappled with a sort of crisis in regional identity, one that continues to this day. Although Oklahoma City was a short drive from places like Dallas, Texas, or Shreveport, Louisiana, some citizens identified themselves as residing in the "Midwest," not the "South." The 1952 Oklahoma A&M College yearbook even lauded its athletic department as among the "most inclusive programs in the southwest"—usually a designation for states like New Mexico or Arizona.[24]

In terms of race, ethnicity, and culture, Native American displacement defined Oklahoma's social climate throughout its history. This too gave many citizens in the 1950s a reason to distance themselves from the controversy surrounding Jim Crow segregation, debates which simmered along black-white binaries. Even the state's most celebrated athlete embodied Oklahoma's traditional ethnic tension. In 1950, the Associated Press named Jim Thorpe the greatest athlete of the first half of the twentieth century. The following year, Burt Lancaster starred as Thorpe in the successful biopic *Jim Thorpe: All-American*. Thorpe's mixed heritage (Irish and Native American) and his constant battle with alcoholism appeared to typify the region's racial tension and social problems more than the African American struggle for civil rights.[25]

Regardless of *McLaurin*, most white citizens in postwar Oklahoma felt that their state was quite progressive when compared to places like Mississippi and Alabama, a view fostered by the African American population's relatively small size and concentration in the state's two largest cities.[26] African Americans remained 7 percent of the state's total population, with active communities in Tulsa and Oklahoma City. The *Black Dispatch* also noted that "a large and considerable number of Negroes" lived in Stillwater, home of Oklahoma A&M College. Editorials encouraged blacks to seek enrollment at OAMC in any graduate program that was unavailable at Langston University, the nearby black college. Oklahoma's NAACP chapter lamented the treatment of George McLaurin at OU, but it celebrated when some black graduate students were allowed to attend OAMC the next summer. "Especially those seeking training in the trades and vocational fields should attend [OAMC]," exclaimed the *Black Dispatch*. "One may unquestionably secure a more practical course in such fields than at Oklahoma University."[27]

Just as Oklahoma's black press considered OAMC more tolerant than OU, OAMC administrators sought to grow a progressive institution that drew international respect and recognition. The number of graduates from Oklahoma A&M increased by more than 50 percent from 1942 to 1948, and the school began to take in a larger number of foreign-born students. Meanwhile, under new leadership OAMC embarked on an impressive international service campaign. After becoming the school's president in 1941, Henry Bennett asserted that "the soundest way we can help in the long run is to assist other countries develop institutions like our Land-Grant Colleges."[28] Bennett visited a number of underdeveloped nations, and OAMC was an integral part of President Harry Truman's "Point Four" program to send graduates to establish agricultural improvement centers in impoverished nations.[29] The 1952 OAMC yearbook even featured a picture of President Bennett and Emperor Haile Selassie of Ethiopia, with a caption proclaiming that Bennett had "traveled millions of miles in the interest of Agriculture and Education."[30] According to Bennett, the Point Four program allowed foreign students to study agriculture under scholarship at OAMC and provided poor countries with "a window into the twentieth century through which they can see the evidence of progress long denied to them and through which they can hear those great ideas of self government, economic progress and social justice."[31] Selassie's agreements with OAMC and Point Four helped bolster an image that Bennett wanted for A&M—a progressive, internationally recognized institution committed to agricultural modernization and social justice around the globe.

". . . A University of Which the Football Team Could be Proud"

Despite the furor over *McLaurin* at OU and pride at OAMC's international outreach, higher education in Oklahoma drew the most attention in the 1950s because of football. Within a context of Oklahoma's uncertain regional identity, rival state institutions trying to solidify their reputations, and a growing public discourse regarding civil rights, Oklahoma A&M College decided to build an athletic program. Although OAMC enjoyed expansion and growing national recognition, the school still lagged its in-state rival on the gridiron. OU competed in the powerful Big Seven—the most prestigious athletic conference in the Midwest—and OAMC struggled to bring about a desired invitation to join the group. The athletic department hoped to overshadow minor opponents in the smaller Missouri Valley Conference and spark a merger that would form a Big Eight.[32] In 1949, Athletic Director Henry Iba was disappointed when the Big Seven voted 5–2 to deny admission to OAMC's football team, the "Aggies." Fans around the state were offended, and sportswriters vented frustration at OAMC being denied a place in the prestigious conference. One *Daily Oklahoman* sportswriter fumed, "The Big Seven should consider joining A&M, not A&M joining the Big Seven."[33]

OAMC invested considerably in promoting football. By 1950, a chartered college airplane flew the team to away games, and television exposed them to viewers around the state. Local fans often gathered at businesses in Stillwater to watch coverage of the games.[34] OAMC had joined the Missouri Valley Conference in 1924, and for the next twenty-five years the MVC struggled to solidify membership and define its own regional identity. By 1950, the conference boasted no major teams, and its schools spanned a huge geographic area: nearly 1,500 miles from the University of Detroit to the University of Houston. In between, OAMC also participated with the University of Tulsa, Bradley University, Wichita University, St. Louis University, and Drake University. Twenty different schools had held membership in the Missouri Valley since its founding in 1907.[35]

OAMC administrators felt that the school was losing out on valuable prestige and investing too much money in athletics not to achieve membership in the Big Seven. According to historian John Watterson, A&M "was known as a 'jock school' that openly gave subsidies" to its players.[36] Not to be outdone, OU President George Cross made national headlines while testifying before the state legislature in 1950. Answering a senator's question about "why he thinks he needs so much money to run the University of Oklahoma," Cross responded that he wanted "to build a university of which the football team could be proud."[37] The president's answer elicited laughs from state lawmakers and drew criticism from the rest of the country. Nevertheless, the benefits of building successful teams were clear. In 1951, OAMC's first Missouri Valley contest versus Wichita drew a paltry 12,000 fans. That same day, the annual game between OU and the University of Texas brought 76,000 people to the Cotton Bowl in Dallas.[38] In addition to gate receipts and local economic stimulus, major conference teams earned recognition, extensive television and print coverage, and the greater potential to play in all-important bowl games.

Thus, OAMC was determined to dominate its competition in the Missouri Valley and win its way into the Big Seven. Despite investing in the creation of a strong program, however, the Aggies did not perform well against smaller MVC schools, some of which barely managed to assemble full squads. In fact, under second-year Coach J. B. Whitworth the 1951 football team opened with a lackluster 1–3 conference record. Whitworth was hired after making a name for himself with successful coaching stints throughout the South. As an assistant coach at the University of Georgia, he built a powerful defense that helped the Bulldogs reach the Rose, Sugar, Gator, and Orange bowls.[39] When the southern coach arrived at OAMC in 1949, the team was struggling in the Missouri Valley. Almost immediately, Whitworth came under pressure to improve the team's standing and create a national image. The new coach carried himself as a true "southerner," and his hardened stare and terse comments gave local fans hope that the man from Georgia could whip the OAMC squad into shape. He emphasized defensive rigor and called on his players to hit "everything that wears the other color shirts" as hard as possible.[40]

At the same time that OAMC was hiring J. B. Whitworth, national observers debated the growing popularity of college football. Many prominent schools were actually deemphasizing athletics in 1951. Along with countless sportswriters and fans, one of football's most famous coaches, Amos Alonzo Stagg, blamed overzealous coaches, boosters, and alumni for ruining the spirit of competition and endangering the future of the game. In Washington, D.C., a group of college presidents met to discuss what they dubbed "intercollegiate sports evils." Michigan State University President John Hannah expressed hope that his conference, the Big Ten, would not renew its contract with the Rose Bowl.[41]

In this context, OAMC's decision to hire Whitworth and seek membership in the Big Seven sent a clear signal: administrators in Stillwater were committed to bringing big-time football to A&M and willing to shape a program that mimicked the success of universities in the South even as the potential for bowl game matchups with integrated teams loomed. Three years earlier, Pennsylvania State University's Wallace Triplett and Dennis Hoggard had integrated the 1948 Cotton Bowl in Dallas, the region's major postseason venue. The following year, bowl officials picked the University of Oregon and its three African American players, including Woodley Lewis, to play in Dallas. Nevertheless, Oklahoma's political leaders and university officials tried to distance themselves from southern racial turmoil—segregated education, African American civil rights, and Jim Crow society. But when it came to college football and regional identity, OAMC and OU wanted nothing more than to join the list of popular "southern" teams.[42]

"The Threat"

Despite fan optimism and the hiring of Whitworth, the Aggies continued to struggle. One month into the 1951 season, the best team in the Missouri Valley was not OAMC but a surprising squad from Drake University in Des Moines, Iowa. Drake's team boasted a 5–0 record, though its success was largely due to one outstanding athlete. Halfback Johnny Bright—an African American student from Fort Wayne, Indiana—was the top player in the MVC and considered among the best in the country. In 1950, his third year on the team, Bright broke the NCAA all-time record for career rushing yards by surpassing Charlie Justice's four-year total at the University of North Carolina. That same season he became the first player in history to gain more than 1,000 yards passing and receiving, averaged more offensive yards per game (266.7) than thirty-nine other college football *teams*, and received several votes for the Associated Press athlete-of-the-year award. With a successful 1951 season, fans anticipated that Bright had a chance to become the first African American awarded the Heisman Trophy.[43] Fay Young and other black sportswriters, helping to bring national recognition to the small university, celebrated Bright's staggering accomplishments on the field. Young, assuming the young man could stay healthy and avoid injury, wrote in the *Chicago Defender* that Bright's prospects for the 1951 season looked even better than anticipated.[44]

Leading Drake to a 5–0 start, Bright's outstanding play confirmed the growing media buzz surrounding him. In a rout over Iowa State Teachers College, Bright ran and passed for 261 yards and scored four touchdowns, all within fourteen minutes. By mid October Drake University and the Des Moines community were officially celebrating Bright's accomplishments. Mayor A. B. Chambers declared a "Johnny Bright Day," and 13,000 fans showed up for "Johnny Bright Night" versus the University of Detroit.[45] Bright's overwhelming speed and 205-pound frame intimidated his opponents, and his uncanny athleticism drew admiration. "I remember him being indestructible," recalled one Indiana sports editor.[46] Nevertheless, race limited Bright's opportunities to pursue athletics at one of Indiana's elite schools. In South Bend, Notre Dame still did not recruit black players in the early 1950s. Purdue University also paid no attention to the young man, while Head Coach Clyde Smith at Indiana University reportedly told Bright he "already had enough black running backs." One Drake official later recalled that Bright's subsequent career marked the high point of athletics at the school. During his second year at Drake in 1950, games brought 21,000 people to overcrowded Drake Stadium in Des Moines; the school scrambled to set up additional seating. In the sixty years since that season, no athletic events have come close to drawing as much attention.[47]

While Drake's star halfback nabbed headlines in the black press and the *New York Times*, OAMC's football team struggled to another disappointing start. The very week that Iowa fans were celebrating "Johnny Bright Day," Coach Whitworth admitted to OAMC's student newspaper, *The Daily O'Collegian*, that he was "scared to death" to face Wichita University. Although the Aggies managed their first win against the lowly Wheatshockers, the team's inability to compete in the Missouri Valley Conference continued to frustrate OAMC's fans and embarrass administrators.[48] As A&M prepared to host Johnny Bright and Drake at Stillwater's Lewis Field, Whitworth voiced more frustration in the press, telling the *Tulsa Daily World* his team was "mentally perturbed" over the prospect of facing the African American star.[49] The *Daily O'Collegian* and local media outlets in Stillwater took the hostile rhetoric toward Bright even further. Two days before the game, the *Stillwater News-Press* announced that Bright was a "marked man."[50] With Whitworth's job in jeopardy and the team struggling, OAMC's program wallowed at the bottom of the Missouri Valley rankings, below smaller schools and nowhere near the caliber of teams in the Big Seven.

Whether or not in jest, the use of such intimidating allusions toward a black football player was backed by the reality of African American segregation in Oklahoma. Bright had visited Lewis Field once before. He was the first black to play college football in Stillwater as a sophomore in 1949—the same year that Yale University's Levi Jackson became the first black to captain an Ivy League team. Bright drew little attention then, as the OAMC team dominated Drake and won the game easily. "Talking to some of the fans after the game," wrote one Drake student who made the trip, "everybody had high praise for Bright. This made one wonder whether or not any racial discrimination actually existed down there. It certainly wasn't shown for Bright."[51] In addition, the 1949 Drake team stayed at a hotel in the nearby town of Guthrie, where Bright was the establishment's first African American guest. However, by 1951 OAMC had hired Whitworth and the attitude toward Bright seemed to change. The same Guthrie hotel now refused to let Bright stay, and while A&M provided dormitory rooms for the rest of the Drake team Bright was housed with a local black minister.[52]

Two photographers from the *Des Moines Register*, Donald Ultang and John Robinson, traveled to Stillwater to cover the game. It was unusual for the paper to fly photographers to a Drake game outside of Iowa, but the gossip surrounding Bright's participation prompted the move. "We had speculated as to what Bright's reception would be," recalled Robinson.[53] Bright was also warned of the trip to Oklahoma by other black athletes at Drake, including Ray Eiland, his friend on the track team. "It was a horrible time for us," remembered Eiland, "we were an integrated team in a segregated conference. The schools didn't even admit African American students. . . . I'd warned John before going down there that I'd run track there . . . and it might be a little hazardous."[54] The *Daily O'Collegian* took pride in the fact that A&M was the only Missouri Valley team to stifle Bright's ability on the field, one of few accomplishments for the struggling football program. Calling Bright "the colored boy" and "The Threat," one student noted how two years earlier "Drake and its sophomore sensation rode into Aggieland but found the welcome mat missing."[55]

After the game, national media even reported that OAMC students were betting how long Bright would last on the field. According to *Life* magazine, "The word was that Drake's Negro halfback, John Bright, the nation's leading ground gainer, would not be around at the end of the game."[56] The *Chicago Defender* reported that Drake players had overheard OAMC students "offering to take bets that the nation's record-breaking collegiate ground gainer would not . . . play the entire game against the Aggies."[57] Rumors of ill intent surrounding Bright's appearance also came from off campus, where two Drake football players reported overhearing plans to injure the star halfback. George Smith, a Drake linebacker, told the *Des Moines Register* that a local barber in Stillwater made ominous comments while giving him a haircut. According to Smith, the barber hoped Bright would finish the game because he had "two bucks bet that he'll make it to the end."[58] Recalled white teammate Gene Macomber, "I can remember . . . on campus words to the effect that the black guy would not finish the game."[59] OAMC students reported that Whitworth had repeatedly screamed at his players to "get that nigger" as motivation during the week's practice sessions, and some fans at the game held painted signs imploring the same.[60] Clearly, much had changed in the two years since Bright had first visited Lewis field. He was now a black athlete considered among the best to play the game, and Bright was drawing to Drake's meager program what little national attention the Missouri Valley Conference managed to generate. Meanwhile, Oklahoma A&M struggled under its new southern coach, and hopes of creating a prestigious football program were quickly fading just as television coverage began to bring valuable publicity into living rooms nationwide.

Yet Bright's story is most significant when considering the broader context of the *McLaurin*, *Sipuel*, and *Sweatt* cases, the growing visibility of Oklahoma's NAACP chapter, and the successful enrollment of black students in graduate programs at OAMC—primarily because his participation sparked more public debate among whites than any of these. Indeed, reaction to Bright's appearance in Stillwater reveals how many midwestern citizens did not take race for granted and instead were ready to engage in dialogue about the unsettling of segregation mores nearly four years before *Brown*. The cultural history of integrated athletics in the region offers historians a unique look at the groundwork for the subsequent reaction to *Brown* and the arrival of full, legislated school desegregation. The day before Bright's appearance, Howard University President Mordecai

Johnson delivered a speech to Oklahoma teachers regarding the problems with focusing only on integrating graduate and professional programs. Meanwhile, debates over integrating Oklahoma's secondary schools permeated the *Daily Oklahoman*. While athletic departments at OU and OAMC were content to model their programs on southern schools, the African American presence in Oklahoma society was growing, and many blacks were starting to draw parallels between segregation in the Deep South and social injustice in their own state.[61]

"A Fist That Was Very Much Intentional": Johnny Bright Visits Stillwater

The question of how Johnny Bright would be received in Stillwater was answered within seconds. On the game's first play, Bright took the snap and handed the ball to Gene Macomber, who rounded the corner and proceeded up the field for a short gain. As Bright stood behind the play and watched, OAMC lineman Wilbanks Smith ran up and landed a forearm blow directly to Bright's face. After crumbling to the ground, Bright got up slowly. According to the *Tulsa Daily World*, Smith had "hit Bright with such force that both his feet were off the ground."[62] With his jaw shattered, Bright struggled to stay in the game. Twice again he was hit viciously, even without handling the ball. The attacks on Bright were so far removed from the ball that many of the 12,000 at Lewis Field did not even notice. Photographers John Robinson and Donald Ultang of the *Des Moines Register* were shocked as they continued to take pictures. "We both looked at one another and wondered whether anyone had noticed what happened," recalled Robinson.[63] After the hit from Smith, Bright remained motionless for several minutes on the ground. Shortly thereafter, he had to be escorted off the field to the dressing room.

Hundreds of African Americans from around the state had traveled to Stillwater specifically to see Bright play; many had passed up the week's black college games. Fordie Ross of the *Black Dispatch* watched as Bright was examined in the locker room. "They hit me in my face with their fists and I just could not ward off their attacks," Ross quoted Bright. "They were out to get me."[64] *Daily Oklahoman* sportswriter Jack Murphy also noted Bright's quick exit from the game, although he attributed it to "Oklahoma A&M's aggressive young football team." "Bright was flattened on the game's first play from scrimmage," announced Murphy, "while serving as decoy on a running maneuver, and remained on the ground for several minutes."[65] Without the services of Bright, Drake lost to OAMC. No longer unbeaten, the team struggled to win a game the rest of the season as Bright remained on the sidelines with his jaw wired shut.

Immediate controversy surrounded what happened to Bright in Stillwater. The local *News-Press* reported that players in the "anger-charged" Drake locker room refused to speak with reporters after the game, although they all agreed

Bright had been maliciously assaulted on the field. "They played a different kind of ball game after they got Johnny out," said one player. "They played clean ball after that."[66] To make matters worse, after the game a ticket agent at the train station prohibited the injured Bright from sitting with his white team-mates. Using time-lapse technology—an increasingly popular tool in sports photography—Robinson and Ultang managed to capture the entire attack on film. The *Des Moines Register* ran the series of photos the next day, under the headline "Ever See a Jaw Broken?" And Iowa residents responded. One thousand "boiling mad" people greeted the Drake team's arrival from Stillwater. The *Register* announced that the assault was "deliberate," an analysis "given support by machine gun and howitzer camera pictures." In particular, John Robinson had used a converted "Bell and Howell Eyemo" movie camera to take still photo-graphs at four frames per second. Although newsreel footage of the game was also widely circulated, Robinson and Ultang's images were far more influential. A poll of Drake's student body found that 40 percent were in favor of the Missouri Valley immediately dropping OAMC from the conference. Many students also called on Drake to relinquish all ties with A&M.[67]

While students at Drake denounced the attack, the school's administrators issued an even stronger response. Within days, the athletic council released an "angry statement" to the public and lodged a formal protest with the MVC. According to the council, Bright had been subject to "three vicious, malicious and intentional attacks . . . which were gross violations of football rules and ethics."[68] In calling for the conference to investigate and punish OAMC, how-ever, Drake officials never mentioned race as a factor in the incident. Sec Taylor, aging sports editor at the *Des Moines Register* and a legendary sportswriter in the region, concluded that Bright was targeted merely because of his ability. "I am glad," wrote Taylor, "that most of the members of the Drake squad are of the opinion that No. 72 assaulted Bright, not because he was a Negro playing in Oklahoma, but because he was a star player."[69]

Yet as letters continued to pour in, it became clear that fans around the region concluded otherwise. One Des Moines woman wrote to "remind Iowans to remember that, as far as racial prejudice is concerned, they are at least 50 years ahead of Oklahoma." Other fans argued that the incident was caused by a con-ference that was willing to include "southern teams" like OAMC. "The dirtiest, yellowest, meanest thing a white man can do," read one letter, "is strike or delib-erately foul a Negro on an opposing team . . . especially true in the South on the home field before partisan fans." With angry sarcasm, another reader exclaimed that OAMC's "'gallant Southern gentlemen' probably would have gotten by with it . . . were it not for the *Register's* machine-gun camera that recorded the action." Many observers concluded that Bright's assault was no different from the kind of daily racism considered commonplace and acceptable in the South, only this incident happened to be caught on camera for the world to see.[70]

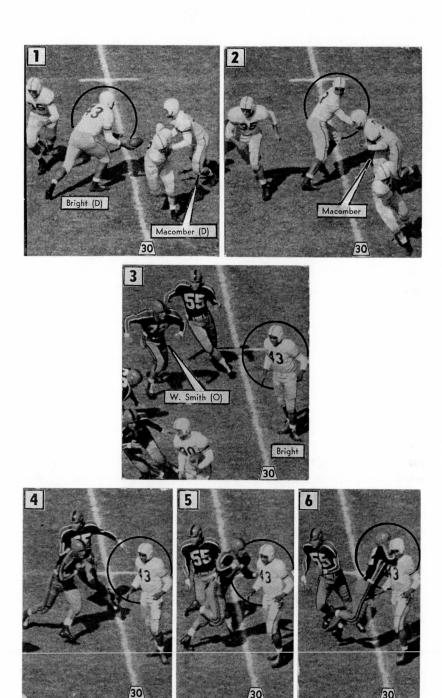

"Bright's Jaw Broken," announced the *Des Moines Register*, which published this sequence of images on 21 October 1951. They were subsequently reprinted in several national publications, including *Life* and *Time*. Photographs by Donald Ultang and John Robinson, Copyright 1951. Reprinted with permission from the Des Moines Register and Tribune Company.

Immediately, reaction to the photographs in Iowa caught the attention of national media outlets. Two weeks after the game, *Life* magazine republished the pictures in an exposé on how athletic emphasis at colleges around the country were generating rough play, violent hits, and outright cheating. "Dirty football has been charged in other games this season," read the story, under the headline "Sluggings Aren't Accidents."[71] Once the images were circulated nationally, scores of letters began arriving at both schools, from every region in the United States as well as distant countries like Denmark and Colombia.[72]

However, in the wake of numerous incidents of point shaving, rules violations, and illegal player subsidies, many condemned Bright's assault in terms not of race but of "dirty play" or "poor sportsmanship." The controversy surrounding football's penchant for inspiring brutal aggression—or even killing and maiming its players—had been percolating for nearly fifty years. As early as 1905, Theodore Roosevelt and Congress had called on schools to limit brutality and unsportsmanlike aggression.[73] However, by invoking the rhetoric of "fair" or "clean" play, even the most understanding observers threatened to eliminate the role of race in Bright's assault. In the *Los Angeles Times*, Iowa Governor William Beardley explained, "I feel sportsmanship must have been at a low ebb when such an outstandingly fair player as Johnny Bright was subject to such physical abuse."[74]

Unlike public statements from figures like Beardley, the reaction of the black press emphasized the role of race in the incident and helped the issue transcend debates over excessive physicality or poor sportsmanship. Writing in the *California Eagle*, black sportswriter Brad Pye wrote that Bright had been viciously taken out of the game by "a fist that was very much intentional."[75] According to the *Chicago Defender*, Bright's assault was emblematic of racial tension in college towns across the Midwest and South: "The fact that Johnny Bright is a gentleman of color goes far to explain the actions. . . . It is indeed regrettable that racism continues to confuse young men in colleges."[76] Black sportswriters wanted to use the incident to shed light on broader social ills at OAMC and within the Stillwater community, not so much to criticize an overemphasis on athletics or a lack of "sportsmanship." After all, the growing importance of sport and the enticement of national recognition convinced some schools to admit black athletes. If college football was one course for eliminating segregation—and the success of athletes like Jackie Robinson and his UCLA teammates had vividly shown it was—many African American sportswriters found it difficult to support the deemphasis campaign. For them, the problem with the Bright incident was not a "jock school" that sought to win at all costs but rather the social barriers that prohibited African American students from participating in the postwar athletic bonanza. "The boys who have been brought up on white supremacy propaganda simply cannot stand to see their illusions threatened," proclaimed the *Chicago Defender*. "[Johnny Bright] struck fear into them, fear that this presumably 'inferior' should make monkeys out of them."[77] While many sportswriters grouped the incident with other examples of rough play on the football field—and even gambling scandals sweeping college basketball—the black press continued to talk about Bright's assault as a stand-alone event with different meanings. By the following week, Bright had personally received from supporters eighty letters, including marriage proposals. When "scores" of letters reached the University of Detroit calling for the team to retaliate by "roughing up" the Aggies, the *New York Times* agreed that the issue was beginning to transcend the sport: "Seldom has a football incident taken on such widespread proportions."[78]

After Drake's athletic council issued its formal protest to the MVC, administrators agreed to wait for a response from OAMC and the conference. Initially, the game seemed to pass with little notice in Stillwater. The *News-Press* reported that "the incident raised barely a rustle of sound" on A&M's campus.[79] Even after viewing the pictures, Coach Whitworth apologized to Drake but defended Smith's assault on Bright. "I want people to look at this boy's record," Whitworth told the *Daily O'Collegian*, "He is not the 'dirty' type of player. He just lost his head for a few minutes. . . . If anything, Smith has never been aggressive enough."[80] Although the new coach admitted that Smith's actions were "illegal" and "vicious," he refused to take any other action. In the *Black Dispatch*, Fordie Ross lampooned the coach's explanation. "Smith 'lost his temper' on the first play!" wrote Ross, " . . . any loss of temper was necessarily born before the game started. . . . His temper mysteriously vanished when Bright left."[81] Like Whitworth, OAMC's athletic cabinet responded to Drake's charges with a short apology regretting "any irregularities that develop in college sports and this is one of them."[82] Athletic Director Henry Iba indicated that OAMC was powerless to do anything else. "I don't see what action we can take," Iba told reporters. "We get kids injured in ball games, too."[83]

Even as Drake pressured the MVC to consider kicking OAMC out of the conference, A&M administrators believed the incident would blow over quickly. According to historian Philip Rulon, President Henry Bennett "refused to attach much significance to the incident or its aftermath."[84] Instead, Bennett took the curious step of leaving the affair entirely in the hands of Vice President Oliver Willham. George Cross, president of the University of Oklahoma, wrote that Bennett was usually obsessed with maintaining his OAMC affairs, even while traveling in the Third World. "I was especially impressed by the way he maintained frequent contact with his institution at Stillwater," recalled Cross, "he . . . telephoned the personnel in his office two or three times a day."[85] Yet President Bennett believed that the furor over a simple football game would soon pass—perhaps the largest mistake in the career of a man otherwise considered among the best administrators in the country. Ironically, his commitment to fostering OAMC's reputation through social justice in places like Ethiopia and Latin America was overshadowed by Bright's assault, an incident that revealed the extent of injustice in Bennett's own hometown. For many fans, Johnny Bright shaped the postwar reputation of Oklahoma's universities more than any Supreme Court case or foreign dignitary.

Some locals defended Coach Whitworth and supported OAMC's decision not to take action. The *News-Press* denounced "quick-fingered sports writers" who were trying to give the school a "black eye" and "make something of it because of his [Bright's] color."[86] Likewise, John Cronley of the *Daily Oklahoman* disagreed that the attack was intentional and denounced the role of race as "pure claptrap on the part of overemotional writers and broadcasters."[87] One letter from Washington, D.C., echoed Cronley's assessment and actually argued that the assault highlighted racial reconciliation in Oklahoma. "Could you not have emphasized the progress this southern school has made," wrote the reader, "in accepting the challenge of a team that had on it a colored youth, and even permitting him on their campus or athletic field, a fact that would not have existed three years ago?"[88]

Like this reader, fans seemed to forget that Bright had already played in Stillwater two years earlier with no problems. Segregation in Oklahoma was not a static entity but rather a loose social system that could manifest itself in different ways and in varying degrees. Whereas legal decisions to integrate college admissions offered a clear example of progressive change, the acceptance of black athletes often depended on the whims of a specific athletic director, the outlook of a new head coach, or fan sentiment during a particular season. Rather than examine the complex reasons behind the change in Bright's acceptance between 1949 and 1951, OAMC critics and supporters viewed the incident within a linear framework of progress triumphed by advancements like the *McLaurin* decision. Yet Bright's assault proved otherwise: some barriers could be rebuilt shortly after they were torn down.

In fact, the migration of major intercollegiate sport to the Midwest and the solidification of athletic conferences sparked the kind of sociopolitical confrontation long associated with the region. A hundred years earlier, the question of slavery had invoked "Bleeding Kansas." It was fortunate that judicial decisions in the 1950s did not engender the same kind of chaos that popular sovereignty had wrought before the Civil War—though in places like Little Rock, Arkansas, they came close. Attempts to organize major conferences with segregated and integrated schools proved a different story. The assault on Bright in 1951 threatened to disintegrate the entire Missouri Valley Conference, which had bent without breaking for forty-four years.

Drake officials made no public mention of race when protesting the incident, but they were certain that tension over black players stood at the heart of the controversy. Even before the game, officials protested the conference's decision to appoint referees from Kansas, Texas, and Oklahoma, a move they called "unwise . . . for this particular game." Curiously, throughout the subsequent controversy no sportswriters targeted the officiating crew, who did nothing while Bright was injured and insisted that they did not see any illegal aggression on the field.[89] After the incident, Drake President Henry Harmon wrote privately to advise the athletic council. "I have some hunch that this may lead to the breaking up of the conference," predicted Harmon. "It is a fine opportunity for the Southern schools to re-introduce the ban on negro athletes or for the Conference to create a situation that would force out some of the Northern schools and allow them to swing the Conference to the South and Southwest."[90] Drake was not only an integrated school, but it was also small, drew little recognition, and hardly emphasized athletics—not the kind of opponent programs like OAMC wanted to schedule every year.

Harmon wrote that the Missouri Valley would quickly agree to remove Bradley and Drake from the conference rather than address the role of race in the Bright incident, and his prediction proved accurate within weeks.[91] After OAMC refused to take any action on the matter, the Missouri Valley issued a statement saying the conference had "no power to take disciplinary action against an individual player."[92] Shortly thereafter, Drake and Bradley withdrew from the conference, and Drake cut all ties to OAMC. Drake's public statement once again hinted at the underlying tension behind its decision without mentioning race. "Recent expansion of the conference to include schools from the Great Lakes to the Gulf of Mexico has created numerous conference problems," read the statement. "Lack of conference action in the Bright case was the culminating event forcing the council to its decision."[93] Bradley officials echoed the sentiment when the school's faculty athletic committee announced that it wanted "to have a part in the formation of a new Conference of a more close-knit nature and covering a considerably smaller geographic area, possibly extending southward a few hundred miles from the Great Lakes region."[94] In deciding to stay with the MVC, only Wichita University issued a statement specifically discussing race; the school contended that "progress has been made on the racial issue not only at Oklahoma A&M but at all schools in the Missouri Valley."[95] Many students at Drake accused the MVC of backing OAMC because it, too, wanted to rid the conference of small schools like Drake and Bradley. "I am confident the Valley will not disintegrate," one University of Tulsa official told the press, "and will look for new and stronger members."[96]

"A True Sport"

Drake's decision to withdraw from the conference brought more criticism from Oklahoma's sportswriters. John Cronley suggested the decision had less to do with race and more with small schools who were deemphasizing athletics. According to Cronley, "a few member schools are traveling a rocky financial road. In this era of large squads and coaching staffs . . . some Valley schools are losing money at a pace that cannot be continued."[97] Certain Stillwater residents were even more condemning. One *News-Press* editorial called Drake's decision a "childish temper display" and accused "the people at Drake" of not recognizing that "football is a pretty rough game and one in which cry babies should not participate."[98] While Jim Crow society traditionally warned of the threat posed by hypermasculine black males, the criticism of Bright proved that African American college athletes were in a unique bind when it came to discrimination. Their physical skills could affirm scientific racism and sexual anxiety, yet they also faced the prospect of being branded infantile, emasculated "cry babies" if they refused to compete in segregated athletics. At OAMC, one campus editorial—headlined "Play My Way, Or I'll Quit"—insisted the Bright attack was merely an excuse for Drake to deemphasize football and leave the conference. Meanwhile, the black press celebrated the decision and applauded Drake officials. In the *California Eagle*, Lester Granger called the incident a "Civil War" that "threatened to break out" between northern and southern rivals and assailed the rhetoric of "illegal" or "dirty" play, "a polite euphony for putting the slug on an opponent."[99]

While the Stillwater community remained silent on the issue, some students at OAMC demanded that the institution salvage its reputation. A group of graduate students signed a petition stating that Johnny Bright "was a fine gentleman" and arguing that the incident should mark the "end of poor sportsmanship at this school."[100] Other students denounced the attack as "un-Christian" and lauded Bright as "a true sport." From nearby Hennessey, Oklahoma, one letter criticized Whitworth and implicitly painted the attack as premeditated by the coach himself. "If that is the kind of coaching they do in the south," warned the author, "I say ship him back down there for he isn't the right kind of a man to be over a group of teen-age boys."[101] The *Black Dispatch* praised OAMC students for speaking out while their administration remained silent. "It is extremely heartening to know that the majority of students at Stillwater are outraged by what has happened and are willing to sign their names and addresses to their protest," announced one editorial.[102]

Nevertheless, some Oklahoma observers who came to the support of Bright did so without having to confront the role of race and segregation in their communities. "Good sportsmanship" was a call for equality, level playing fields, and fair contests, but the concept also completely bypassed the fact that race undoubtedly stoked the agitation surrounding Bright and the Drake squad. Meanwhile, the black press applauded Drake's decision to withdraw from the conference. In December, the *Chicago Defender* added the school to its top-ten list of people or institutions benefiting integration during the year.[103]

Reaction to Bright's assault revealed a significant gap between OAMC campus culture and the dominant ideology of the surrounding community. In the midst of all the controversy and negative press, the state's sportswriters still honored Whitworth as "Sportsman of the Year."[104] Building on his popularity, the coach later returned to the Deep South and spent three seasons at the

University of Alabama, after which he was fired and replaced by Paul "Bear" Bryant in 1958. Ironically, Johnny Bright's visit to Lewis Field created more tension than the *McLaurin* case or the overall integration of classrooms at OU and OAMC. For many students, it revealed the extent to which their university was not on the cusp of equal rights. Even with the tide of formal integration beginning to sweep Oklahoma's schools—with far less fanfare and opposition compared to other states—the Bright incident and college football brought the greatest public introspection regarding the true status of civil rights in the region. "The extreme intolerance of the past had vanished," wrote historian Philip Rulon, "but perhaps the Johnny Bright case tempered racial attitudes in the state even more."[105] Yet for most Oklahoma citizens, condemnation of Bright's attack was couched in terms of "poor sportsmanship" instead of race. Although some used the incident to rethink civil rights and Oklahoma's image on the national stage, others could just as easily use it to cloud the issue of segregation and reinforce the false notion that Oklahoma was racially progressive.

Repercussions from the attack also resonated across the country and helped bring important reforms to college athletics. Shortly after the season, the NCAA issued a new code of ethics and mandated that conferences include committees "to investigate incidents deemed detrimental to intercollegiate athletics." *New York Times* sportswriter Allison Danzig, who twelve years earlier was on hand to witness Coach Major Neyland and Tennessee officials celebrate a segregated Rose Bowl, continued to recognize the role of race in stoking ethical abuses. "Undoubtedly those drawing up the amendment," wrote Danzig, "had in mind such incidents as the fracturing of the jaw of Johnny Bright of Drake."[106]

Not only did Bright's treatment signal the successful migration of big-time college football from the South to Midwest, it also helped further minimize the game's popularity in the Northeast. By 1954, the same Ivy League schools that had created the modern game—and made it big business—formally committed themselves to deemphasizing. The "Ivy Agreement" effectively curbed football in the Northeast and further opened the door to teams in the West that wanted to build winning programs. The effects of the agreement still exist today, as few Northeast schools have managed to rank nationally in the past thirty years. In addition, Johnny Bright's assault sparked reform in the way the game itself was played. According to the *Journal of Blacks in Higher Education*, the Bright assault forced the NCAA to mandate that college players wear face guards over their helmets (a staple in today's game). The following year, the NCAA also imposed new penalties on deliberate blows and acts of aggression on the field—precursor to the more euphemistic "personal foul" penalty.[107]

However, what happened to Johnny Bright was much more than a "personal foul," for the incident changed the trajectory of the young man's life. With a healed jaw and large amounts of public sympathy, Bright finished fifth in voting for the Heisman Trophy—an immense accomplishment considering Drake was relatively unknown and Bright missed a number of games. Nevertheless, the country had to wait another ten years before an African American player was awarded the Heisman Trophy. Just three years after Wallace Triplett (Pennsylvania State University, 1946–1949) and George Taliaferro (Indiana University, 1945–1948) became the first black players to be drafted into the National Football League (UCLA's Kenny Washington and Woody Strode were signed directly), the Philadelphia Eagles chose Bright as the fifth pick in the first round of the 1952 NFL draft, ahead of future stars like Frank Gifford and Hugh McElhenny.[108] "I would have been their first Negro player," Bright later told the *News-Sentinel*, "but there was a tremendous influx of Southern players into the NFL . . . and I didn't know what kind of treatment I could expect."[109] Bright instead chose to leave the country, where he signed with the Canadian Football League and still holds numerous CFL career records. After retiring in 1964, he became a respected teacher and principal in Edmonton, Alberta.

In yet another testament to the disregard of black collegians, the men who photographed Bright's assault earned more recognition from the incident than Bright himself. John Robinson and Donald Ultang's pictures for the *Des Moines Register* were published in several leading periodicals. After *Life* magazine received more than three hundred letters in response, *Time* magazine also ran the photos with a telling caption: "the year's most glaring example of dirty football."[110] While Bright was unable to play for the Heisman Trophy, reaction to his pictures gave Robinson and Ultang a 1952 Pulitzer Prize for journalism photography.

The subsequent history of athletics at Drake and OAMC is just as pointed as Bright's personal story. In 1957, OAMC changed its name to Oklahoma State University, a reflection of the continuing growth in student population and a broader curriculum. The following year, OSU finally achieved admission to the coveted Big Seven Conference. Two years after the Bright incident, the conference had sent a strong signal to member schools that resisted integration (including the University of Oklahoma and the University of Missouri) by signing a major contract to have the Big Seven champion compete annually against the Atlantic Coast Conference (ACC) champion in the Orange Bowl. It was a move that made intersectional, integrated match-ups in Florida virtually certain. Two years later, a Big Seven team from the University of Nebraska became the first to integrate the game, bringing two black players to the 1955 Orange Bowl against Duke University.[111]

With the newly christened Big Eight Conference embracing a clear position on race and intersectional play, Oklahoma State found a home in the organization and built one of the most successful athletic departments in the country. By the 1980s, numerous black athletes—including Barry Sanders, a celebrated running back and winner of the 1988 Heisman Trophy—played successfully at Lewis Field. Oklahoma State was also the first school in the conference to hire an

African American coach. Unfortunately, the institution continued to carry its reputation as a "jock school" and again found itself at the center of athletic scandal in the 1980s. In 1989, Dexter Manley, a successful black quarterback at Oklahoma State, broke down in tears before a Senate Subcommittee on Education and acknowledged what sportswriters had long rumored: he had managed to graduate from OSU without learning to read.[112]

Nevertheless, sparked by a private, $165-million gift, OSU announced in 2003 a fundraising program dubbed "The Next Level." The plan included construction of an entire "athletic village" on campus and expansion to seat 60,000 at Lewis Field, a capacity 50 percent larger than Stillwater's total population. Not to be outdone (as in the 1950s) rival University of Oklahoma averaged 85,000 spectators at its home games in 2005, ninth highest in the nation. Meanwhile, by 1987 Drake University had deemphasized football to the NCAA's Division III—a minimal, less expensive, and completely nonscholarship program. Before a homecoming crowd of 3,234, the school renamed Drake Stadium "Johnny Bright Field" in October 2006 with Bright's daughters and former teammates in attendance. After a Drake alumnus notified the school that there had never been any reconciliation or apology from OAMC, both university presidents met in 2006 to "thoughtfully discuss the 1951 Johnny Bright incident" and "bring closure to the event."[113]

Why for over fifty years had there been no closure? Perhaps administrators hesitated to place importance on a small football game between small schools in Oklahoma, especially in the midst of a civil rights historiography that emphasizes legislative wrangling, judicial precedence, grassroots activism, and organized student protest. Yet an analysis of Johnny Bright's assault reveals otherwise. Some locals veiled the discussion in terms of sportsmanship, brutality, safety, and fair play, yet the centrality of race was not lost on the majority of observers both inside the state and nationwide. As the popularity and importance of football increased after World War II, a single, vivid moment of violence directed toward a black athlete in 1951 generated a public examination of race in the Midwest that no civil rights rally, court case, or speech had ever managed. For the rest of the decade, it remained to be seen how intercollegiate football would function in the region where it was most cherished and where the most controversial battlegrounds over civil rights were emerging—the Deep South.

4

"We Play Anyone"

Deciphering the Racial Politics of Georgia Football
and the 1956 Sugar Bowl Controversy

> . . . The spirit of the cheering throng
> Resounds with joy revealing
> A brotherhood in praise and song,
> In the memory of the days gone by.
> Oh, Scion of the Southland!
> In our hearts you shall forever fly!
>
> –Alma Mater, Georgia Institute of Technology

> There is no room for politics in the sports pages . . .
>
> –Johnny Hendrix, *Augusta Chronicle*, 6 January 1956

On the night of 2 December 1955, 2,500 hundred students from the Georgia
Institute of Technology marched through downtown Atlanta, broke into the
Georgia state capitol, and later marched to the Governor's Mansion, where
they congregated on Governor Marvin Griffin's front lawn. Streaming out of
every dorm and fraternity on campus, the crowd carried signs reading "Griffin
Sits on His Brains" and "To Hell with Griff." After burning an effigy of the governor, the students broke through a cordon of police officers surrounding the
capitol. By two o'clock in the morning, the mob had overturned trash bins and
broken windows inside the building as Atlanta mayor William Hartsfield and
dozens of police stood by. Griffin anxiously paced inside his home and watched
students, assembling on the lawn, sing "We'll hang Old Marvin from a sour
apple tree." The following day, 200 protesters at Mercer University followed
suit, marching through downtown Macon and singing the Georgia Tech fight
song. That Monday, 2,000 students at the University of Georgia in Athens rallied behind a banner that read, "For Once, We're for Tech." The next night,
Athens police used tear gas to dispel a crowd of 1,500 after one UG administra-
tor called the mob "a sorry bunch of boys." Meanwhile, at Emory University in

Atlanta, administrators found a Griffin doll burning on the front steps of the library.[1]

Anger over Georgia's new governor spread quickly across the country. Nearly three thousand miles from Griffin's home, students burned yet another effigy at the University of Oregon, this one pinned with a Confederate flag. White Georgians directed overwhelming disdain toward their governor. In Los Angeles, the African American *California Eagle* called it "the first time in the recent history of the South that any sizeable segment of white people have uttered a defiance of lily-white policies."[2] Yet most intriguing about the uproar was the issue that sparked it: a single college football game.

The day before Georgia Tech students marched through Atlanta, Governor Griffin asked that the state Board of Regents reconsider allowing schools to schedule athletic contests with racially integrated teams. What sparked the governor's move was next month's Sugar Bowl, where Georgia Tech and the

Georgia Tech University students protest Georgia Governor Marvin Griffin on 2 December 1955. Afro-American Newspapers Archives and Research Center.

University of Pittsburgh were planning to meet in New Orleans. Griffin initially celebrated Tech's invitation to the prestigious event; that is, before he discovered that the Pitt squad included a lone African America player, fullback Bobby Grier. For most observers around the country, student interest in football produced this extreme reaction to the governor's request to the Board of Regents. Many protest signs simply read "Sugar Bowl," while others proclaimed "We Play Anyone."[3]

However, the centrality of race could not be ignored. Even in making mundane assertions about their love of sport, students and citizens around the country were articulating their visions of an integrated (or segregated) America. Whereas civil rights historiography turns to political activism in the mid-1950s, the 1956 Sugar Bowl controversy was an important, overlooked cultural confrontation. The episode offers historians an example of critics who wanted to separate "sport" from "politics," particularly white southerners who envisioned that a public discussion about race could take place when filtered through the lens of a college football game, but not when examined in the political arena. In other regions of the country, including Los Angeles, the growing participation of African American college athletes embodied the tenor of transformed race relations and the slow progression of civil rights, both prior to and following World War II. For schools in the Deep South, intercollegiate athletics posed a false reality. Even if teams from around the country agreed to bench their black players while in Georgia, Governor Griffin realized that the game's popularity—and the visibility of black athletes on the national stage—had reached a point where intercollegiate football damaged the fight to preserve his region's status quo.

In the five years after Johnny Bright's assault, dramatic developments continued to shape the course of African American civil rights. One year before Governor Griffin's request, Martin Luther King Jr. began his public ministry in Montgomery, Alabama. For many, King's debut at the Dexter Avenue Baptist Church—and the subsequent black boycott of the city's buses in 1955—signaled the opening salvo of the modern civil rights movement. At a time when Congress inserted the phrase "under God" into the Pledge of Allegiance and 94 percent of Americans reported a belief in the Almighty, King and the black church provided the spirit, leadership, and grassroots organizing essential to sustaining these early economic battles.[4]

Yet the appearance of a renewed, coordinated movement in the South was not the only new threat to segregation emerging in the 1950s. In the realm of public housing, blacks made significant progress in breaking down some initial barriers erected by the Federal Housing Administration (FHA) after the war. More of the country's local housing projects were opening spaces to black families, and a Supreme Court decision outlawing the use of "restrictive covenants" translated into meaningful gains in some places, including northern cities, where large numbers of blacks migrated after 1945.

The early 1950s also witnessed real gains in black political power and economic clout. When the American Federation of Labor (AFL) merged with the Congress of Industrial Organizations (CIO) in 1955, African Americans A. Philip Randolph and Willard Townsend were elected vice presidents of the nation's largest labor organization. By 1956, there were forty blacks in state legislatures throughout the North and West, while Illinois, New York, and Michigan sent black representatives to Congress. According to historian John Hope Franklin, no other city spoke to the progression of civil rights in the early 1950s more vividly than Washington, D.C.—where in five years the nation's capital eliminated segregation in hotels, movie theaters, public parks, restaurants, and schools. As the decade progressed, civil rights agitation permeated a number of different discourses—from religion and politics, to labor and public education. Yet Georgia's Governor Griffin identified another serious threat to Jim Crow from a realm few anticipated could be so meaningful: intercollegiate football.[5]

Postwar College Football and the Deep South

All sport is infused with symbol and meaning, yet scholars have particularly argued that football in the American South embodied transcendent values. Notwithstanding hyperbolic assertions that dub the sport a "religion," most agree that southern observers infused the game with cultural values and used it to reinforce identity in the twentieth century. "The upwelling of feelings about athletic rivalries has helped mark the boundaries of a distinct regional identity," writes the historian Patrick Miller, who connects the rising popularity of football to the political rhetoric of Huey Long. "In similar fashion, the rituals and spectacles of sporting competition have often played into the values, ideals, and popular images of modern southern culture."[6] Andrew Doyle and Michael Oriard also note the importance of college football in the 1920s and 1930s, when the region was beset by fundamental conflicts between rural, agrarian values and an "emerging urban society built upon the secular gospel of progress and innovation." According to Doyle, southerners "used college football as a symbolic reconciliation of progress and tradition."[7]

In his studies of the postwar South, Doyle uncovers an illustrative case in the popularity of Alabama football Coach Paul "Bear" Bryant. He claims that Bryant was celebrated as an icon of the past and "singled out by the national press as a fascinating but unsavory oddity produced by a region not fully assimilated into the mainstream of American culture."[8] Nevertheless, "Bear" Bryant represented more than just southern "tradition"—and its implicit white supremacy. By the late 1960s, his popularity in Alabama exceeded that of the state's political leadership. At the 1968 Democratic National Convention, two Alabama delegates even cast votes for Bryant to succeed Lyndon Johnson. After Alabama introduced its first black football player (John Mitchell, who earned All-American honors in 1972) stories circulated about Bryant's influential role in educating Governor George Wallace on the benefits of racial integration. Two years earlier, Bryant had invited the University of Southern California and its black fullback, Sam Cunningham, to play against his team in Alabama. Although Cunningham's performance was influential, stories about Bryant's plan to use the game to convince Alabama society to integrate are overblown. Southern author Willie Morris, noting that Bryant's teams "provided a diversion from the old compulsions" and "gave the state at least one thing to be proud of when Wallace was making it an object of opprobrium," also posited Bryant as a more progressive figure. Bryant ran his team with scientific precision by observing practices in Tuscaloosa from atop an infamous ninety-foot tower, "like the Old Testament Jehovah assaying the whole of his creation." With pseudo-industrial allusions, Morris wrote of Alabama football as personifying the region's ongoing social and economic transition, not its "traditional" values.[9] Yet, according to the historian Charles Wilson, the massive outpouring of grief and "ceremonial reaction" to Bryant's death and burial in 1983 signaled the deep meaning southern fans attached to the man and the game he coached.[10]

Whether college football represented the past or the present, by the 1950s it was central to southern life and culture. Newspapers devoted extensive coverage, with lengthy features covering the personal stories of coaches and players. In many communities, football games were the most important social or civic events on the calendar. By connecting the sport to broader festivities—parades, exhibits, the crowning of homecoming kings and queens—football in the postwar South was a part of nearly everyone's life. Although the game enjoyed popularity in the North and West, southern citizens, in general, had fewer outlets for sport and urban entertainment. The lack of professional leagues and teams in the region further emphasized the role of universities and colleges in shaping identity. By equating "lost-cause" imagery with team mascots and schools, like the waving of Confederate flags or the use of "rebel yell" cheers, the game offered yet another testament to the permanence of the antebellum South in twentieth-century southern culture. By 1970, *Sports Illustrated* continued to dub the rivalry between the University of Mississippi and the University of Alabama "The War Between the States." A 1969 game drew 50,000 fans waving flags "not designed by Betsy Ross," announced the magazine. "[It was] college football's answer to *Gone With the Wind*, an Old South spectacular awash with melodrama, madness and more passes than Rhett Butler ever threw."[11] Young or old, male or female, black or white, a Georgia resident in 1955 could not ignore football, even if he or she had no interest in the sport or knowledge of the game. This was especially true after Governor Griffin's demands made front-page headlines.

The 1955 public debate surrounding the governor's attempt to bar Georgia Tech from the Sugar Bowl—and the subsequent backlash of most whites in the state—reveals tension not only between progress and Jim Crow but also among segregationists themselves. According to historian Thomas Dyer, rioting students in Georgia "were saying that race was not as important as football."[12] This may have been true for some; however, to uncover the role of race in the controversy—to what extent these were rallies against segregation or for football—it is necessary to examine how Georgians (white and black) argued about the governor's intrusion of politics into what they considered a depoliticized arena. It is also important to illuminate the role of the national media and black press in celebrating the incident as a milestone of progress. Meanwhile, prosegregationists considered it an overall victory for their cause and used the controversy to help solidify negative reaction to the Supreme Court's 1954 ruling in *Brown*.

In the middle of the turmoil stood Bobby Grier himself, a young man from Ohio who came to Pitt as an ROTC student. His high school coach encouraged him to play football simply because he "had a chance to make the team." Grier was not a particularly talented athlete, nor did he have any desire to play professionally. "I thought I wasn't good enough," he later recalled, and he was careful not to overemphasize the role of sport in his life. Unlike Jackie Robinson or Johnny Bright, football for Grier was simply a positive extracurricular activity on the road to a college degree. Yet for two months in 1955 and 1956, he was thrust into a world of social upheaval, political squabbling, and national press coverage well beyond his years. His is perhaps the most important perspective.[13]

Historians Robert Dubay and Charles Martin have both addressed the 1956 Sugar Bowl. Dubay focuses on the Griffin archives in Bainbridge, Georgia, which feature revealing, heated correspondence between the governor and various southern politicians.[14] While Dubay is most interested in the governor, Martin addresses Grier's story within his excellent attempt to contextualize the commercial rise of "bowl games" as centers of intersectional play and inevitable conflict.[15] Although both provide clear and valuable narratives of the incident, it is important to draw larger comparisons to the broader transformation of civil rights historiography, the relationship to the 1955 Montgomery bus boycott, reaction of the national black press, and the perspective of Bobby Grier himself.

Football in the Wake of *Brown* and Montgomery

Four years after Oklahoma A&M players attacked Johnny Bright on the field in Stillwater, athletics in the Sooner state underwent dramatic transformation. Having played (and hosted) integrated teams from around the nation, the University of Oklahoma was the country's most celebrated team in the mid-1950s. In 1955, the Sooners invited an integrated team from the University of Pittsburgh—including Bobby Grier—to play on the OU campus in Norman. Grier recalled that Pittsburgh had already played in segregated North Carolina and Virginia. In both states, athletic departments had arranged for him to stay at local black colleges. However, in Oklahoma he was housed with the rest of the squad. "Everybody noticed that," Grier recalled more than fifty years later and noted that the Pitt students "didn't consider Oklahoma a southern state" because of their experience. Driving into Norman, he saw "black players on the Oklahoma freshman team. I thought, 'Wow, they are really going to start integrating here.'"[16] In 1959 a black halfback named Prentice Gautt, from "the ghetto of Oklahoma City," was a featured All-American at OU. By 1960, OU and OSU were engaged in bidding wars over African American talent in the state, and both schools offered large scholarships to black players less than a decade after the Johnny Bright scandal.[17]

Meanwhile, highly visible schools in the Northeast and Big Ten continued to field talented black players after World War II. Defensive back Emlen Tunnel integrated the NFL's New York Giants in 1948 after playing at the University of Toledo and the University of Iowa (1946–1947), while Claude "Buddy" Young earned accolades at the University of Illinois and was named the Player of the Game at the 1947 Rose Bowl. Legendary Coach Woody Hayes recruited running back Robert Watkins to Ohio State University, where he played from 1952 to 1954 and led the Buckeyes to the 1954 national championship. At the University of Illinois, James (J.C.) Caroline was an All-American running back who led the nation in rushing yards in 1953, while Roosevelt Grier was a celebrated, four-year starting lineman at Pennsylvania State University from 1951 to 1954 before beginning a professional career with the New York Giants and Los Angeles Rams. Jim Brown (Syracuse University, 1954–1956) was a unanimous All-American in 1956, finished fifth in voting for the Heisman Trophy, and had one of the most successful professional careers in football history with the Cleveland Browns. Brown also participated in the 1957 Cotton Bowl in Dallas, Texas. Following in the steps of UCLA, schools on the West Coast also recruited more black students to participate, such as All-American Ollie Matson (University of San Francisco, 1950–1951).

Just as the acceptance of black college athletes convinced sport fans that Oklahoma was not a "southern state," *Brown* helped codify the lines between Midwest and South. Regions with local officials willing to abide by the ruling contrasted with the legislative backlash unleashed throughout the Deep South. For many states, "compliance" with *Brown* meant only an assurance to eliminate *de jure* segregation from state and local laws; this could mean little or no actual difference for black citizens. The 1957 "Little Rock Nine" standoff between Arkansas Governor Orval Faubus and the federal government highlighted entrenched segregation in certain areas outside the Deep South. Yet it also revealed the relative failure of segregation politics and white "citizens' councils" in midwestern states like Oklahoma and Kansas. Within a few years of *Brown*, civil rights legislation informed the nation which states were prepared to fight integration at all costs.

As a result, postwar civil rights historiography spotlights the Deep South by revealing the legislative and grassroots battles over education and transportation in the wake of *Brown*. Unfortunately, the centrality of leisure (including sport) has received far less attention. This oversight neglects the intriguing story of an athlete like Bobby Grier, whose participation in the Sugar Bowl drew threats from not only Governor Griffin but also the Georgia States' Rights Council and various segregation groups throughout the region. The result was a rare, dramatic public debate among white residents over integration. While the story of Rosa Parks and the burgeoning Montgomery, Alabama, bus boycott receives far more attention from historians, many southerners at the time attached considerable and equivalent significance to Grier and the desegregation of the Sugar Bowl.

Beginning with the 1955 boycott, scholars have emphasized the growing role of "local people" in civil rights campaigns throughout Georgia, Mississippi, and Alabama. As the historian Kevin Gaines notes, most of these histories were "guided by the view that movements predated and created leadership."[18] Often, the narratives explicated the stories of activist cadres at the city and county levels—for example, regional grassroots heroes such as Rosa Parks—and wove them into a national narrative. This focus on the transformation of southern society at the community level has been vital in deepening our knowledge of race in postwar America; however, it is centered mainly on the same political issues that the national civil rights leadership campaigned for in the 1950s—including voting rights, education, and transportation. Yet the Sugar Bowl controversy offers a clear example of these same racial politics infiltrating popular culture with very different consequences. Glenda Gilmore and other scholars of the nineteenth and early twentieth centuries, drawing from cultural history to expand the definition of "political," uncovered politicized encounters in the mundane, everyday lives of southern citizens.[19] By examining popular culture, scholars of the postwar South can do the same, for the Sugar Bowl controversy was an important politicized episode that enriches our understanding of the struggle to integrate schools, buses, and voting booths. Most observers criticized Governor Griffin not for his racism but for his intrusion of politics into what they considered to be an apolitical situation—Georgia Tech's football schedule. Ironically, historians and the governor should agree that the racial politics of college football were real and meaningful.

In December 1955, the local boycott by African American citizens in Montgomery began making national headlines. Following Parks's arrest, the story was a catalyst for the civil rights movement, an example of nonviolent citizen action that drew immediate attention throughout the South. As early as 6 December, the *Atlanta Constitution* declared that the boycott was 90 percent successful, "one of the largest and most effective economic reprisals by either race in recent years in the segregated South."[20] The *New York Times* immediately picked up on the boycott, while the national black press lauded a gathering of 5,000 black citizens at the Holt Street Baptist Church.[21] The boycott received overwhelming support from the NAACP, whose E. D. Nixon served as principal architect. By the end of 1956, the boycott became one of the most symbolic and important episodes in the civil rights struggle—an event fully embraced by the black press. Yet in December 1955 the movement was in its infancy, and even sympathetic media outlets withheld editorial coverage. In addition, few columnists addressed the boycott and public letters of support (or opposition) were rare, even though the NAACP hoped to use the incident to bring national attention to Alabama.

Ironically, in December 1955 and January 1956 Bobby Grier received more attention than Rosa Parks or the bus boycott. For many, even pending civil rights legislation took a back seat to the controversy over Grier, Governor Griffin, and the Sugar Bowl. As Americans analyzed race relations in the South through the lens of college football, many who had never shown any interest in sport used Grier's story to voice their political opinions and make personal statements about the meaning of racial integration. Nevertheless, although the NAACP carefully micromanaged economic boycotts and legislative challenges to Jim Crow, Bobby Grier received little assistance, even as his every action and word made national headlines. "I was on my own," he later said, when recalling how journalists from around the country swarmed him in the weeks before the Sugar Bowl.[22]

"The South Stands at Armageddon"

Governor Marvin Griffin believed that Georgia citizens who wanted to preserve "the southern way of life" were also on their own. Elected in January 1955, Griffin ran on a platform devoted to Jim Crow and promised to continue the fight waged by previous prosegregation Governor Herman Talmadge. During his first year, the governor felt empowered with a mandate from the people. After entering office his racial rhetoric was direct, forceful, and often apocalyptic. Griffin vowed "to take whatever steps necessary to preserve segregation," including the use of force by the Georgia highway patrol and state militia: "the police powers of the state."[23] In November 1955, Griffin, proclaiming it "would serve no useful purpose," made headlines when he turned down a request from a moderate biracial organization that wanted to study Georgia schools. Although the group insisted it was not advocating integration, the governor offered a harsh rebuke, claiming that "if it's wrong now, it'll be wrong ten years from now."[24] Griffin shared his racial philosophy with other Georgia politicians, including Secretary of State Ben Fortson. Fortson harassed the Georgia NAACP, called it an "illegal organization," and claimed it failed to register as a corporation.[25] In September 1955, Griffin, Talmadge, and other local leaders cofounded the States' Rights Council of Georgia. Under Griffin's direction, Georgia was second only to Mississippi in mobilizing grassroots organizations committed to fighting *Brown*.

In his 1956 "state of the state" address, Griffin articulated the policy of "massive resistance" that many southerners soon embraced and pressured moderate leaders throughout the South to take a firm stand on segregating public schools. "There will be no mixing of the races in public schools, in college classrooms in Georgia as long as I am Governor," he announced. Later, Griffin addressed the States' Rights Council directly and proclaimed that "the rest of the nation is looking to Georgia for the lead in segregation."[26]

After the Supreme Court ruled again in 1955 that that the desegregation of public schools had to proceed "with all deliberate speed," Griffin assailed the moderate *Atlanta Journal* and *Atlanta Constitution* for conducting "one of the most abusive personal campaigns against me."[27] Calling the Atlanta media a "monopolistic combine" and "trojan horse," Griffin went on statewide radio and pleaded with citizens not let them "sell us down the river to the NAACP and the liberal pinks who would destroy all the guarantees of constitutional government." The governor complained that Atlanta newsmen "were for the mixing of races, though the editorial staff does not have the courage to come out and say so."[28]

Locked in this fierce battle with the state's moderate press, Griffin appealed to his supporters with claims of two important achievements: an influx of new business and increasing prestige for the state's universities. In particular, he lauded the success and national recognition achieved by the Georgia Institute of Technology. Georgia Tech stood as a powerful symbol of the "New South," one that segregationists could use to combine the rhetoric of progress with the fight to preserve the social status quo. The same week Tech was invited to the Sugar Bowl, the school unveiled a new million-dollar computer center. The same Georgia press that attacked Griffin called it "a long step forward" in the engineering and scientific development of the South.[29] Regardless of political persuasion, a majority of Georgia citizens and many outside observers celebrated the relative strength and prestige Georgia Tech had earned during the previous thirty years.

The school's athletic program had also achieved unprecedented success, including the football team's thirty-one-game winning streak. From 1951 to 1957, Georgia Tech was invited to six consecutive national bowl games and won them all. Contests versus rival southern teams engendered regional pride (like a victory over the University of Mississippi in the 1952 Sugar Bowl). But games against popular teams from outside the South truly solidified the school's reputation and brought pride to a state otherwise bemoaned in the national press. Initially, Tech was reluctant to abide by the so-called "gentlemen's agreement"—the compromise of segregating participants for games in the South and integrating contests at northern locales. Top football programs routinely benched their African American players when visiting southern schools. Yet in 1934, Tech administrators even convinced the University of Michigan to bench a black player for a game that took place in Ann Arbor.[30] Nevertheless, by the 1950s Georgia Tech regularly faced black opponents in numerous sports as long as the games were scheduled outside the segregated South. These included a popular 1952 game against Notre Dame in South Bend, Indiana, where the Fighting Irish (with their first two African American players) ended the Yellow Jackets' famed winning streak. By 1955, Georgia Tech had also become the first team in the nation to have won all four major bowl games—Orange, Sugar, Cotton, and Rose.

Moreover, the positive media coverage associated with football helped assuage the growing national criticism toward segregated politics in the region. No other figure represented this counterbalance like Head Coach Bobby Dodd. While state segregationists, including Marvin Griffin, faced a barrage of criticism from outside the South, Dodd achieved notice as a popular "player's coach." A 1952 feature in *Time* magazine announced that players at Georgia Tech "come as close as any big-league squad can to playing football for fun." Four years later, the magazine called Dodd "The Happy Coach" and celebrated his mellow, happy-go-lucky approach to winning, while *Sports Illustrated* dubbed him "a low pressure engineer."[31] Dodd's young, all-American look and soft personality presented a stark contrast to Bear Bryant, whose crotchety demeanor in the 1960s played into northern stereotypes about the region's aging and obdurate segregationist leadership. Yet Dodd was a lifelong southerner and even played quarterback at the University of Tennessee under Coach Bob "Major" Neyland, the man who did not want to face the integrated UCLA Bruins in the 1939 Rose Bowl.

At Georgia Tech, Dodd was aware of the gentlemen's agreement and never attempted to arrange contracts for games in Atlanta versus integrated teams. Yet for games outside the state he did not think twice about the opponent. When the Yellow Jackets received the invitation to face Pittsburgh in New Orleans, Dodd was "tickled to death" and immediately accepted the bid. The game "will have a good intersectional flavor," the coach told the *New Orleans Times-Picayune:* he recognized that a successful game against one of the North's finest teams was probably worth more to his program than a game versus an opponent closer to home. Foreshadowing the impending controversy, pictures of a smiling Dodd appeared on front pages in New Orleans, directly below the story of a violent assault on an NAACP official by members of a Mississippi citizens' council.[32]

Governor Griffin and many legislators were perturbed that Georgia schools were scheduling contests with integrated teams outside the region. Nevertheless, Bobby Dodd and Tech administrators were unprepared for the harsh response to the Sugar Bowl invitation. Within days of accepting the bid, Dodd ignored a plea from the States' Rights Council of Georgia not to play in the game. Formed in the wake of *Brown*, the council was a new and fledgling group with little organization or direction. Griffin and former governor Herman Talmadge had cofounded the association just two months earlier. Secretary W. T. Bodenhamer— a local Baptist preacher whom *Time* magazine later dubbed a "rabid racist"—said the council rarely gathered and had no scheduled meetings. The protest telegram sent to Bobby Dodd was probably one of the first actions ever taken by the group. Most likely, Dodd did not even know that its members included Governors Griffin and Talmadge, as well as Roy Harris, a member of the state's Board of Regents.[33]

The following week, from the governor's office, Griffin himself sent a personal telegram, which he publicized, that denounced all integrated athletics. The governor asked that the Board of Regents consider a complete ban on Georgia schools scheduling *any* contests with integrated teams, regardless of the proposed location. "The South stands at Armageddon," the governor explained. "There is no more difference in compromising integrity of race on the playing field than in doing so in the classrooms."[34] Coach Dodd was "surprised" at the governor's demand and told the *Atlanta Journal* he had already ignored the earlier request from an "unofficial source."[35] Clearly, the coach and other Georgia citizens did not recognize that members of the Board of Regents (including Roy Harris) were in constant contact with the governor over the issue.

The episode offers an interesting look at the initial stages of organization in response to *Brown*. Within a year, citizens' and states' rights councils became powerful, coordinated political machines throughout the South; some had already reached that level of sophistication in Mississippi. But in Georgia, the subsequent embarrassment over the governor's actions and the lack of clarity and organization behind them illuminate an initial period in which the States' Rights Council of Georgia was a weak and divided organ with members unsure of which integration battles they wanted to fight. The governor probably talked with few people before acting, perhaps only Talmadge and Regent Harris. Only after Griffin himself went public with the fierce, apocalyptic statement did Georgia Tech officials, Bobby Dodd, and the Board of Regents take any notice. Moreover, within months, states' rights councils would no longer be "unofficial" sources that one could ignore.

The prospective game also drew the governor's ire because the Supreme Court's most recent segregation ruling centered on public leisure. Local officials in the South reacted decisively after the court released a sweeping decision outlawing racial barriers at public parks, beaches, and golf courses. On 7 November, the court ordered Atlanta to integrate its Bobby Jones Municipal Golf Course. One city commissioner in Birmingham, which had an ordinance banning all interracial sporting events, warned that the court's ruling over integrating public parks and swimming pools would "lead to bloodshed." In Leland, Mississippi, authorities simply "sold" the town's park to a private club for $1. Soon, Griffin emerged as the South's most outspoken critic of the ruling. "Comingling of the races in Georgia state parks and recreation areas will not be permitted or tolerated," he told the national press. "The state will get out of the park business before allowing a breakdown in segregation in the intimacy of the playground."[36] In a radio address to Georgia citizens, Griffin called the decision "the most recent attack on our social traditions" and insisted that Atlanta mayor

William Hartsfield keep Georgia golf segregated.[37] Meanwhile, local activists sought to test the new ruling. Readers of the black press were outraged by reports of middle-class black men arrested on golf courses throughout the South before they reached the first tee. In Atlanta, Dr. Hamilton M. Holmes, a seventy-one-year-old black physician, was plaintiff to one of the original cases when he sued for the right to play on the Bobby Jones Course. "All we want is a chance to play golf," Holmes told *Time* magazine.[38] Most likely, Griffin and the States' Rights Council of Georgia responded so strongly to the Sugar Bowl invitation because the fight against Jim Crow had turned public attention to sports and recreation in the preceding month. If whites were going to fight for segregated golf courses, swimming pools, and public parks, then how could the state allow its collegians to participate in integrated athletic contests, especially a game that drew the attention of millions? (Griffin was right to see the link between leisure and education; Dr. Holmes's grandson was one of the first two black students admitted to the University of Georgia in 1961.)

"The Hub of Everything That Lives and Breathes in New Orleans"

For New Orleans citizens, the Sugar Bowl was one of the largest events on the city's calendar. Scheduled for 2 January, the game climaxed a week of festivities that jammed downtown hotels with spectators and participants. Events included a Sugar Bowl parade, a full collegiate basketball tournament, and a tennis tournament featuring some of the world's best players. The inaugural game in 1935 before 24,000 spectators at Tulane Stadium was an instant success. Within five years, the game's sponsor—the New Orleans Mid-Winter Sports Association—was scrambling to expand seating at the stadium, first to 69,000 in 1940 and then to 81,000 in 1955. "By American standards, New Orleans is an ancient and conservative city," remarked the president of the Chamber of Commerce at a celebration marking the game's twentieth anniversary. "Yet, in a span of twenty years we have seen this carefree, fun-loving, backward city transformed, and the Sugar Bowl was the first step on this long journey that again will make us one of America's greatest and most dynamic cities."[39]

According to sportswriter Furman Bisher, what began as "a minor affair" had become "the hub of everything that lives and breathes in New Orleans" during the holidays.[40] Each year local newspapers, devoting entire "women's" and "fashion" sections to the Sugar Bowl, outlined the extensive list of politicians, dignitaries, administrators, and players' wives headed to New Orleans for the festivities. Traffic jams and congestion did not stop residents from embracing the game, along with the added influx of dollars. The Sugar Bowl brought so many from outside the state that the *Times-Picayune* traditionally devoted its front page to news from the home regions of the two teams participating in the game. Other schools eagerly waited should Governor Griffin and the Board of

Regents pull Georgia Tech from the festivities. The organizing committee contacted the University of Texas as a potential replacement immediately after the governor's outburst, an inquiry that stimulated excitement for students and fans in Austin.[41]

The last time an integrated team had participated in the Sugar Bowl, it was the unbeaten 1941 Boston College Eagles, which played the game without star African American halfback Lou Montgomery. The black press remembered Montgomery's treatment (a few sportswriters actually criticized the young man for agreeing to sit out) and waited anxiously to see how citizens in New Orleans would react to the decision to invite Bobby Grier and the Pittsburgh squad.[42] Bill Keefe, sports editor at the *Times-Picayune*, was the city's most respected authority on athletics. Keefe thoroughly praised the committee and made no mention of Governor Griffin's protest. He announced that Pittsburgh was playing the "invading role" and seemed certain that the home crowd would root for Georgia Tech. "It wouldn't do to have an Eastern team come down here and show up our league," he wrote. Nevertheless, he praised Bobby Grier, "the big Negro fullback," and applauded the invitation of the Panthers.[43] Echoing the broader gains won by blacks after World War II, Keefe's coverage of African American athletes likewise changed considerably. He had been the most outspoken critic of Joe Louis in the late 1930s. While most southern sportswriters tacitly approved the idea of a black boxing champion, Keefe wrote scathing denunciations of Louis, whom he called the "black terror" in 1936.[44] Yet by 1955, Keefe's softened response to black athletes and the desegregation of the Sugar Bowl spoke to the general ebbing of strict segregation in New Orleans's spectator sports.

Many in the black press admitted the city was more tolerant than other regions in the South, although this was hardly a ringing endorsement. "New Orleans is relatively liberal but no less opposed to desegregation," wrote Roi Ottley in the *Chicago Defender*. "The climate is by no means as brutal and violent as in next door Mississippi."[45] Indeed, the city experienced its own backlash to the *Brown* decision, including the passage of renewed school segregation laws in 1954. Even after the Interstate Commerce Commission barred segregation in interstate travel, black passengers in 1955 still reported discrimination at the city's Moissant International Airport.[46] In addition, most of the city's upscale establishments, including the historic St. Charles Hotel, where many Sugar Bowl teams traditionally stayed, barred black patrons. One *Chicago Defender* columnist predicted Bobby Grier would receive an overwhelmingly negative reception should he attend and challenged the young player to remove himself from the team in a protest of his own. Yet Grier never once thought about boycotting the game. "We all knew there were only six or seven bowls, your chances of playing are a thousand to one," he recalled. "To be part of the championship, that's part of every kid's dream and nobody wants to give up that chance."[47]

Black sportswriters applauded the decision to invite Pittsburgh yet remained cautious about what restrictions might be placed on Grier and his teammates.

Although the Sugar Bowl was segregated on the field, organizers in recent years had relaxed Jim Crow restrictions. Since the 1940s, seating for the game at Tulane University Stadium had been strictly segregated. A printed disclaimer on each ticket even warned that admittance was "issued for a person of the Caucasian race."[48] However, by 1956 the disclaimer was removed, and visitor sections in the stadium were opened to unrestricted seating. While the players remained all white, the U.S. Naval Academy had its integrated student body sit together for the 1955 contest versus the University of Mississippi. Organizers for the upcoming 1956 game also informed black sportswriters that the stadium's press box would be opened to them for the first time.[49] In addition, the Cotton Bowl in Dallas had already hosted several black players since 1948, and in 1952 College of the Pacific halfback Eddie Macon integrated the Sun Bowl in El Paso after the University of Texas system previously resisted having black players compete against Texas College of Mines and Metallurgy (known now as the University of Texas at El Paso).[50]

In New Orleans, Sugar Bowl organizers and most local residents were reluctant to speak out publicly about the idea of a black athlete in the 1956 game. Yet plenty of citizens agreed with Governor Griffin and criticized the committee for loosening segregation rules at the stadium. In particular, activists from the New Orleans Citizens Council applauded the governor's stand. The council incorrectly announced that a "great majority" of residents was opposed to the game and "disappointed at the Sugar Bowl committee's decision to invite Pittsburgh to play." Although the council supported the game, it warned the *Times-Picayune* that "New Orleanians have always whole-heartedly supported the annual classic but if the Sugar Bowlers persist in agitating the segregation issue by permitting a game where the races are mixed and the seats sold on a non-segregated basis, the Sugar Bowl will soon lose the support of the people."[51] Other segregation groups asked Louisiana's Governor Robert Kennon to stop the game. "We have state laws for segregation . . . in our schools and institutions," the governor responded, noting that "every official act of mine has been in favor of segregation." Nevertheless, Kennon refused to intercede and left the decision to "those that control the Sugar Bowl and city authorities in New Orleans."[52] In Georgia, Roy Harris, a member of the Board of Regents and the States' Rights Council, claimed that the Mississippi Citizens Council sent 1,000 telegrams of protest to the Sugar Bowl Committee. Harris also announced that segregation groups were planning a full boycott of the game if Grier participated.[53]

Despite this sympathy from segregationist groups in the South, Governor Griffin's demands only sparked more interest in the upcoming game. Georgia Tech officials reported a noticeable spike in ticket requests from around the country, "despite injection of the racial issue."[54] In Pittsburgh, the African

American *Courier* encouraged its readers to purchase tickets in the unrestricted seating areas, and Jimmy Brown of the *Philadelphia Tribune* announced that Pittsburgh's athletic department was "flooded with calls" from blacks seeking tickets.[55] Nevertheless, publicity surrounding the protests of Georgia's white students stimulated the most interest in the game. Thousands had marched around Georgia, and in Atlanta it took an impromptu speech from State Representative M. M. "Muggsy" Smith—a Tech alumnus and former football star—to calm the crowd at the governor's mansion. At the capitol, students linked Griffin's demands to the activism of former state leaders. The crowd defaced a statue of John Gordon—former Confederate general, early Ku Klux Klan leader, and governor from 1886 to 1890—and placed an ashcan over the figure's head. In addition to the protests at Emory, Mercer, Georgia Tech, and the University of Georgia, spontaneous student outbursts were reported around the country. At Wake Forest University, 500 students used the Georgia Tech incident to spark their own demands for "big time athletics" while protesting the administration and chanting, "Why can't we get great athletes like we used to?" Ironically, the only school that stopped students who wished to protest was the University of Pittsburgh itself, where unrest remained centered on race and the proposed exclusion of Bobby Grier. Hundreds of Pitt students planned a large demonstration against Griffin before administrators cancelled the event.[56]

Student outburst sparked nationwide attention. Within days, Sugar Bowl organizers and the city of New Orleans remained steadfast that the football game would go on regardless of Georgia Tech's attendance. What remained to be seen was whether Georgia citizens, the Board of Regents, or Tech administrators would respond to Governor Griffin's demands and how they would interpret the actions of their own state's collegians.

"The Solid South Is No Longer Solid"

The decision of the Georgia Board of Regents was a striking juxtaposition to the overwhelming student response on campuses across the state. The group declared that it would meet and consider Griffin's proposal, which it did within days. Along with Roy Harris, others on the board seemed in sympathy with the governor. Regent C. L. Moss told the press he was for Griffin's request "100 percent," while Regent John Spooner claimed integrated athletics "should never have been tolerated in the past, and I'm not in favor of them playing against Negroes now." Regent Quimby Melton, a close friend of Griffin, suggested that Tech be allowed to play in the upcoming Sugar Bowl but that schools adopt the governor's suggestions for future athletic contracts. Meanwhile, the board's chairman, Robert Arnold, generally distanced himself from the controversy but declared that it was "no innovation" for Georgia teams to play African American opponents. The board's only female regent, also opposing the governor's request, noted that her son "played football against Negroes" twenty years earlier at a northern school and she "never thought anything about it." Yet the governor's most vocal opponent on the board was Atlanta resident David Rice, who immediately told the press Griffin's request was "utterly ridiculous."[57]

Not surprisingly, when the regents met to decide the issue, Roy Harris advocated forcefully on the governor's behalf. Before the meeting, Harris announced that he would vote to bar Tech from participating in the game but predicted that the board would side against him, Griffin, and the States' Rights Council. In a lament that seemed to indicate a football game was more important than segregated schools, Harris bitterly said the board would "show the world that Georgia stands for segregation where there is no money involved but will sell out when it is."[58] Harris and Rice clashed incessantly during the meeting, which Georgia Tech President Blake Van Leer and Coach Bobby Dodd also attended. Rice called for a resolution that condemned the governor for "interfering" with regents' affairs and asserted that the board be "unchangeably independent."[59] Meanwhile, Harris observed that he regularly read the *Pittsburgh Courier* "and other Negro newspapers." "Negroes are determined to break down segregation through the invasion of the fields of entertainment and sports first," he warned the group.[60] The two also clashed over how to describe the student unrest that had taken place on the streets of Atlanta and around the state. Rice objected to the term "riot" and tried to downplay the protests by noting that the governor himself called the events "just a bunch of college boys having a good time." Charles Bloch, a committed segregationist, disagreed and claimed that "a gang" breaking into the state capitol and "restrained only by police" indeed qualified as a riot. "If that's not a riot, what is?" he asked.[61]

After lengthy debate, the board voted 14–1 to pass a curious, confusing set of resolutions. The board praised Griffin's "courageousness," hinted at future compliance with segregated athletics, but completely rebuked his immediate demand and allowed Georgia Tech to participate in the Sugar Bowl. Another resolution condemned the student marches and implored Georgia schools to locate and punish those responsible for organizing them.[62] The lone dissent did not come from the board's ardent segregationists, but rather from David Rice— the most "liberal" voice on the panel. Nevertheless, because Tech was allowed to play, observers nationwide interpreted the decision as a complete rebuke of Governor Griffin and the state's segregationists, though it clearly was not. In fact, more interesting than the resolutions was the way in which all sides of the political spectrum, including Griffin, claimed victory from them.

As college students in the state celebrated the success of the demonstrations, many retreated from the discourse of equality voiced by protestors. Tech's student body president called Griffin's actions "unwarranted" and apologized to the Pittsburgh community for the governor's remarks. Yet despite being "morally certain" that the Yellow Jackets should be allowed to play, the young man later made it clear to Atlanta residents that the demonstrations "were not against segregation but against political forces . . . trying to prevent us from going to the Sugar Bowl."[63] Indeed, reaction from most students lacked any real criticism of the racial status quo. "Denying a team the right to play in a bowl is carrying the issue too far," said one University of Georgia student, who again implied that football schedules had a greater impact on the lives of white Georgians than public schools and buses. Another student even insisted that lessons learned from the incident would strengthen Jim Crow. "Segregation is a good thing as long as it does not cramp the lives of the forces which are keeping it in effect," wrote James Wynn. "Most Georgians are for segregation as long as it does not interfere with their athletics."[64]

Many students berated the governor not for his hard-line stand on segregation—or his virulent racism—but for trying to earn political favor through a situation that they felt held no political meaning. "Griffin and Company had better wake up," announced one student editorial. "The school system of Georgia, and particularly the University system, should not be brought into politics."[65] Yet the overall reaction of most students betrayed such broad statements. The segregation of public education (both secondary and collegiate) was a completely acceptable political platform for the governor, and practically no one spoke out against Griffin's suggestions that student bodies remain segregated. Nor did students use the issue to rally support for admitting blacks at Georgia universities. In essence, "University system" was little more than a euphemism for scheduling football games. There were obvious arenas within Georgia public education where political wrangling was expected, even welcomed, but sport was simply not one of them.

Few had ever questioned how white students at segregated schools would react if administrators were forced to shut down intercollegiate athletics to preserve Jim Crow. In 1939, the *New York Times* assumed that Tennessee fans and citizens would support a boycott of the Rose Bowl should UCLA attend. With segregation under full attack by 1955, national media and local politicians were shocked at the reaction from some of Georgia's supposedly finest white students. "I personally have no objection to playing a team with a Negro member on it," announced Tech's starting quarterback. "And, as far as I know, the rest of the boys feel the same way."[66] Although Griffin backed down after the regents denied his request, other politicians were not ready to give in. State representative John Drinkard called the student demonstrators "mobsters and hoodlums" and proposed that the state dismiss them from Tech and cut off funding to the school if administrators insisted on participating in the game.[67] Drinkard also argued that every prospective college student in the state be required to "state truthfully . . . whether or not he or she favors mixed races"; administrators could then legitimately deny admission to those who did not support segregation.

Even in condemning the political attack on football, some students actually supported Drinkard's proposal. Student editorials called it "sheer stupidity," but others noted that "a so called 'loyalty oath' . . . is a good idea." "It would state that the prospective student was dedicated to upholding the principles in which Georgia and the South as a whole believes," responded one University of Georgia student.[68] White students had challenged the governor's boycott of the Sugar Bowl and voiced their weariness of prosegregation politicians, yet they ultimately marched for the freedom of football, not the freedoms of speech, thought, or political equality. Sport stood as a separate, almost mythic, ground when compared to the mundane realm of race politics. Griffin brought "shame and disgrace upon all citizens of our state," announced an editorial in the UG *Red and Black*: "[He] stepped out of bounds in making an issue of segregation in sports, where there has been no controversy under similar circumstances in the past."[69] College football represented such a false reality that fans were required to have short memories.

Moreover, the reaction of media outlets outside Georgia tended to misrepresent the meaning of the student protests. The students were "demonstrating that not all people in Georgia or the South share the bigotry of some of their political leaders," proclaimed the *Philadelphia Inquirer*.[70] In particular, the black press celebrated the students as symbols of the South's crumbling racial hierarchy and the emergence of a new, more progressive generation of white leaders. The *Pittsburgh Courier* announced that the riots proved there was a "large body of white people in the South which is indifferent about the issue" of race yet still "secretly welcomes the opportunity to do [what] the Supreme Court's desegregation decree offers."[71] The *Afro-American* celebrated the "wrath" of Tech students and even linked the episode to segregationist threats to close public schools in the wake of *Brown*. If they attempted to do so, southerners "are going to find this same reaction among parents of school children," warned the paper.[72] According to the *Chicago Defender*, the spontaneous demonstration was a "heartening development" because the "youngsters represent the south's future leaders." In California, the *Eagle* echoed the optimism of blacks nationwide who hoped that the incident revealed the true desire of young white Georgians to limit racial segregation: "The solid south is no longer solid."[73]

Even in Atlanta, the black press claimed that the student protest held meaning beyond football. "We must admit," read one *Atlanta Daily World* editorial, "that we did not think that the Yellow Jackets of Tech would respond so quickly, vigorously, and numerously with their stings of protest."[74] Black sportswriter Marion Jackson announced that local students in Atlanta proved that "the politicians are speaking from a ghostly grave on the whole racial question." Mistakenly blurring sport and education—a common error for those who praised the students—Jackson insisted that the young people had torn down the "academic curtain which had corralled their liberalism and open-mindedness on mixed sports and desegregating schools."[75] Other blacks insisted that "Northern white boys enrolled at Georgia Tech" refused to "buy all of that cheap, anti-Negro political propaganda."[76] Writing in the *Pittsburgh Courier*, only Benjamin Mays—president of Morehouse College and mentor to Martin Luther King Jr.—recognized the discrepancy between the reality of the protest and the idealism of northern progressives by noting that black students had tried to gain admission to Georgia Tech and the University of Georgia for years without a single student demonstration.[77]

Northern politicians and white liberals also looked for more than just a love of football in the student response. At the Harlem YMCA, New York's Governor Averell Harriman and Jackie Robinson both praised the Tech student body for "knowing what's right."[78] In Pittsburgh, the American Civil Liberties Union announced that "it is the students of Georgia Tech who speak for the people of Georgia and not a demagogue governor."[79] ACLU executive director Patrick Malin insisted that "Tech's spontaneous outburst" was a "dramatic instance showing that the younger South wants to deal with people on terms of individual merit, not on terms of accidental membership in a racial group."[80] Even at the groundbreaking AFL-CIO merger convention in New York, CIO President Walter Reuther used the occasion to address the football controversy. In citing civil rights reform as a major objective for the new union, Reuther condemned Griffin's request to boycott the Sugar Bowl. "That kind of attitude is un-American, it's immoral," he charged. "You couldn't help the Communists more if you were on their payroll."[81] Only the *New York Times* downplayed the student marches as "largely influenced by the desire to 'save a football game' rather than a protest against Governor Griffin's segregation policy."[82]

Similarly, in 1962 some observers claimed that football helped "defuse racial crisis" at the University of Mississippi. Ole Miss Coach John Vaught wrote that football "saved the school" during the riots surrounding James Meredith's admission and even noted that Attorney General Robert Kennedy contacted him during the controversy because a football coach could "keep the situation calm."[83] There was a certain charm in envisioning college football as somehow occupying a higher moral ground, and many in the North romanticized southern college students as a fifth column waiting to overthrow segregation in the region. Northern media reshaped Georgia Tech students—who had largely marched in support of the racial status quo—into symbols of progressive change.

Likewise, many claimed that the Georgia Board of Regents had rebuked and embarrassed the governor. The *Pittsburgh Post-Gazette* announced that the regents had "thrown . . . bigoted Marvin Griffin for a loss" and were even "piling on" with the 14–1 vote, forgetting that the dissent had come from David Rice, who actually wanted a harsher resolution and called the governor's request "asinine."[84] The Pennsylvania state legislature immediately debated a formal protest of Griffin's actions, and editorial cartoons nationwide had their own field day. Some images characterized Georgia's governor as an immature, weak little man while others depicted an overweight, bloated football player run over by opponents. One of the most popular featured Griffin as a football-clad donkey, "Georgia's All-American Ass."[85] In New York, the *Post* announced that Griffin had injected "a deadly note of burlesque into the Southern defense of the segregation system," while the *Daily News* called the Board of Regents "a group of outdated fuddy duddies."[86]

Meanwhile, in Atlanta the *Constitution* rejoiced that the regents had "emphatically refused" the governor. Not only did the governor's demand clash with his recent trips to northern cities to attract business, but his demand had instead disgraced the state's reputation. "I have never been so ashamed and humiliated," wrote one *Atlanta Journal* reader.[87] On the GTU campus, administrators announced that hundreds of alumni had contacted the school to voice their disapproval—with only one demanding that Tech refuse to play. After the regents' decision, the Tech faculty gave President Van Leer a standing ovation at their next meeting. Meanwhile, Mayor Hartsfield used the swirling controversy to divert attention while he quietly desegregated Atlanta's public golf courses against Griffin's wishes.[88]

The black press also commended the board for its decision and announced that blacks in Atlanta were "quietly cheering the mess . . . Griffin has made for

Georgia Tech students continue to march in the early morning hours of 2 December 1955. The sign reads, "To Hell With Gov. Griffin." Courtesy Georgia Tech University Archives.

himself." One black historian at Atlanta University announced that the governor had committed political suicide.[89] The *Afro-American* thanked Griffin for "performing a more useful service for our side than if he had written his check for a life membership in the NAACP." Even mild-mannered Bobby Grier was depicted as mocking the governor of Georgia. A popular picture of Grier and his white teammates, smiling with their "thumbs down for Marv," appeared in black newspapers across the country.[90]

"Someone Needs to Write a Handbook on Segregation"

All of this positive reaction stemmed from the fact that Grier would be allowed to integrate the Sugar Bowl against Georgia Tech. In celebrating, however, many overlooked how much the Board of Regents, white students, and Georgia citizens had actually agreed with the governor's rhetoric. Indeed, the very fact that the board had decided to meet and discuss Griffin's proposal—something it was not required to do—belied the sentiments of those who saw a progressive university system publicly rebuking the state's backward leadership.

In the aftermath of the decision, comments from some regents confirmed that the board supported the governor. Regent Charles Bloch claimed the resolutions reinforced the status quo embodied in the "gentlemen's agreement": Georgia schools would never play African American opponents inside the state. In a veiled reference to Johnny Bright, Bloch claimed the policy was a "safety measure" to "prevent riots that might result if a white boy injured a Negro boy in a game, or vice versa."[91] While the resolutions rebuffed Griffin's attempt to block the game, they also praised him for "keeping the faith" of his administration and applauded his "inspiring leadership in protecting inviolate the sacred institutions of our people." Bloch also told the *Atlanta Journal* he thought the Board of Regents should require its approval for all future bowl invitations.[92]

Griffin himself even celebrated the regents' decision and claimed victory for the segregationists. Congratulating the board for being "forthright," the governor said the resolutions would "serve to prevent breeches in our traditions in the future."[93] Although Tech would participate in the Sugar Bowl over his objections, Griffin still maintained that the debate solidified a future of segregated athletics in the state. The governor's office also claimed that hundreds of Georgia citizens had voiced their opinion, and 2–1 favored the governor's crusade to stop the game. "I will give no comfort to negroes and white folks playing on the same field," Griffin announced. "But if other people want colored folks sitting in their laps, we'll have to abide by it if we go there to play."[94]

Winning football games had achieved such a degree of meaning that participants were now more important than spectators. Although Griffin had agreed to budge on integrated seating in the stands, he continued to oppose integrating the actual players on the field. Such a response, echoed by segregationists throughout the state, revealed the complexities of sport that separated it from other forms of leisure and entertainment. Traditionally, the racial separation of spectators had been paramount to systems of social inequality—including venues for music concerts, movies, and theatrical plays. By the 1950s most segregationists had opened themselves to African American performers as long as audiences remained strictly separated. While the Sugar Bowl drew an integrated crowd of 80,000 spectators, the continued racial separation of the performers was most important to segregationists and integrationists alike. The participants were young men—not professional artists—who represented the future of Georgia, and their status on the field was more important than anything else. The segregation of twenty-two college students on the gridiron (that is, eleven from each team) became more significant than the 80,000 who watched.

After the board's ruling, Griffin continued to announce that citizens would "have to make sacrifices" in the fight to preserve the social status quo, by which he meant football fans should prepare to give up future opportunities to see celebrated teams play in the state.[95] And many white Georgians were ready to make those sacrifices, regardless of student sentiment at the universities. Without a single professional sport franchise, fans in Georgia embraced intercollegiate athletics to support regional identity. Only in 1965 would citizens vote to construct Atlanta Stadium and finally lure major league baseball to the South. Without other teams to support in the 1950s, most University of Georgia and Georgia Tech football fans were not current students, and many were not even alumni.

Like those who celebrated the incident as a symbolic rebuke of segregation, historians have also underestimated the tacit support for the governor, even from those who wished to see Georgia Tech compete in the Sugar Bowl. Perhaps not as swayed by the lure of prestigious football games, many white women in Georgia stood with Griffin and used the opportunity to speak out against both integration and an overemphasis on athletics. "He is only protecting my children and yours in years to come," wrote one Atlanta woman.[96] The Tech students exhibited "bad breeding," wrote another female *Atlanta Constitution* reader. " All that sort of rot reflects on their homes and their school and gives football a prominence it does not deserve."[97] In particular, the governor's office reported that three-quarters of Atlanta residents who telephoned their opinion voiced disapproval of his stand, while every other correspondent from around the state offered overwhelming support. "Governor Griffin has it right," wrote one Augusta resident. "This is not just a Georgia Tech matter . . . when every single institution and right is being invaded by the NAACP."[98]

The state's rural press criticized Griffin for drawing negative publicity to the region but still celebrated the ideology behind his actions. Playing up accusations of bias in the Atlanta media, the Jackson County *Herald* claimed the city's newspapers had "incited" the demonstration of "irresponsible students" and applauded the regents for complying with the governor's more general (and important) requests.[99] If not for the board's rational decision, supporters argued, David Rice's proposal would have "liberalized" athletics in the state.[100] Other sympathizers criticized the governor's tactics, including the request sent to Coach Bobby Dodd by the States' Rights Council of Georgia. "The football team belongs to Georgia Tech, not to Coach Dodd," read an editorial in the *Macon Telegraph*, "and he should no more be faced with the questions of declining this issue than a teacher should be called upon to set the racial policy of a school system."[101]

Griffin had indeed received a mandate from white Georgians to preserve segregation at all costs, and his election proved that the majority of those allowed to vote were attracted to his confrontational rhetoric. Nevertheless, both the governor and the state's image were smeared in the national press, too much for even his admirers. "It was expected he [Griffin] would represent the problem of segregation as what it is," wrote one embarrassed supporter, "and handle it without turning it into a nationwide scandal."[102] Many segregationists felt that the attacks on Griffin in the national press exceeded the standard criticism directed toward southern politicians during the 1950s. Some even claimed that Griffin acted only after his office was "flooded" with complaints from white citizens in the state. There was no "animosity evidenced" against Bobby Grier himself, reported the *Ledger* in Columbus, Georgia. "But for the Supreme Court decision, it is unlikely that the protests against the Tech-Pitt game would have arisen."[103] Even the ardent segregationist *Macon News* called the regent's decision "consistent with Georgia's position on states' rights" and argued that integrated contests within Georgia itself "would not tend to break down the color line."[104]

Still, the controversy publicly exposed rifts in segregation's political base, which historians have too often characterized as solid and unchanging. Many supporters of Jim Crow saw no threat in the celebration of athletes breaking color barriers in sport. While some segregationists ignored the rhetoric of meaning and progress used to describe these events, others felt that such high-profile incidents were the most important battles segregationists had to fight; just as Regent Harris had pleaded with the board, they believed segregation would be dismantled first through sports and entertainment. These divergent interpretations of the governor's actions created a dramatic split that played out in the public sphere. One prosegregationist assailed Griffin for "making us appear to be an ignorant bunch of louts and practically sub-human to the rest of the world."[105] Another wrote that "someone needs to write a handbook on segregation for white Georgians" on how to fight for their cause. After all, Georgia's college students grew up rubbing elbows with "Negro chauffeurs . . . janitors . . . cooks . . . and baby sitters," how was a back-up football player any different? According to many segregationists, a boycott of the Sugar Bowl because of

Grier was not an important symbolic stand; it was "the rankest sort of hypocrisy and two-faced gobbledygook." The fight to maintain segregation should instead "confine itself to the real and important color line that needs to be held."[106] Just as the souring reaction to Johnny Bright in Oklahoma from 1949 to 1951 revealed the shifting, uncertain nature of segregation, Georgians also struggled to define which color lines were most "real" or "important."

Other segregationists went even further in their critique of the governor. "There are an abundance of broader fronts on which the issue of segregation can be fought," announced the *Augusta Chronicle*, "without descending to a petty, picayune level and stultifying the reputation of our two great state universities whose football teams have brought fame, and glory, and prestige to Georgia."[107] Overnight, segregationists turned the rhetoric of honor and tradition inward and directed it at the man who was specifically elected to represent those very ideologies. Indeed, the "southern way of life" was a euphemism for enforced racial segregation, but by 1956 it was also a celebration of big-time college athletics. To these fans, sacrificing one to save the other was a cowardly retreat, not a noble stand.

In a curious sidelight to the controversy, many tried to equate Grier's actual role on the team and his physical skill with the overall impact his participation would have on southern society. To minimize the conflict, one Tech spokesman claimed that "this boy Grier hasn't played except a few minutes since mid-season." Others noted that he was only a "third string substitute" running back.[108] There was a chance that Grier would not even enter the game or at most participate in just a few plays. If the former occurred, he would spend the game on the sidelines, and the whole controversy appeared meaningless. Somehow, the difference between a black student either playing a minimal role in the contest or potentially being a key factor in the game's outcome apparently defined the spectacle's overall mark on racial politics. One columnist told Atlanta readers that Grier was just an "innocent bystander who probably won't play more than five minutes," a "liability" player with a "moderate reputation."[109] Even some in the black press indicated that Grier's small role on the team would likely minimize the meaning of his participation, especially because Pittsburgh had featured several more accomplished African American players in the past. Just a few years earlier, Grier had played behind a high-profile black running back named Bobby Epps, who later played professionally for the New York Giants in the National Football League.[110]

However, after the regents decided to allow Georgia Tech's participation, news began to circulate that Grier would play a larger role in the game. Because of injuries to other players, Pitt Coach Johnny Michelosen announced that Grier had been bumped up on the roster and would start for the Panthers. The prosegregation *Savannah Morning News* ominously reported that Grier would "sleep, eat, practice and play" with the team and noted that his skills had improved over the season.[111] Ironically, the argument over Grier's effectiveness on the field made unlikely fans out of Georgia's most ardent segregationists. While sportswriters in the North emphasized Grier would have no major impact on the actual game—further lampooning Griffin's overreaction—supporters of the governor convinced white Georgians that Grier was physically accomplished and integral to his team's success. The result was a surreal spectacle, as various factions politicized a young man's physical skills in order to gauge what broader impact the incident would have. This included many Americans who knew little about the game of football but who cared deeply about either the elimination or the preservation of Jim Crow segregation.

"Football or Sociology?"

Bobby Grier participated in the 1956 Sugar Bowl, and he played an important role in the game's outcome. Along with increased police presence because of the controversy, 80,174 fans were treated to perfect weather and a close game. Although Georgia Tech pulled out a 7–0 victory, Grier finished with fifty-one rushing yards to lead his team.[112] On the game's pivotal play, officials called an interference penalty on Grier in the end zone, which lead to a Tech touchdown and the game's only points. The call had him in tears afterward as he insisted that he had done nothing wrong. Some black sportswriters even saw prejudice in the penalty, indicating just how pertinent race was in the minds of most casual observers. Future Secretary of State Hodding Carter III, then a student at Princeton University, recalled he was "sick to my stomach" after white southerners expressed jubilation over Grier's "mistake" on the field. "They loved it," Carter explained. Fifty years later Grier still claims a "bad call" cost Pittsburgh the game and fondly remembers how his white teammates were nearly ejected for coming to his aid and arguing on his behalf, "mad as heck."[113] The *Times-Picayune* praised Grier's demeanor and announced that he was a "trailblazer." Sports Editor Bill Keefe congratulated him on a "whale of a game" and noted that the capacity crowd gave Grier "a thunderous round of applause from both sides of the field." In Atlanta he was praised for "weathering a difficult assignment."[114]

From Grier's perspective, the episode was a once-in-a-lifetime achievement that remains vivid in his mind. Even greater than his accomplishment as a player was his ability to handle the controversy off the field. A young black student from Ohio took on Georgia's governor in a public relations battle and won handily in both the North and the South. Grier said he was "sorry about the trouble" when first informed of Griffin's challenge: "I heard it [Georgia Tech] has a real good team." When notified of the regents' decision, he announced that he was "glad to play the finest team in the south."[115] Grier also relied heavily on his white teammates and the support of Pittsburgh's coaches and administrators, many of whom told the press they were outright "mad" at the governor and that Griffin "couldn't have picked a nicer, more quiet fellow" to pick on. Pittsburgh's players shielded Grier from public scrutiny and tried to lighten the mood in the weeks before the game. "To loosen him up and try to take the pressure off him, we played some practical jokes on Bobby during practice for the Sugar Bowl," recalled one of the Panther's cocaptains. "One night some of the players dressed with white sheets over their heads, and we burned a circle outside our dorm."[116] Whether such tactics were in good taste, years later Grier insisted that his teammate's support was crucial to helping him get through the experience.[117]

The black press also noted that Grier was an excellent student and religiously devoted.[118] He humbly thanked the city of New Orleans after the game by proclaiming that the "crowd was wonderful" and he "would be happy to have any son of mine go through the same experience."[119] Segregationists assailed their top spokesman for his inability to articulate their position, while all agreed that Grier had shown an uncanny ability to say the right words at the right time, especially while in Louisiana. Years later, one local disc jockey noted that for many New Orleans residents Grier was "regarded as just as much of a trailblazer as Jackie Robinson was in his debut in Brooklyn."[120]

Overall, the black press praised the reaction of white fans in New Orleans as a further rebuke of Governor Griffin. Ralph McGill of the *Atlanta Constitution* counted "several hundred" African Americans in the integrated Pittsburgh stands alone. One black columnist celebrated that Grier had been "slammed to the ground with the same tactical force that greeted other . . . players." All the while, "throngs of Negroes who heretofore had only passing interest" in football "came from everywhere and sat on an unsegregated basis."[121] Grier's movement off the field was watched as closely as the game itself. Pittsburgh Coach Johnny Michelosen claimed he had no intention of keeping his players isolated from the week's festivities, and journalists probed how Grier's participation would influence the scheduling of social functions, housing, and transportation. One Atlanta columnist bemoaned the "hordes of race-baiting journalists" following Grier's every step.[122] Was the game "football or sociology," asked a sarcastic editorial in the *Augusta Chronicle*. The segregationist press criticized northern media for sending reporters to the game who "confessed their ignorance of football," "made no pretense of being sportswriters," or, worst of all, "weren't even interested in sports."[123] "A lot of yankees . . . came down and evidently were disappointed because there wasn't a racial angle to write about," claimed one southern sportswriter.[124] Yet plenty of respected sportswriters, who had proven themselves interested in sport, knew exactly why the game was so important. "Over all the folderol of greetings and parties loomed the figure of a dark-skinned young reserve Pitt fullback . . . named Bob Grier, first Negro ever to play in a Sugar Bowl football game," announced *Sports Illustrated* after the contest. Furthermore, sportswriters from the North defended their decision to focus on Grier's race based on Governor Griffin's actions. *SI*'s report continued:

> Made a *cause célèbre* by the earlier racist ravings of Georgia Governor Marvin Griffin, Grier came to New Orleans amid trumpeting by Pitt officials and Sugar Bowl big shots that he would be treated just like a white boy. . . . While the Georgia Tech team quartered at the downtown St. Charles Hotel, the Pitt squad forsook its Hotel Roosevelt headquarters to stay in dormitories on the Tulane campus. Georgia Tech players were given a free hand to do what they wanted downtown—even tour the French Quarter joints—but Pitt stayed in seclusion.[125]

From the perspective of southern sportswriters, those who were interested only in writing "along racial lines" were guilty of infusing politics where it did not belong; the southern writers were angry at their northern colleagues for injecting race into their stories about the Sugar Bowl. Yet Governor Griffin proved right in thinking otherwise, and he, ironically, was one of the few southerners who refused to follow any coverage of the festivities.

Despite the positive reception, Grier's participation did alter some of the week's events. While Georgia Tech's team stayed downtown at the St. Charles Hotel, Pittsburgh players were housed near the Tulane stadium. After the game, Grier attended a private gathering for both teams at the St. Charles, although he skipped a formal ball and instead went to a function in his honor at Dillard University, a local black college. Some sportswriters noted that Grier never intended to appear at the ball, while others asserted that officials had encouraged him not to attend.[126] The *New York Times* announced that the St. Charles Hotel and Sugar Bowl committee agreed not to raise any questions over Grier's participation in any functions related to the game. Nevertheless, the hotel's manager told one prosegregation paper in Georgia that Grier would "definitely not go dancing" at the St. Charles. "If he shows up I won't block his way to dinner," the man said. "But he would never come . . . you know the custom around here."[127]

An immense level of surveillance surrounded the young man. One reporter actually followed Grier around the lobby and asked other patrons for their reaction to a black man at the St. Charles. "Anybody with his ability should be able to go anywhere," replied one woman.[128] Ironically, black sportswriters criticized the northern media for hounding Grier during his time in the city, especially for bringing out what one called "the old social dance riot-provoker as a scarecrow."[129] While Grier's participation seemed to indicate that New Orleans was moving toward integrated athletics, there would be additional altercations in the next ten years. In 1964, twenty-one black professionals voted to boycott the American Football League's (AFL) All-Star game after being barred from restaurants and hotels throughout the city. When the National Football League (NFL) finally established a New Orleans franchise in 1966—ten years after Grier's Sugar Bowl—Commissioner Pete Rozelle was still hesitant about black athletes playing in front of the city's fans.[130]

"We Will Never Surrender"

Nor did the battle to keep Georgia segregated end in 1955. The bad publicity generated for Marvin Griffin and the States' Rights Council of Georgia ironically helped encourage segregationist groups to organize and communicate more effectively. Instead of fading away, the council was able to regroup and launch an even broader campaign. Within two years, politicians in the Deep South were debating all-out sport segregation bills. Grier's publicity certainly helped Louisiana pass Legislative Act 579, which banned all interracial sports in the state for the next three years. Although the Supreme Court's decision in *Dorsey v. Louisiana State Athletic Commission* declared the act unconstitutional in 1959, it was enough to frighten the Mid-Winter Sports Association from inviting another nonsouthern team to the Sugar Bowl for the next decade.[131] That same December, Mississippi Citizens' Council President Bill Simmons cited the Georgia Tech controversy when his group attempted to bar a local school from playing in the Junior Rose Bowl against Compton College in Los Angeles. On 1 January 1956— the day before Grier's debut in New Orleans—the *New York Times* reported that local states' rights organizations were beginning to "coordinate their efforts." This included a meeting of top segregation leaders in Memphis, Tennessee, that emphasized better communication and a united public front.[132] Griffin's failed, solo attempt at tackling the Sugar Bowl was an immediate factor in this stepped-up effort to solidify and coordinate the political backlash to *Brown*. One week after the game, the governor appeared more confident than ever before the cheering Georgia legislature. "We will never surrender," he proclaimed.[133]

Nevertheless, one *Afro-American* editor called the integration of the Sugar Bowl the second most important event of 1955, behind only the murder of Emmett Till. "In less than five years," wrote Marion Jackson, "Negroes are going to be playing on Tech's Grant Field and Georgia's Sanford Stadium or both will be out of the football business."[134] Jackson's prophecy proved accurate, and while Georgia Tech remained segregated for the next six years the school's quiet integration in 1961—two years after Griffin left office—contrasted with the violence at the neighboring University of Georgia. Tech President Edwin Harrison called an open meeting with the student body to discuss the issue, and a vote of 2,500 attendees revealed that only 10 were opposed to integrating the campus. Tech's first black professor joined the faculty in 1968, and in the subsequent forty years no other institution in the country has graduated more African American engineers.[135] Today, Georgia Tech's football team remains among the most popular in the country, and games draw regular crowds of 55,000 to Bobby

Dodd Stadium. By the 1980s, integration allowed a young Herschel Walker of Wrightsville, Georgia, to attend college in his home state and become one of the best players in the game's history. Fans at the University of Georgia commonly cheered "God Bless Earl Warren" as Walker led his team to the national championship in 1980.[136]

5

"Beat the Devil Out of BYU"

Football and Black Power in the
Mountain West, 1968–1970

Where the western lights long shadows
Over boundless prairie fling.
And the mountain winds are vocal!
With thy dear name, Wyoming,
There it is the Brown and Yellow
Floats in loving loyalty,
And the college throws its portals
Open wide to all men free.

—Alma Mater, University of Wyoming

He is a dictator! He pushes the buttons and we just act, according to his rules!

—Joe Williams, UW football player, Black Student Alliance meeting,
October 1969

"Athletics were a real nemesis to me," recalled William Carlson, former president of the University of Wyoming. The accomplished D.V.M. and radiology professor took office on 1 January 1968—the same day the school's football team went to the Sugar Bowl, and excitement surrounding the achievement surged throughout the state. According to his memoir, Carlson recognized the importance of athletics to the institution he now governed, yet he realized that the athletics department struggled to recruit successful athletes to the quiet university nestled 7,200 feet high in the cozy town of Laramie. Athletic officials "were often dealing with inner city kids who hoped to play professional football to get out of the environment in which they were trapped," Carlson wrote. And by 1968 many of the school's top potential athletes were African American. Carlson sympathized with coaches who labored to woo black athletes to Wyoming, often with elaborate tactics, such as taking recruits on snowmobiling trips outside town. Carlson recalled how numerous footballers came through his office, shook his hand, and talked of their desire to play for Head Coach Lloyd Eaton, most of whom he never saw again.[1]

African Americans comprised only 1 percent of UW's entire student body, yet the athletics department did manage to convince dozens of black athletes to stay in Laramie. Several talented black football players from around the country led the 1967–1968 Sugar Bowl team, and only one was a native of the state. In his memoir, President Carlson fondly recalled star tailback Joe Williams, a senior from Lufkin, Texas, who seemed to thrive at UW even though he was one of few African Americans in the community. In October 1969, Carlson sat with Williams in the back of a university vehicle en route to a meeting of the Cheyenne Quarterback Club. The ride took them through fifty miles of breathtaking high plains—isolated, rural, and seemingly endless. Before presenting themselves to the boosters in Cheyenne, Carlson and the twenty-two-year-old Williams visited on the drive. "He told me with great sincerity, I believe, that his goal was to be an elementary school teacher," the president wrote thirty years later. Williams talked about his family back in Texas and how he was sending money home from his summer jobs in Wyoming to help his sister through college. Carlson was impressed with the young man's character—he was "soft spoken" and "sincere."[2]

Two weeks later, President Carlson was embroiled in a firestorm of controversy: the largest scandal he faced in his eleven years as head of Wyoming's only university. National headlines spoke of countless crises that galvanized radical youth, including the Chicago Seven trial, My Lai, and a Vietnam Moratorium that threatened to shut down college campuses. Of all the problems he anticipated, President Carlson never imagined that football Coach Lloyd Eaton would throw his fourteen African American players off the team or that the subsequent fallout would flood Laramie with national attention and trigger the state's largest racial confrontation in decades. He was under the impression that the players had asked to engage in a small protest by wearing black armbands during their upcoming game against Brigham Young University—and Coach Eaton immediately responded by dismissing them.

Carlson's biggest surprise was when the students brought their demands directly to him. He was shocked to find that Joe Williams served as the group's spokesman. "This was no revolutionary person," he lamented, "but an honest American with solid goals using the means available to be a success for his family." Football was the means, and success meant either landing a professional contract or perhaps returning to Texas to teach elementary school just as the two had talked about on the drive to Cheyenne. Either way, Carlson wondered why Williams would throw it all away by initiating a "protest," one that would accomplish nothing except to get him and his peers removed from the university. "Joe," the president recalled saying as the young man entered his office, "this just doesn't figure with your goals and aspirations for yourself and your sister."[3]

In his memoir, Carlson wrote that he felt betrayed and confused. To him, black athletes had been given the opportunity to obtain a quality education at UW. Thus, the only explanation for their action was clear: they had been duped by outside agitators, race antagonists, and seasoned political radicals. "It looked like many times we had the players ready to compromise," wrote the president. "Each time . . . an unknown force crept in and we couldn't consummate the reconciliation."[4] Soon, Carlson, state officials, and many Wyoming residents had identified the source: Black Panthers. One local reporter announced that "remote Wyoming and its previously sacrosanct campus has been caught in the backwash of a revolution."[5] It was October 1969, and the revolution had finally reached the Equality State, brought by fourteen black college football players.

Revolution, Sport, and the "New Individualism"

American society changed drastically in the decade after Georgia Governor Marvin Griffin attempted to ban integrated athletics. Beginning in the mid-1950s, relentless opposition to integration in the South plunged the freedom movement into crisis. African Americans became increasingly impatient with mere economic boycotts, and by the 1960s they began to adopt more direct, confrontational tactics, including "sit-ins" at segregated facilities and "freedom rides" on integrated buses throughout the region. The movement also encountered a renewed wave of violence. The high-profile murders of black leaders (such as Medgar Evers in 1963) and sympathetic whites (such as Andrew Goodman and Michael Schwerner in 1964) challenged the nation's willingness to enforce its own laws. When Congress passed the landmark Civil Rights Act in 1964—ten years after *Brown*—the bill symbolized real progress yet reminded the nation that the elimination of de facto segregation was an ongoing struggle.

The movement made significant progress weakening Jim Crow in the South, but by 1968 nearly 50 percent of African Americans lived outside the region. From 1950 to 1970, the number of blacks in cities like New York, Detroit, Los Angeles, and Chicago grew at a rapid pace. This continued dispersion of African Americans, combined with the violent reaction to desegregation, helped popularize new, more radical movements in the black community. African American unrest in the urban North and West Coast energized groups such as the Black Muslims (who had been active since the 1930s) and the Black Panthers (founded in 1966). In addition, a new generation of activists clashed with the freedom movement's most formative establishments: black Christian churches and the NAACP. Young leaders like Malcolm X and Bobby Seale came to define new ideological platforms, which ranged from those who questioned Martin Luther King's doctrine of nonviolence to those who embraced the black separatism advocated by Elijah Muhammad. Beginning in Rochester, Philadelphia, New York City, and (most notably) Watts, urban riots erupted in the country's North and West after 1964. By the time King was assassinated in April 1968, the postwar civil rights movement threatened to become a revolution. This emergence of black radicalism coincided with new student movements fed by the period's unrest. With nearly 150,000 American troops in Vietnam by 1966 (including 22,000 blacks), radicalism targeted the very tenets of state formation and the nature of war. And 1960s "social revolutions" also challenged fundamental ideas about American society, including sex, gender, and religion.[6]

By the end of the decade, athletics were also under attack from critics who questioned the traditional value of sport. In education, cynics disputed the belief that participation built "character," helped socialize diverse groups, or instilled discipline and responsibility in America's future leadership. For a century, educators and administrators had trumpeted these basic values in sport participation. Even the media backlash to football's brutality in the early 1900s or the movements to deemphasize athletics that gained traction in the 1930s rarely attacked the fundamental notion that organized sport, if structured appropriately, helped develop well-rounded young people. Along with the burgeoning social movements of the 1960s, however, emerged what one historian has called a "new individualism" in sport.[7] Like much of the social transformation evident in the period, student unrest played an essential role in shifting the discourse of athletics toward a critical analysis of race.

Dissension also percolated from unlikely sources, including the players themselves. During the 1960s, professional black athletes in the NFL went public with complaints about discrimination, and some even sought NAACP assistance in taking legal action against their own teams. In the National Basketball Association, African American star Bill Russell criticized the league's racism in his 1966 memoir *Go Up for Glory*. And former college standout Lew Alcindor (Kareem Abdul-Jabbar) made shocking allegations that he had faced prejudice from 1965 to 1969 at UCLA, a school that still considered itself among the most race-blind campuses in the nation. In 1968, celebrated journalist and *Sports Illustrated* contributor Jack Olsen published *The Black Athlete: A Shameful Story*. According to Olsen, African American college athletes were not reaping the benefits of increased access; instead, they encountered "social vacuums," "cruel delusion," and "unconscious prejudice." Most important, Olsen railed against white coaches for the very traits that many Americans had once celebrated: confidence, no-nonsense discipline, and the ability to command young men. "Who is this Big Daddy who strolls around campus in spiked shoes and sweat socks," wrote Olsen, "with whistle dangling around his neck, while Ph.D.s stand aside and point him out as a celebrity?"[8] Sportswriters began to challenge the authority of coaches and administrators, especially in terms of race, and Head Coach Lloyd Eaton at Wyoming was a prime candidate for such criticism. Eaton's national reputation was based on his iron discipline, strict leadership, and ability to push young players to their physical limits.

This burgeoning attack on sport frustrated conservative fans, many of whom believed that athletics would emerge unscathed by the social turmoil at American universities. Observers could blame grassroots elements at "radical" campuses for sparking the antiwar and free speech movements, but athletic protest was also emerging from elite professionals and celebrated figures in the sporting world. "Negroes Seem Unsatisfied Despite Bigger Rewards" read one typical headline in 1970.[9]

For Joe Williams and the rest of Wyoming's black players, unrest was fed by a call for African American student athletes to protest at schools throughout the West. It began with one man, Harry Edwards—a black sociologist at San Jose State College whose 1969 book *Revolt of the Black Athlete* articulated the merging of black power and popular sport.[10] At the age of thirty, Edwards (himself a former college basketball player) earned national attention by denouncing discrimination in sport and what he considered the blatant exploitation of black athletes by white America. The *New York Times* dubbed him a "typically angry young black man," but others were less measured. In *Sports Illustrated*, Jack Olsen wrote that Edwards was a "fanatical superblack" who successfully took over San Jose's athletic department after organizing its majority black athletes.[11] In 1967, Edwards issued a list of grievances on behalf of fifty-nine African American students at the school. Many cited discrimination in athletics: overbearing coaches, a lack of academic assistance, and exploitative demands made on black participants. Others addressed prejudice outside of sport, including hostility in the campus Greek system and the local community. During the football season, Edwards and his supporters threatened to "physically interfere" with a game at SJSC, a threat that prompted the *New York Times* to announce the first ever cancellation of a college football contest "because of racial unrest." California Governor Ronald Reagan deemed the young professor unfit to teach and called San Jose's decision to stop the game "an appeasement to lawbreakers."[12]

Nevertheless, Edwards's popularity at SJSC continued to build, and his attempt to address the problems faced by black athletes on predominately white campuses spread throughout the West. After the University of California, Berkeley suspended a black baseball player, Edwards launched a demonstration that led to the resignation of the school's baseball coach and athletic director.[13] The agitation at Wyoming and the protest over BYU eventually marked the pinnacle of Edwards's influence in intercollegiate athletics. By 1968, the militant sociology professor decided to turn his attention to the Olympics. That year's Summer Games in Mexico City solidified him as a prominent face in the new black power movement, but it also meant that black collegians were left to themselves to organize agitation on overwhelmingly white campuses like the one in Laramie.

Specifically, Edwards's attempt to galvanize black athletes culminated in his call to boycott the Mexico City games, which historians Amy Bass and Donald Spivey have analyzed extensively. Plans to target the Olympics for black protest were not completely new, similar ideas had circulated before the 1964 games in Tokyo.[14] Edwards's grievances included a myriad of prominent issues in international and professional athletics. According to Bass, "1968 proved to be a year when the International Olympic Committee (IOC) could hardly settle on a workable definition of . . . 'black,' and remained seemingly blind to how issues of media, decolonization, and black militancy might mingle to produce an Olympics unlike any before."[15] Edwards assailed the antagonism of IOC chairman Avery Brundage toward black athletes as well as the committee's refusal to bar apartheid South Africa and Rhodesia from participating. The boycott also earned broader appeal by citing grievances within American professional sports, including Muhammad Ali's punishment for refusing the Vietnam War draft and the dearth of black coaches or owners in professional leagues.

Not all black athletes supported the boycott—former boxer Jimmy Carter warned fans that communists had "brainwashed" young sportsmen. But Edwards publicly denounced those who refused to support the effort. He called aging 1936 Olympian Jesse Owens an "uncle tom" along with baseball superstar Willie Mays and numerous others. Any African American who overemphasized sport "becomes a caricature of his race," Edwards warned. His classroom wall featured pictures of the "traitor (Negro) of the week," a prominent black athlete who refused to support the boycott and was content with the demeaning nomenclature that many had started to denounce. Edwards's movement did win the endorsement of some moderate figures, including Jackie Robinson and Martin Luther King Jr. (before his April assassination).[16]

Nevertheless, dozens of minority athletes opted to participate in the 1968 Olympics and Edwards's movement ultimately failed. UCLA's Alcindor was the most prominent black athlete to boycott. Once it became apparent that most would participate, Edwards instead encouraged black athletes to capitalize on the media spectacle by displaying their frustrations before an international audience. In one of the Olympics' most memorable episodes, former San Jose State runners Tommie Smith and John Carlos did just that: bowing their heads during a medal ceremony and raising gloved fists in a black power salute. According to Bass, "Despite the division within the boycott attempt . . . the action taken by Smith and Carlos on the victory dais in Mexico City largely solidified a politicized notion of the 'black athlete.'"[17]

Nevertheless, while the Olympic protest signaled the influence of the new black power in sport, many African Americans competed in Mexico City without incident. To Edwards's disdain, nineteen-year-old-boxer George Foreman celebrated his gold medal by circling the ring wrapped in an American flag. It is easy to overestimate the significance of a link between black protest and sport, one

that was noticeably weaker than similar connections in popular music, entertainment, and art. On many campuses in the 1960s, athletes (including African
Americans) remained relatively square compared to their peers. In particular,
football maintained its traditional reputation for conservatism throughout the
decade and into the 1970s. Black or white, football players were less likely to
protest the Vietnam War, join groups like Students for a Democratic Society
(SDS), and engage in social activism. Reports even circulated that athletes were
acting as ad hoc campus security, physically confronting radical demonstrators
on some campuses.[18] Yet a brief wave of black protest, sweeping through college
football beginning in 1968, culminated in the controversy at the University of
Wyoming. Such agitation from black student athletes, especially in communities
that figured to be immune to the burgeoning radicalism and counterculture, was
all the more significant considering the sport's traditional conservatism. Like the
historian Beth Bailey's explanation of how a more tame sexual "revolution" influenced rural college towns, the story of athletic unrest at the University of
Wyoming extends our knowledge of black protest from the standard narratives
emphasizing either California's Bay Area or the urban Northeast and reveals how
the specter of black power functioned "in the heartland."[19]

Black Athletes in the Western Athletic Conference

By the late 1960s, intercollegiate athletics were of critical importance to the
University of Wyoming and the rest of the schools in the Western Athletic
Conference (WAC). National rankings and television contracts, interregional
rivalries, and select major conferences were now firmly entrenched in college
football and an established part of the game's business. No longer were universities merely courting the idea of big-time athletics. By 1970, schools had
developed a serious reliance on sport to provide expected revenue, facilitate
undergraduate recruitment, entertain alumni, and aid in the development of
campus community and "spirit." Total live attendance at football games jumped
from fifteen million in 1956 to more than thirty million by 1971, and NCAA television revenues went up nearly 600 percent in the same period.[20] Most schools,
including the University of Wyoming, enjoyed a spike in football revenue
throughout the 1960s. At Indiana University, fielding one of the least successful teams in the Big Ten Conference, the team's earnings increased 160 percent
in the ten years after 1959 to top nearly $636,000 in 1968. Even low-profile
teams experienced financial success; for example, the University of Maryland
saw its revenue rise by 55 percent during the decade despite the team's relative
obscurity.[21]

Black student athletes—hitherto considered direct threats to social stability
at southern universities—were now crucial to the imagined communities these
very schools desired. And at some institutions, black players were moving from

acceptance to celebration as white fans in the 1960s began to embrace African American collegians for their achievements both on and off the field. The career of Ernie Davis, running back at Syracuse University from 1959 to 1961, embodied this transformation. In 1961, Davis became the first black student to win college football's top honor, the Heisman Trophy; he also received the Most Valuable Player Award in the 1960 Cotton Bowl. Yet Davis did not represent change merely because he was allowed to participate; Pennsylvania State University's Wallace Triplett and Dennis Hoggard had already integrated the Cotton Bowl in 1948. Nor was Davis even the first black student to lead the Syracuse team and earn national notoriety; Jim Brown, graduating in 1956, had already achieved NFL success. Instead, Davis's story was new because his popularity was based on his status as the top player in the game, his compelling demeanor, and his unsuccessful battle with leukemia. His success proved that fans had gone beyond celebrating the meaning of black participation merely for the sake of victory. Northern football fans and media were now beginning to embrace individual black students as compelling human interest stories, emphasizing their accomplishments off the field, their experience as students, and their individual personalities.[22]

Some fans were spiritually moved by the story of Davis's untimely death, and beginning in the 1950s many universities and boosters consciously replaced their institutional religious heritage and symbolism with the cult of football. Instead of weekly chapel or mass services, football provided a new activity that could bind diverse students together. In the secularizing world of higher education, the sport was central to corporate identity formation—a powerful tool of campus socialization and an advertising bonanza. By the late 1960s, football had also transformed the architectural environment at America's most celebrated schools. At the University of Notre Dame's Hesburgh Library, administrators in 1964 installed the massive "Word of Life" mural depicting a resurrected Christ with arms outstretched to heaven. Officials designed the image so it could be seen from the football stadium, and fans immediately redubbed the work "Touchdown Jesus"—a mark of secularization and a name the university soon embraced in its own literature.

As college sport grew in importance, black athletes discovered that fostering campus community and solidarity could be a burden more than a privilege. Gone were the days of blatant segregation, although a few institutions, including the University of Mississippi, still did not have a single African American football player by 1970. Most other schools recruited black athletes vigorously, but promises of scholarships and additional "help" for players (in the form of unreported gifts or "slush fund" payouts) were not yet common. Still, a 1968 government study of schools with major athletic programs found that 6.5 percent of sport scholarships were awarded to black athletes, more than four times the total percentage (1.5 percent) of black students enrolled. In essence, the recruitment of minority athletes helped African Americans obtain what little access universities granted them in the wake of the 1964 Civil Rights Act. By 1970, 378,000 black students attended predominately white schools in the United States.[23]

The 1968 Olympics defined an era of black athletic protest and convinced many observers that African American dominance in mainstream sport could not be brushed aside as an apolitical phenomenon, especially during a period of heightened social tension and unrest. Harry Edwards's message to collegians like Wyoming's Joe Williams was simple: black student athletes should wrest control of their experience from white educators, coaches, and administrators and use it as a positive tool for individual empowerment and community formation. Although participants were insulated from other student groups and campus society, including separate housing, Edwards's philosophy resonated with an increasing number of student athletes. Black footballers especially followed his standoff with Governor Reagan and the campaign at SJSC. Thousands of African American players faced little hope of parlaying their talent into professional success, and many relied on tenuous athletic scholarships to obtain a college degree. Despite athletes' penchant for avoiding radical protest, footballers at San Jose State successfully transformed the school's athletic department. In response to Edwards's demands, administrators eased the team's strict rules and hired a black alumnus (a former athlete) to assist the athletic director in addressing the players' grievances. Officials also eased restrictions on hair, dress, and clothing and provided an increase in academic assistance for the athletes.[24]

The Mormon Protest

The unrest that culminated at the University of Wyoming began with a specific victory achieved by Edwards and the San Jose State players: a shift in school policy regarding athletes and protest. In 1968, SJSC football players introduced the idea of wearing black armbands during a game against Brigham Young University (BYU). The bands were meant to protest the Church of Jesus Christ of Latter Day Saints (the Mormon Church), which prohibited black congregants from membership in the "priesthood," a status all other males in the church were expected to obtain.[25] In response to the protest, officials at SJSC ironed out a "right of conscience" agreement that granted players the right to sit out games or express themselves on the field. Administrators also permitted the wearing of armbands, and Head Coach Joe McMullen even helped the demonstration with his own criticism of BYU in the press.[26] To observers around the country, what happened at San Jose was remarkable; black athletes had united their voices with campus organizations—most notably the Black Student Alliance (BSA)—to gain significant leverage over the school's administration and athletic program.

Although the most dramatic incident occurred at the University of Wyoming, Edwards's success at San Jose sparked a wave of black protest that swept through college football from 1968 to 1970. Fourteen players at Berkeley refused to participate in spring practice amid allegations of "stacking"—the claim that schools were overrecruiting blacks for certain positions (usually running backs, wide receivers, or defensive backs) and subsequently cutting scholarship support to many.[27] Players were also frustrated over the lack of black quarterbacks, long considered the most important position on the team and one that coaches claimed required more "cerebral" skills, like the ability to memorize a playbook. At Iowa State University, twenty-four black athletes submitted a list of grievances to the Athletic Council in 1968; these included requests to be called "black" or "Afro-American" and demands that the school hire more black coaches and administrators. Two football players subsequently dropped out over the controversy, including the vice president of ISU's Black Student Organization (BSO).[28] Meanwhile, thirty-eight footballers at Michigan State University called on their school to hire a black coach and provide more academic counseling to players, as did nine participants at Syracuse University. Five players at Princeton University made headlines after accusing Coach Dick Coleman of "racist tendencies in coaching," particularly in denying them playing time on the field. And at Oregon State University, a statewide controversy erupted after a coach's insistence that a player shave his goatee; the meager bit of facial hair led OSU to appoint a Commission on Human Rights and Responsibilities.[29]

Sometimes coaches shrouded the suspension of black players in indefinite, vague terms. The University of Washington football team was briefly left without its thirteen African American participants after they were suspended for "not expressing a 100 percent commitment to Huskies football"; that is, apparently they refused to take a loyalty oath. On other occasions, the subject of tension was quite clear. Fourteen black footballers were dismissed from Indiana University's team after boycotting practices because of a coaching atmosphere that was "mentally depressing and morally discouraging to blacks." At the University of Kansas black football players refused to play until the school recruited an African American cheerleader, which it did within days. Complaints resurfaced after coaches sang "Dixie" and waved Confederate flags at the team's banquet, while the squad's twenty black players watched in stunned silence. And sixteen years after Bobby Grier had faced scrutiny at the St. Charles Hotel, African American players at the University of Oklahoma complained publicly after organizers invited only one black woman to the social events surrounding the 1972 Sugar Bowl. Overall, examples of black college athletes registering complaints in 1968 alone exceeded one hundred, and most involved football players.[30]

None of these movements was as organized as San Jose State's demonstration against Brigham Young University and the Mormon Church, which soon spread to black athletes at BYU's rival schools in the Western Athletic Conference (WAC) before it reached the University of Wyoming. In summer 1968, eight black athletes on the track team at the University of Texas, El Paso (UTEP), refused to participate in meets with Brigham Young. "The Mormons teach that Negroes are descended from the devil," one told *Sports Illustrated*. "Who . . . wants to go up there and run your tail off in front of spectators who think you've got horns?" The eight were stripped of their athletic scholarships and pressured to leave the school. Officials even told Bob Beamon's wife she could no longer keep the job her husband's coach had acquired for her. Beamon—short on funds, kicked off his college team, and unsure if UTEP would let him register for classes—still managed to qualify for the Mexico City games, where he shattered the world long jump record by two feet.[31] After Jack Olsen highlighted the situation in *Sports Illustrated*, faculty launched a fundraising campaign to replace the athletes' scholarships. Just two years earlier, in 1966, UTEP (then known as Texas Western College) received a major boost when black athletes led the school's basketball team to a national championship over an all-white squad from the University of Kentucky. That team was (and still is) credited with hastening the desegregation of college basketball in the South, and national headlines trumpeted El Paso and the UTEP community. Yet the happy ending was premature; the school's faculty only managed to raise $200 to support its endangered track athletes. According to the *Nation*, "the drive was met with granite indifference . . . from the city's intellectually balding businessmen, upset over the bogy of Black Power." Only 250 of 10,000 UTEP students (or 2.5 percent) were African American, yet El Paso residents pegged the small BYU protest as the arrival of a much larger social movement.[32]

Although the issue of blacks in the Mormon Church received little attention from most Americans, controversy had been brewing for some time. In 1963, *Time* magazine warned that the church's "Negro Question" threatened the presidential aspirations of Michigan Governor George Romney, a devout LDS member, even though Romney publicly supported civil rights legislation. Younger Mormons were more adamant in demanding that the church renounce its position on blacks and the priesthood. "The change will come, and within my lifetime," asserted one former bishop. "The Mormon liberal has for years felt a deep uneasiness over his church's doctrine that Negroes are not worthy to hold the priesthood."[33] BYU, the shining jewel of Mormon higher education, was not immune to the controversy. The school insisted that LDS theology had no bearing on its admissions process and that officials never discriminated against minority students. Nevertheless, administrators rigidly enforced the church's ban on interracial dating and all but warned prospective black students not to attend the university. Some African American applicants in the 1960s received a letter notifying them that the city of Provo housed "no families of your race."[34] Only one or two black students enrolled at BYU each year, and none participated on the football team. Nevertheless, Brigham Young, asserting that it was doing its best to recruit black students and athletes, claimed that the school's location and lack of diversity in Utah were hindering its effort to recruit minorities.[35]

Unlike other institutions, racial controversy and big-time sport did not sneak up on BYU. Beginning in the late 1950s, administrators deliberately made a decision to build a major athletic program, form a large conference with other schools in the West, and use sport to "enhance the national image of the university."[36] The school played a key role in forming the Western Athletic Conference in 1961. Along with six charter members—Brigham Young, Arizona State University, the University of Arizona, the University of New Mexico, the University of Utah, and the University of Wyoming—the conference subsequently welcomed UTEP and Colorado State University in 1967. The WAC schools were committed to using football to enhance their national profiles, and in 1969 the conference's football games drew nearly one million spectators. Yet black athletes found little support or diversity outside of sport. At the University of Utah, *Sports Illustrated* reported that only eleven of forty-six African American athletes had even graduated and only one in four years.[37]

Wyoming's "Black 14"

Within this context, the most significant confrontation of all occurred when the BYU protest reached President Carlson and the University of Wyoming in fall 1969. The graduation rate for black athletes at the school was low (approximately 20 percent), but Wyoming had the most success in the early years of WAC competition, thanks in large part to its African American players. Under Coach Lloyd Eaton, the football team was 50–20–2 in the first seven years of conference play, including trips to the 1966 Sun Bowl and 1968 Sugar Bowl. Local citizens in Laramie particularly celebrated the Sugar Bowl appearance. Although the city and state population actually dropped between 1960 and 1970, officials approved plans to upgrade the school's football stadium to seat 33,000. By 1970, half of Laramie (and 10 percent of all Wyomingites) were able to watch the Cowboys play football live.

Such community support for a rural college team was impressive even by postwar standards. The *Laramie Daily Boomerang* was disappointed when "only" 12,000 showed up for a game in October 1969, despite blowing snow and temperatures that dipped into the teens. The playing field was among the most contentious political issues in the regional press that year, as citizens debated whether to upgrade the existing stands or construct a brand new stadium. Local media hardly mentioned the reports of black athletes protesting around the country, and in Laramie residents applauded how football helped bring pride to the state and bind students together. After a 4–0 start, the team was ranked twelfth in the nation and poised to complete another exceptional season.[38]

To achieve its success, Wyoming's athletic officials vigorously recruited players from around the nation, including Joe Williams and thirteen other African Americans. Athletes came from as far as Hawaii to play football in the unforgiving Wyoming winter, and of the sixty-two players on the 1969 squad only three were native to the state.[39] Like Williams, all but one of the other African American players also came from outside Wyoming; they hailed from Oklahoma, Massachusetts, California, Ohio, Nebraska, Colorado, Tennessee, Michigan, and Arkansas.

Most had turned down other opportunities in order to play for Coach Eaton's successful program, but life on the team was difficult. Black offensive tackle Mel Hamilton went to Laramie after saying no to a full scholarship at Cornell University, only to discover that his coach "was a tyrant," "not a fair man," and had serious "control issues." Eaton's discipline was infamous in the world of football. While the state embraced him, UW's black players had a very different relationship. He forbade them from wearing mustaches and enforced strict rules regulating the length of sideburns. "White players can make all sorts of mistakes and they just get pats on the back," recalled John Griffin, a junior lineman from San Fernando, California. "The black athletes make a mistake and they are out of the game." Others complained that Eaton placed unrealistic, racist expectations on his black players. "If you are black and get hurt, you are told you are supposed to heal right away," noted Ron Hill, a sophomore health education major from Denver. Another player, junior Tony McGee, was upset when Eaton responded to his separated shoulder by telling him he was "too big to get hurt." The players also found little academic support, and no tutors supplemented the many hours spent on the practice field. Of all the participants, Hamilton had perhaps the most troubling personal experience with Eaton. As a sophomore on the 1966 team, the Nebraska native courted a white girl and was urged by his coach to drop the relationship.[40]

Along with the football players, the other black students on campus reported similar dissatisfaction with the institution as a whole. "The social environment was a bad environment for all the blacks . . . ," recalled another player, Ivie Moore. "We stayed amongst ourselves by choice."[41] One African American student, Willie Black, came to UW in 1968 and founded a chapter of the Black Student Alliance (BSA). A married, thirty-six-year-old father of four, Black was in his first year working toward a Ph.D. in math when he decided to form the organization.[42] Several football players joined the group, where they found an outlet to voice their frustrations, especially over Coach Eaton. "He is a dictator, he pushes the button and we just act according to his rules," vented Joe Williams at one BSA meeting. "He has wild eyes." Williams complained that Eaton was stricter with black players than whites on the team. Even worse, there were few understanding faces in Laramie: "You can walk across campus and see one black person and thousands of whites," Williams told his peers. The BSA did find some minimal support in Laramie, including a local barbershop that offered to host the group's meetings. Like most railroad towns, the city also had its own small African American community with deep roots.[43]

The formation of UW's small BSA chapter and the agitation of Wyoming's African American players echoed the activism of other student groups, many of whom were sympathetic to the black protest movement. The campus also had its share of antiwar and free speech demonstrations, and some students participated in October's Vietnam Moratorium, to which the university responded with relative understanding compared to other campuses. UW's student association also approved efforts to lure counterculture figures like Abbie Hoffman and Tom Hayden to the school, and a December appearance by Yippie leader Jerry Rubin drew a hundred cheering students, along with hundreds more angry telegrams from Wyoming residents.[44]

The social tension and student activism that has come to define the period certainly existed in Laramie, but the campus was relatively quiet compared to institutions of similar size. Ultimately, the student senate rejected the Vietnam Moratorium because of what it called "a lack of interest." "Amid a contemporary sea of collegiate unrest and even violence, the University of Wyoming has long maintained a reputation for quiet and stability," the *Laramie Daily Boomerang* told local residents.[45] Despite a number of successful events put on by the BSA, most white students and Laramie citizens paid little attention to the recent surge in black protest. "Although quite a few people showed up for BSA educational programs in the spring of 1969," recalled Philip White, a UW law student and editor of the school's newspaper, "the Black 14 incident that fall indicated that nobody in leadership positions in the state or the university had made any effort to understand what young blacks were thinking."[46]

Yet just as the period's social revolutions (including the transformation in sexual mores) did not sneak up unannounced on the heartland, so too were university and conference officials prepared for a movement of Black Power among athletes at rural, predominately white institutions. Most Laramie residents did not realize that Coach Eaton and Wyoming administrators were already taking steps to prevent players from participating in any form of protest. Eaton made it clear to the team that they were not allowed to participate in campus demonstrations, even on their own time. In 1968, the coach dispatched his assistants to an ROTC protest to see if any of his players were participating.[47] Before the Vietnam Moratorium, he gathered his team again and warned them that participating in the march was not allowed. The coach also enforced a rule that prevented players from "forming factions or groups within the team," an obvious attempt to keep the black athletes from taking collective action.[48]

Moreover, UW administrators and WAC officials specifically supported Eaton's stance and agreed to grant him the power to control his players on and off the field. Eaton brought his position to the trustees in the summer before the 1969 season. He "talked about all the problems surrounding black athletes at the different campuses" and "wanted assurance that he was completely in charge of team discipline," recalled President Carlson. Although some administrators

were concerned about "effectively precluding the administration from question-
ing any rules the coach might lay down," they approved Eaton's request "loudly
and clearly." At a time when many Americans feared the nation's college campuses were slipping into anarchy, wimpy administrators were as much to blame
as radicalized youth. Although Wyoming's campus was largely free of such agitation, its new president and trustees must have found the simple, iron discipline
of a football coach appealing. After all, wrote Carlson, "Wyoming was effectively
a law and order state and there was little or no tolerance for this kind of activity."[49] Moreover, other schools in the Western Athletic Conference were essentially doing the same, positioning themselves to respond to any form of black
protest behind the scenes, especially demonstrations against BYU. That same
summer, athletic officials from each WAC member school discussed the "problems of the black athletes and student dissidents" at a closed-door meeting.[50]

Meanwhile, Wyoming BSA leader Willie Black and the school's African
American footballers were well aware that students at other institutions, includ-
ing San Jose State, were calling on teams to protest Brigham Young. One player,
Melvin Hamilton, even claimed that BYU players had used racial slurs against
Wyoming's squad in the past.[51] Echoing the San Jose State protest, the players
decided that they, too, would wear black armbands on the field during a game
versus BYU in Laramie on 18 October 1969. The BSA's faculty advisor—Professor
Roger Daniels, a nationally recognized historian of American racism—informed
President Carlson that the black players were going to defy Coach Eaton's ban
on establishing factions and participating in demonstrations.

The morning before the contest with BYU, the fourteen players went to the
athletics department and asked to meet with Eaton. Without prompting, the
coach took the players out to the field house and sat them down in the bleach-
ers. "I can save you fellows a lot of time and a lot of words," he began. "You are
all through."[52] When the players attempted to plead their case regarding the
armbands, Eaton told them to "shut up" and verbally assailed the fourteen with
the vigor they were accustomed to on the practice field, but the subject was now
race and education, not the X's and O's of a game. According to Willie Hysaw—
a junior philosophy major from Bakersfield, California. Eaton said, "You can get
on negro relief or colored relief and then maybe at these Morgan States and
Gramblings they'll put up with this kind of stuff. You're with a bunch of black
people so they might tolerate this action, but here it's not going to be tolerated."[53] Another player from California, junior tailback Ted Williams, emphasized the sincerity of the protest by stating that he was thinking of joining the
LDS Church. "Isn't that something," responded the coach sarcastically. "You plan
to join that church and abide by its beliefs for the rest of your life but you plan
to demonstrate against it tomorrow."[54] Eaton later claimed he gave the players
ten minutes to present their ideas before dismissing them from the team. "Like
hell he gave us ten minutes," Joe Williams told *Sports Illustrated*. "He came in,

sneered at us and yelled that we were off the squad."[55] Despite disagreement over the racial rhetoric he employed, all sides later agreed that Eaton was determined to enforce his ban on players participating in protest, on or off the field. "You're not going to use the legislature's money to demonstrate," he announced.[56]

Coach Eaton dismissed the black players twenty-four hours before the Saturday contest with BYU. A subsequent attempt by President Carlson, other Wyoming administrators, and the state's governor to address the disagreement in time for the game revealed the sheer importance of football in the state. When first notified of the controversy, Governor Stanley Hathaway was actually attending the opening ceremony for a new Union Pacific rail service meant to bring weekend football fans to Laramie. While California's Governor Reagan was content to denounce Harry Edwards from Sacramento, Hathaway—future secretary of the interior under Gerald Ford—drove from Cheyenne to Laramie in a blinding snowstorm to attend an emergency meeting between Wyoming's black athletes and the university trustees.[57] Like Georgia Governor Marvin Griffin a decade earlier, Hathaway recognized both the importance of sport to the state's communities and its usefulness as a political tool. The fourteen players asked that the board meet with Eaton and their entire group, but the coach refused to talk unless they ceased to be a "faction."

The subsequent meeting was remarkable, not just for its longevity (it lasted until 4:30 in the morning) but because fourteen college football players confronted Wyoming's most influential leaders. President Carlson and Governor Hathaway continued to ask the players whether they intended to wear the armbands and if they would return to the squad with Eaton as coach, at which point many refused to rejoin the team unless he was sanctioned or fired. Yet there was "no give and no leverage since the coaches were heroes in the state," wrote Carlson. "The alternative would have been dismissal of the coaches which would have blown up the state and not accomplished anything."[58] As the night wore on the discussion became increasingly candid; the black players answered appeals from Athletic Director Glen Jacoby by accusing him of not taking them seriously and constantly referring to them as "boys." The grievance confused Jacoby, who was unaware of the racial dynamics inherent to such terminology. For his part, Eaton refused to attend the meeting and only talked to Hathaway and Carlson after they came to his home that evening. According to the coach, the rule was in effect because the players were C-average students and "didn't have time to demonstrate."[59]

President Carlson and Governor Hathaway felt they had obvious control of the situation, yet, like many black athletes in rural towns by 1970, the players recognized that their athletic skills provided them with real power as well. The simple threat of ruining Wyoming's football season had assembled the state's most powerful men in the middle of the night; this was no mere budget crisis. Just as Harry Edwards had advocated, this power seemed to embolden the players. They refused to back down, and not just against their coach. Sometime after midnight, junior flanker Willie Hysaw looked across the table and asked the governor of Wyoming if he, too, was a racist.[60]

"The Bogy of Black Power" in Wyoming

President Carlson and Governor Hathaway informed the players that the trustees were backing Eaton and his coaches "because they were legally and morally correct."[61] Spectators arriving at War Memorial Stadium for that morning's game with BYU were met with confusion. The BSA handed out thousands of fliers addressed "To All Loyal Wyoming Fans"; these papers announced that the black players had neither "quit" nor "demanded" anything but instead were "unceremoniously" kicked off the team by Eaton.[62] The police presence was heightened, although most protest emerged in the following weeks after news of the school's decision spread. Nevertheless, signs from black and white students were confiscated before fans were allowed to enter the stadium. The most visible symbol was a large Confederate flag one local resident managed to bring in, which he waved from the back of the stands. Police did not respond when some students complained that the flag had the potential to incite just as much violence as a protest sign or black armband.[63] The fourteen players, soon dubbed the "Black 14" by the national press, were seated immediately behind the team's sideline. The stadium's announcer chimed in with a clarification: "Our coach has had to expel fourteen players but we think he has done the right thing so let's stand up and give him a cheer." Thousands of fans did just that, cheering and chanting "We love Eaton" throughout the game. The stadium erupted again when the all-white Cowboys managed to beat BYU's Cougars.[64]

The back of the BYU-Wyoming program featured a large advertisement for Chevrolet, with a smiling O.J. Simpson standing next to a new 1970 Impala Coupe.[65] The juxtaposition of Simpson and the Black 14 spoke volumes. America was now convinced of the benefits and opportunities athletics offered young black men. The barriers of Jim Crow were gone. As long as a player abided by a coach's rules, football was a one-way ticket to riches, fame, and a free education. After all, just months earlier "The Juice" was an amateur student athlete winning the Heisman Trophy at the University of Southern California. Football had lifted him out of what *Life* magazine called an "aimless, street-corner kind of existence."[66] Within days of graduating, Simpson turned pro and landed the massive endorsement deal with Chevrolet, enough for him to hold out for a better football contract before he even stepped on the field as a professional. "Prepared to sit out the season, O.J. Simpson isn't about to lower his asking price for shuffling off to the Buffalo Bills," announced *Sports Illustrated*. "He has all sorts of deals in the works."[67] The following year, Simpson published his first autobiography, *O.J.: The Education of a Rich Rookie*. "I am twenty-two years old, black, and lucky enough to be very talented at running with a football," wrote

Simpson: "I'm enjoying the money, the big house, the cars; what ghetto kid wouldn't? But I don't feel that I'm being selfish about it. In the long run, I feel that my advances in the business world will shatter a lot of white myths about black athletes—and give some pride and hope to a lot of young blacks."[68] The distinction between amateurism and professionalism had become a blur, and in the minds of many fans it was nonexistent. Times had changed for black athletes, and, after being bombarded with success stories like Simpson, most fans found it difficult to sympathize with young men who refused to follow coach's orders.

Fans continued to support their Wyoming Cowboys, even after the dismissal of the Black 14 destroyed the program. The team had won thirty-one of thirty-six games, including the BYU game and a subsequent contest against San Jose State. Yet the squad lost every other game of the 1969 season, and thirteen of the next sixteen. Within days, national media outlets descended on Laramie. While the disruption at San Jose State had brought the ire of California's governor, Coach Eaton's harsh restrictions and Wyoming's relative conservatism drew far more interest to the issue of black protest and college athletes. Both ABC and NBC broadcast stories from the school on the evening news, framed in terms of black radicalism creeping into the nation's heartland. In doing so, national media managed to oversimplify both black power and Wyoming's citizens. "The team is the town's industry, the state's pride—until last week, football, cattle, and minerals were the main topics of talk in Wyoming," ABC news informed viewers. "And until last week, racial problems were something folks in Wyoming only read or heard about." Behind anchor Frank Reynolds was the image of a football superimposed over a map of the state, the ball slowly enveloped by blackness. The depiction of a dark menace taking over the state echoed the interpretation of many observers. "The issue is not just a standoff between a hard-headed coach and some racial firebrands," said the reporter in Laramie. "The issue is that, even in Cowboy country, you cannot hold back the racial revolution."[69]

Nationwide, sympathy for the players grew after President Carlson and Wyoming administrators bumbled through several days of media scrutiny. There had been plenty of eloquent pundits who clambered to denounce the Olympic black power salute, the mass agitation of blacks in the streets of Oakland and Chicago, and the aggressive rhetoric of black radicalism, but to account for a small-town football coach who furiously punished his players for asking to wear armbands was not going to be easy. One major press conference was abruptly cut short after a reporter got President Carlson to admit that "football came first and civil rights second" in Wyoming.[70] Coach Eaton, too, struggling to defend the school's actions, told the media what he had told UW officials earlier in the summer: there was simply no time for anything but football. "There is no demonstration that is not demanding on time," the coach said. "You're here to get an education through athletics. . . . It's time consuming, that's why we have that regulation on demonstrating."[71]

Adding embarrassment, the school promptly back-pedaled on Eaton's strict policy. Just eight months earlier, anti-Vietnam armbands were at issue in *Tinker v. Des Moines*, the landmark Supreme Court decision that vindicated three high school students who were suspended for wearing the symbols at a public high school in Iowa. The University of Wyoming clarified that its student athletes were now allowed to participate in similar activism when off the field, but not while playing football; thus, the armbands were still out. "We've all made errors in this thing," Carlson told the *Laramie Daily Boomerang*.[72] The school even defended itself by noting that a group of Eaton's white players had also been denied permission to participate in the Vietnam Moratorium, yet the fact that Eaton did not unilaterally dismiss his white athletes only reaffirmed that the African American students had indeed received unequal treatment. Wanting to avoid the media scrutiny, Governor Hathaway simply proclaimed that "demonstrators cannot be permitted to run a university" and pledged his full support to Coach Eaton and President Carlson.[73]

The school's official response was characterized by two conflicting rationales, both of which lie at the center of how Americans configured black footballers by 1970. Wyoming had provided the young men a special opportunity; in essence, the university had done the players an immense favor by letting them participate on the team and attend the school. "What we were trying to do . . . was give them that chance to really do something for their people by getting that education," Eaton explained to the *Daily Times*.[74] Most Wyoming residents were ignorant (or forgot) that their school vigorously courted the Black 14, many of whom turned down offers at other prestigious institutions. Fans now agreed that participating in football, working for a tough-as-nails coach, and attending the university were free gifts that were given to blacks on a silver platter. According to one sportswriter, even "living up to rules" was a "privilege" that universities bestowed on their black athletes.[75]

At the same time, schools like the University of Wyoming also defended the suppression of players' rights by framing the relationship as one of employer and employee, a false distinction picked up by the media. On *NBC's Nightly News*, Chet Huntley mistakenly told viewers that the Black 14 had been "fired" by their coach, as did *Jet* magazine.[76] Some critical editorials even mentioned that the students had signed contracts to play for the team, another false allusion to professionalism. These helped generate a sentiment that universities struck deals with their African American athletes, complete with contractual commitments that unruly blacks were now breaking.[77] Even the discourse of team play and character building—so central to the amateur and educational model that provided the foundation for modern college sport—was now laced with the language of professionalization. According to one *Laramie Daily Boomerang* editorial, black players had at least entered into a "moral contract" with schools when they agreed to play football, a contract that required them to play by the "rules of the game." Apparently there was no room for distinction between rules enforced on a playing field—offside, false start, interference—and rules laid down by overbearing coaches and institutions—length of hair, engagement in protest, and so on.[78] One sports editor from the *Denver Post* articulated what most Americans now believed: "a college football player is just as much a professional athlete as Joe Namath. The only difference is the pay scale."[79]

Even if it brought increased criticism of black athletes, the professionalization of collegiate sport at least should have allowed for greater freedom of expression. After all, *actual* professional athletes who were subjected to overbearing coaches drew sympathy from fans. At the same time that the University of Wyoming dismissed its Black 14, many Americans condemned the NFL's Chicago Bears after quarterback Virgil Carter was fined and punished for speaking out against his coach. Some even offered to pay for Carter, who happened to be a Mormon and BYU graduate. "The Bears had no right to fine a man just because he's got guts enough to speak his mind," exclaimed one Chicago resident.[80] In terms of race, football fans were also proving themselves sensitive to the difficulties professional black athletes faced while playing in predominately white communities. In the late 1960s, the NFL's Green Bay Packers, led by Coach Vince Lombardi, were the most popular football team in the nation, and sportswriters hailed Lombardi's efforts to reach out to his black players. "Green Bay is an isolated community with no significant Negro population," Jack Olsen informed *Sports Illustrated* readers. Nevertheless, Lombardi "insisted that his Packers be a family."[81]

Even with such praise, understanding, and sympathy heaped upon racially sensitive coaches and black athletes at the professional levels, many fans still berated college athletes who complained. Critics began to circulate the idea that African American collegians were spoiled and pampered and that the college experience was somehow meant to break down black athletes before they moved on to the riches, fame, and greater racial equity that awaited them in professional leagues. Little attention was given to the fact that most college players never reached success as professionals. Although many of the nation's traditional institutions were under fire in the late 1960s, fans particularly questioned how anyone could find fault with the all-American game of football. "Too many black athletes have become prima donnas," wrote Roger Stanton in *Football News*. "It is ironic they have selected football—the last place in the world to harbor discrimination."[82] By the 1980s, such sentiments coalesced into a full-scale backlash against black college athletes, especially as reports of illegal payments and academic fraud escalated.

However, Wyoming's Black 14 were treated as professionals only insofar as it helped control their activities and suppress their right to free expression. In essence, the school argued that athletes on the field were virtually no different from employees representing the university, a contention many schools echoed in their attempts to halt black athletes from speaking out. Yet at other times, university administrators also insisted that black athletes were anything but professionals. Schools argued that not only were African American players more amateurish than other students because many came from farther away, but also their sporting commitments required stronger discipline, more surveillance, and the need for schools to take a greater role *in loco parentis*. Like Bob Beamon's uncomfortable relationship with UTEP officials, coaches and administrators often helped players find housing, secure employment, and receive academic support, given their demanding schedules.

In addition to the conflicting notions regarding their relationship to the Black 14, Wyoming officials also told the nation they were under a black power assault. Coach Eaton was fully convinced that he was the target of an organized, political plot. "We've had Negro players since 1960," he told *Sports Illustrated*. "Why haven't we had a demonstration before?"[83] The school even sent out an official letter warning that 2,000 Black Panthers were headed to Laramie, and its Alumni Association issued a statement sympathizing with athletes "who must suffer the consequences of their actions . . . urged upon them by a group which does not truly have their welfare in mind." One sportswriter at the *Laramie Daily Boomerang* pleaded with the black athletes "not to fall for this overworked hogwash."[84] Vice President Spiro Agnew had denounced the Vietnam Moratorium as the work of "hard core dissidents and professional anarchists" and warned of "wilder, more violent" demonstrations. For some Wyoming residents, the controversy surrounding the Black 14 was just that. "Outside influences know Wyoming is close enough to be reached," read one ominous editorial. Other residents went so far as to insist that black athletes throughout the West were under the influence of mind control, or worse. Hate letters proclaimed that the armbands smacked of Nazi propaganda, worn by "black bigots" and "intolerants."[85]

Echoing the refusal of most Americans to give agency to college athletes, school officials and Wyoming residents were certain that the Black 14 had been influenced by outside agitators. The weekend after the BYU game, the football team from San Jose State came to Laramie. Convinced that busloads of Black Panthers were coming from Denver and California, Governor Hathaway called in the National Guard and stationed troops under the stadium for the season's remaining games. Such claims only frustrated the students further. "I am not a troublemaker and I was not sent here by some subversive organization," announced Willie Black, who eventually left the Wyoming BSA chapter he founded and later become a math professor at the University of Chicago.[86] The players agreed and continued to reject the idea that they were pawns of the black power movement. Although influenced by other students—the movement to protest BYU clearly began with Edwards and Bay Area radicals—the actions of black athletes around the West took place with minimal guidance. No major black power figures or members of the radical leadership even mentioned the controversy.

"We don't need outside influence to tell us what we already know," vented junior Willie Hysaw to the press.[87]

The idea of black power infiltrating football stirred fear in regions nearly devoid of African Americans, and rural residents had little problem transposing the specter of urban riot to their own world. Referencing Watts, New York City, Detroit, and Chicago, Wyoming's largest insurance association issued a notice warning that "the violation of rules and regulations" in other parts of the country had caused millions of dollars in property damage.[88] The NCAA itself also contributed to the hysteria surrounding the connection. The organization's official publication ran a sweeping story, "Militant Groups Doing Great Disservice to Black College Athletes," in which it claimed that the Black 14 were acting under the auspices of the Black Panther Party in Denver.[89] In addition, black protest in college sport lent credence to even more outlandish fears about the general counterculture and liberal movements. Some warned that Mountain West states would be targeted for protest precisely because of their isolation. One rumor warned that 100,000 hippies were planning to establish a Wyoming compound to take over state politics and elect their own senator. After black athletes made headlines with the BYU protest, such stories emerged from obscurity and appeared more frequently in residents' conversations. Thirty years later, President Carlson still insisted that Wyoming's black football players were "probably" threatened with physical harm by Black Panthers, a "few hard-core members who somehow controlled the group."[90]

"Xenophobic Pontifications and Ludicrous Hero Worship"

Nevertheless, reaction to the Black 14 by some faculty and students at the University of Wyoming proved that rural campuses were anything but isolated from the context of the times. Within days, a faculty meeting to address the issue drew at least 750 people, more than any of the state's previous antiwar marches. Seven faculty members said they would resign if the school did not reverse its decision and reinstate the players, including one English professor who denounced UW's willingness "to place black people in chattel slavery for the good of a football corporation." While some faculty supported the administration, professors from the College of Arts and Sciences issued a resolution calling the players' treatment "a mockery of academic freedom."[91] The players were surprised to learn that most of their professors backed them. "I naturally assumed the faculty would support the athletics department," said Mel Hamilton. "It is amazing that they are willing to throw away their whole careers for our beliefs."[92] Wyoming residents and members of the UW community were also taken aback at the reaction from instructors at the state's institution—something they expected from radical faculty at campuses such as Berkeley, but not in Laramie.

Amidst the turmoil of 1960s higher education, UW's dismissal of its black athletes was the campus's most tense moment of the decade. "I question if Wyoming even wants a true university," wrote one professor in an open letter to President Carlson. Another sent his basketball season tickets back to the athletics department with a message that he refused to promote sports at UW. Two days later the note was returned to the professor with a simple inscription: "good!"[93] Along with many faculty members, some UW students, usually those from outside the state, were outraged as well. One freshman from California told a local newspaper that Coach Eaton was "unjust" for not listening to his own players, while graduate students formed a "Committee for the 14" and staged several marches on campus.[94] Other athletes voiced additional frustrations. The school's basketball team threatened to quit until their coach agreed to let them participate in demonstrations, and several track members (including a white student) left the team while claiming that their coach had told them to quit if they thought civil or constitutional rights were more important than an education. "Either you're my boy, or you go home," he reportedly told one of his black athletes.[95]

As news of the controversy spread, students and fans at schools throughout the WAC expressed shock at Wyoming's treatment of its own players. Following the dismissal of the Black 14, every member of the San Jose State football team (white and black) wore armbands on the field during their game in Laramie—this

Students at the University of Wyoming protest the suspension of the "Black 14." The sign reads, "The Black Ball Players have fought for you, fight for them NOW!" Irene Schubert Collection, American Heritage Center, University of Wyoming.

time protesting Coach Eaton and the UW administration.[96] Wyoming residents responded with their own show of force. Fans cheered a private plane that circled the stadium pulling a banner with the words "Yeah, Eaton." The crowd's deafening roar was enough to halt the game for several minutes. "It was like they were worshipping an idol," recalled Philip White, editor of the student newspaper.[97]

The protest of black athletes galvanized other forms of campus activism at WAC schools, including Wyoming. "It's building all over the country," announced Bill Watterman, a Detroit civil rights attorney who arrived in Laramie within days to help the Black 14 file a civil rights lawsuit.[98] One student's picket sign cynically asked the school to completely finish professionalizing intercollegiate athletics: "Fire Faculty, Burn Books, Hire Green Bay Packers." Other white students picketed Coach Eaton's home.[99] In response to the incident, some students and faculty launched a new underground publication, *Free Lunch*, which featured articles supporting the players interspersed with news from the antiwar and free speech movements. Campus activists assailed what they considered the university's failure to defend the athletes, the conservatism of Wyoming residents, and the general complacency of the UW student body. Willie Black, founder of the BSA, particularly urged the antiwar and free speech crowd to speak out on behalf of the black athletes. "The Black man's fight against the day-to-day manifestations of racism in this country and the plain struggle to survive make the war by comparison seem terribly remote," he wrote. When the BSA brought in civil rights leader James Farmer, cofounder of the Congress of Racial Equality (CORE) to speak on behalf of the athletes, hundreds of students and Laramie residents attended.[100]

Such attempts to unite campus activism were largely successful in the immediate weeks of the controversy, for the national media spotlight on Laramie signaled a rare moment in which the campus had the nation's attention. Faculty and students launched another radical newsletter, *Revelations*, in which they called the state's mainstream press an "unending supply of xenophobic pontifications and ludicrous hero worship."[101] Ironically, none of the progressive literature on campus addressed the role of gender in the equation; that is, athletic recruitment brought few black women to the university. For that matter, virtually no media coverage surrounding the BYU protests as a whole mentioned that Mormonism enforced even stronger regulations against women serving in the church. Because male athletes were leading the charge, the BYU protests centered exclusively on race, yet numerous women participated in picketing subsequent football games in Laramie and athletic events on other WAC campuses.

"Beat the Devil Out of BYU"

Despite this renewed activism on the part of some students and scrutiny in the national media, Wyoming was distinguished from other campuses facing black athletic unrest because most students continued to support their beloved coach and the school's administration. A campus poll found that students supported Eaton's form of discipline two to one; a Cheyenne sophomore told the *Daily Times* he would stand behind any coach no matter what he did to his players.[102] In the weeks that followed, an overwhelming number of Wyoming residents also supported the administration's decision to dismiss the Black 14. Of the 25,000 petition signatures, telegrams, and correspondence the school received from residents, only 1 to 2 percent were from citizens denouncing the school's action.[103]

Nevertheless, while residents appeared to stand in solidarity against the threat of black power, the controversy still managed to reveal deep divisions in a state where issues of race and equality were rarely discussed. Weeks after the incident, a Casper judge agreed to postpone a black man's murder trial because of the "serious racial issue which has divided the state into two areas: those for the blacks and those against the blacks."[104] Numerous grassroots booster clubs held meetings, rallies, and fundraisers to express their satisfaction with the team's stance against the black players, groups like the Carbon County Quarterback Club, the Touchdown Club of Casper, and the Cheyenne Quarterback Club—the very same organization of 400 that gave Joe Williams a standing ovation several weeks before the BYU game. In response to UW faculty threatening to leave over the administration's decision, one club offered money to help get the radical professors out of Wyoming as soon as possible. Sport "has done more to unite the state than anything else," wrote one Laramie booster. "It's not northern ranchers against southern mineral interests when it comes to Wyoming football."[105]

The overwhelming response affirmed the centrality of football in shaping civic identity in Wyoming. Residents specifically rallied around Coach Eaton as an embodiment of what many saw as the state's "values." In response to student protesters at War Memorial Stadium, fans wore armbands emblazoned with the word "Eaton." [106] There was also a connection between the state's condemnation of the Black 14 and national segregationist politics. One Casper man who showed up at games offering "Eaton" bumper stickers turned out to be working with the American Independent Party, state manager for George Wallace's fledgling presidential campaign; the stickers were seen around Laramie for weeks.[107] Messages hailing the coach and his rules arrived from hundreds of miles away and all corners of the remote state. Citizens in tiny northern towns like Basin (pop. 1,000), Worland (pop. 5,000), and Ten Sleep (pop. 300) gathered to sign and send telegrams of support. Pro-Eaton petitions circulated everywhere. Within a few hours, one group of Cheyenne residents gathered signatures from 3,500 people (nearly 9 percent of the city's population). In the state's far northeast, Campbell County legislators threatened to withhold funds from the university if the school reinstated the players, while the Rotary Club in Rawlins denounced UW's faculty and issued a resolution celebrating Coach Eaton.[108]

Supporters of Coach Eaton's decision to dismiss UW's black football players attended subsequent games wearing armbands and hatbands. Irene Schubert Collection, American Heritage Center, University of Wyoming.

Whereas coaches like UCLA's Babe Horell or Georgia Tech's Bobby Dodd were celebrated for personalities that seemed to soften institutional and regional images, Wyomingites embraced Eaton's personification of merciless justice and stern discipline.

Residents even linked the coach's iron will to the kind of strong conservative leadership they longed to see running the nation. "It is unfortunate that the leaders of our country have not taken a stand against riots and demonstrations," read one letter to the *Laramie Daily Boomerang*. Perhaps Eaton's courage could "stimulate the legislators of our country to take a stand and maintain it."[109] The coach's name was included in discussions about Goldwater, Nixon, and Reagan— conversations about what was wrong with America and who could fix it. Within weeks of his decision to throw Wyoming's black players off the football team, and despite the criticism circulating in the national press, Eaton was the most

An "Eaton" bumper sticker. Irene Schubert Collection, American Heritage Center, University of Wyoming.

popular man in the state. "You gentlemen and your counterparts . . . have saved football," he told a roaring crowd of boosters in December. To them he had saved much more.[110]

Joining other fans confronted with the BYU protest, Wyomingites proposed an easy solution to the controversy: play more football. Because athletics were the domain of African American talent, black students could articulate their frustration and activism through sheer physicality within the confines of a game. This assumed, of course, that players controlled the various meanings audience members took from winning or losing sporting contests, which they did not. Nevertheless, according to one local editorial the black players' strongest protest would have been to simply participate in the system and "beat the devil out of BYU." Football was so privileged that many Wyomingites claimed the school could not be racist precisely because the ratio of black players on its team was larger than the actual ratio of African Americans who lived in the state or attended UW. Either way, residents urged black athletes to voice their frustrations by winning more games. "A good old-fashioned football game is much more satisfactory than a new-fashioned Love-in," exclaimed one editorial from the little town of Thermopolis.[111] Other editorials appealed to the black athletes with stories of Jesse Owens and his decision to run in front of Hitler and the German people in 1936; evidently the writers did not realize that Owens was Harry Edwards's favorite "uncle tom" or that the comparison of 1960s Wyoming with fascist Germany was probably counterproductive. Also, the Black 14 had never refused to play; the players only wanted to wear armbands while they competed (and hopefully beat) Brigham Young. Even worse, in calling for the players to make their statements on the field, many fans were asserting that black athletes had to earn their civil rights by playing a game well. According to one *Denver Post* reader, the Black 14 "had the unique opportunity to prove on the football field their right to equal treatment."[112]

Support for a crackdown on unruly athletes in the WAC also trickled in from around the nation. "Bear" Bryant at the University of Alabama—also infamous for his no-nonsense discipline—contacted Eaton to offer his encouragement.[113] Unlike *Sports Illustrated* or the *New York Times*, some national publications echoed Wyoming's support of its coach. While many criticized how college sport created prima donna black men, others maintained that coaching and the games themselves had nothing to do with it. "The educational value of playing football is based on selfless submission to discipline, the will of the group and the authority of the coach," wrote one sportswriter.[114] Thus, despite the intention of Harry Edwards and certain athletes, sport protest could further racialize black students. No matter what went wrong, games like football could maintain their traditional, all-American purity as long as Americans blamed young black men for infusing them with their own innate hypermasculinity and overaggression. Although football supposedly incorporated America's most cherished values, it was surprisingly unclear what those values were. Fans were far more certain about what they were not: "Football is not a democracy," wrote one editor at the *Denver Post*.[115]

"The Fruits of Permissiveness"

Ironically, Wyoming's crackdown on the Black 14 helped stimulate the overall movement of black athletic protest in the West. Led by Willie Black, BSA representatives from a number of WAC schools asked to plead their case before a meeting of the conference in Denver. After WAC officials denied the request, some fifty protestors disrupted the event. "It has become clear the Western Athletic Conference is no place for Negro athletes," Black told the press.[116] Students at Utah State staged a demonstration during a BYU game the following month. Like San Jose State, black players on the University of New Mexico's football squad wore armbands supporting the Black 14 during another November game against Wyoming, and dozens of student protesters demonstrated on the field at Albuquerque's University Stadium. In January, scores were arrested at the University of Arizona after a large demonstration (including players wearing armbands) took place during a basketball game versus BYU. Meanwhile, at Colorado State University and the University of Washington students shut down wrestling matches with BYU.[117]

Building on the furor surrounding Wyoming's Black 14, BYU and the LDS church faced its most damaging threat in decades. President Ernest Wilkinson thought it would help sway public opinion by announcing again that Provo had only one black family living in its city limits. In remarks before the whole student body, Wilkinson also hinted that the athletes were manipulated by the mysterious hand of black power—"Leaders, such as Hitler, regardless of their cause can always find followers," he warned.[118] Nevertheless, BYU and LDS officials fought a losing battle. Although Wyoming residents largely denounced the Black 14, administrators around the West were starting to lose patience with BYU's tepid response.

Still, the WAC refused to intervene. In the tradition of the Pacific Coast Conference (PCC) in 1939 and the Missouri Valley Conference (MVC) in 1951, another organization meant to govern regional intercollegiate athletics simply ignored a racial controversy. Several coaches demanded that WAC officials consider the issue, but the conference refused to embark on a discussion that it felt would involve "theological precepts." In November, the scandal peaked when Stanford University President Kenneth Pitzer formally announced that the school was severing athletic relations with BYU. Despite having its own vibrant LDS group on campus, Pitzer exclaimed that Stanford's new policy was "not to schedule events with institutions which practice discrimination on a basis of race or national origin." Soon after, the University of Washington also cut ties with Brigham Young.[119]

The backlash to Stanford's decision was furious. One professor called it "easily the sharpest criticism of the Mormon religion in this century," while many LDS members reacted with less restraint. "Stanford is just another garbage dump for intellectual trash," wrote one Ogden, Utah, resident.[120] Max Rafferty, California state superintendent of public instruction and a former Republican candidate for the U.S. Senate, likened the move to the Third Reich's stifling of Judaism. In one of the few overt references to Jim Crow segregation, a Provo sportswriter announced that the "fruits of permissiveness" threatened to bring harm to BYU's athletes and suggested the problem could be addressed by forbidding black fans from sitting near the field of play.

The controversy convinced the LDS Church—long known for its secrecy—to engage in an unprecedented amount of public dialogue, as church officials tried to clarify the policy by releasing numerous statements and granting interviews.

"The seeming discrimination by the Church toward the Negro is not something which originated with man; but goes back into the beginning with God," read one letter officials released to the public. "Sometime in God's eternal plan, the Negro will be given the right to hold the priesthood." Overall, the LDS public response tended to backfire on the Mormon leadership. Few black athletes were in a mood "to wait for revelations, divine or otherwise," proclaimed the *Denver Post*, the region's only major publication to come out in support of the Black 14.[121]

Seeking to force their reinstatement to the team, Wyoming's black players and civil rights attorney Bill Watterman took their case to district court in Cheyenne. In defending itself, UW once again found it useful to classify black college athletes as professionals. Wyoming Attorney General James E. Barrett argued that the players were acting as representatives of the state and university, in the same way as any other employee of the school. The state, firing back at Watterman himself, even argued that he had subjected Wyoming to "ridicule, abuse, and scorn by means of press conferences, TV appearances, and public statements designed to inflame the public." Under riveting examination, Watterman pressed President Carlson to clarify what it meant to be a "representative" of the school. For example, were members of the marching band also officials of the university?[122]

Judge Ewing T. Kerr's ruling affirmed what many Mountain West fans believed: football coaches indeed had absolute power over their players. Kerr indicated he had "serious doubts" that a court had jurisdiction over "the verbal directive" of a coach. In his own way, the judge did invoke inalienable rights, which at the time was so central to the ongoing debates over free speech and civil rights. "Any coach has certain inherent powers to discipline, regulations, and training," wrote Kerr.[123] While freedom movements were burgeoning around the country, Wyoming's judiciary spawned perhaps the most curious one: the inalienable rights of a football coach. Watterman and the players immediately appealed.

The case, *Williams v. Eaton*, was the culmination of Wyoming's most serious postwar racial incident and one of the state's few civil rights cases. It dragged on until October 1972. While the players lost on appeal, ten of the fourteen managed to graduate from college, including two who returned to UW. Four also went on to play professionally, including Joe Williams, who returned to his native Texas not to teach elementary school but to play for the Dallas Cowboys. Tony McGee, a talented defensive end from Battle Creek, Michigan, transferred to Bishop College and subsequently played fourteen seasons in the National Football League for the Bears, Patriots, and Redskins.[124] Today there is little memory of the Black 14 on Wyoming's campus, other than a small commemorative statue that sits in the basement of the student union, engraved with the players' names. Ironically, it depicts a single arm raised high in a Black Power salute, just like Carlos and Smith in Mexico City. The players' connection to the "bogy of Black Power" is fixed in bronze.

As for Coach Lloyd Eaton, he went from being the most popular man in Wyoming to complete obscurity. Even though UW briefly promoted him to assistant athletic director, Eaton never recovered from the Black 14 incident. The national media painted him as hopelessly backward and racially intolerant, and he struggled to recruit athletes. Wyomingites embraced him in the immediate aftermath of the controversy, but he left the state two years later and never coached again. Subsequently, the coach known for his orneriness became increasingly withdrawn and bitter. Although he never returned to Laramie, one writer managed to track him down in 1982, where he was living alone in rural Idaho and refused to own a telephone. Eaton had no regrets about dismissing all the black players on his team and was still unsure why so many around the nation criticized him for confronting black power head on. "They were biting the hand that feeds them," he said. "Music—entertainment especially—and athletics have been the great areas for the black man."[125]

The BYU scandal was the most prominent black protest movement in the history of college football. It started from a likely source: college athletes at a progressive campus in San Jose, under the direction of a man who articulated the 1968 Olympic boycott. And it eventually returned to the Bay Area, with Stanford's controversial decision to cancel athletic contests with Brigham Young. Yet this important movement of black college athletes was solidified in an unlikely place—on a quiet mountain campus in one of the nation's most isolated and rural places.

The story of Wyoming's Black 14 reveals how rural Americans perceived the black power movement; in many ways they assigned it far more influence and control than it actually exercised. African American footballers in Laramie organized and agitated largely on their own terms, but by 1969 many Americans were ready to categorize any collective response as an expression of militancy. Certainly images of the antiwar movement—most notably the previous summer's televised coverage of the Democratic National Convention—helped feed such reaction. Yet from the perspective of many white fans, black football unrest was most significant because protest, however mild, had infiltrated the traditionally conservative realm of college football. Furthermore, as many parents feared that minorities—particularly black culture—were influencing white youth to embrace sexual and moral revolution, black athletes who spoke out on integrated teams questioned the basic tenant that amateur sport built cooperation and character in America's youth; black athletes challenged the popular myth that sport had helped unite and integrate the nation.

By attacking the system, black protest in college football threatened to rewrite history itself. After all, what was significant about Jackie Robinson integrating major league baseball in 1947 if the predicament of many college athletes thirty years later was worse than Robinson's own experience at UCLA? Examining black athletic unrest in tandem with political and social movements in the late 1960s illuminates how discourses of militant revolution and response impacted popular culture in unique ways. More important, it also reveals how those movements reached far more Americans than historians have previously considered. Indeed, contrary to what the University of Wyoming had predicted, 2,500 Bay Area Black Panthers never showed up in Laramie to foment black power. Nevertheless, most Wyomingites still insisted they had encountered the militant nationalists head on.

The movement of black athletes in the Mountain West came to a quiet and abrupt end. At 2:45 P.M. on 1 June 1978, LDS President Spencer W. Kimball received a revelation from God. It confirmed "the wishes of the Brethren" and eliminated the prohibition of "African blacks" from the priesthood. From 1976 to 1986, BYU's football team won ten straight WAC championships; in 1984, they were national champions. The school survived the period of athletic protest and emerged as one of the top football programs in the West. Yet access to the LDS priesthood did not translate into significant growth in minority admissions at Brigham Young, except among student athletes. In 1996, a total enrollment of 26,553 students featured just 75 African Americans, 20 percent of whom were football recruits. Only 2 of 1,339 faculty members were black; of those, one was a physical education teacher hired to work with the football team.[126] And although divine, the new revelation simply confirmed what many Americans had already known for decades: God himself was a football fan.

Epilogue

In the forty years since Wyoming students criticized the pressure white society placed on black athletes, college fans have continued to rely on sport to represent their institutions in ways that transcend mere "school spirit." According to media reports, in 2007 Virginia Tech University turned to football's "healing power" in the aftermath of one student's rampage, when he gunned down thirty-two people on campus in the largest mass murder in the nation's history. Four months later, the press announced that the Hokies opening home game against East Carolina University was "more than the start of a new season" when 66,233 fans gathered at Lane Stadium in Blacksburg to watch the school take its "biggest step towards a return to normalcy." One alumnus told the Associated Press that the game was "like a funeral service . . . like a memorial." Faced with incredible expectations, the team (fielding 85 percent African American players) delivered victory, and spectators reacted with both "tears and cheers." "It's a relief that we made the community proud," said Victor Harris, a twenty-one-year-old black cornerback from Richmond.[1]

Much has changed in the sixty years since Harvard's Chet Pierce became the first black to play football against a southern university in nearby Charlottesville, Virginia. What has not changed, however, is the meaning that schools and fans tie to their athletic teams. Although this volume has tried to illuminate the varying reactions to black athletes in different places and at different times, one consistent theme is the immense pressure intercollegiate sport has always placed on students, especially blacks who realized that the meaning behind their accomplishments transcended school sprit, regional pride, and economic gain.

Another theme has been the continual shift between amateurism and professionalism at the collegiate level, which often influenced Americans' responses to black athletes and their grievances. African American students like O.J. Simpson were considered professionals well before they graduated, and in achieving immediate financial success at the professional level they reinforced the idea that intercollegiate sport rescued African Americans from inner-city poverty and taught them how to succeed in "mainstream" society. Many Americans also believed that sport provided amateur collegians simple life skills, familial support, and an education. As criticism of the black family grew in the 1970s, some white fans embraced the idea that collegiate teams gave young black males the family structure they lacked at home, especially through white coaches who filled the gaps left by delinquent black fathers.

Since then, amateurism and professionalism have continued to blend together, and by the 1980s many schools embraced the idea that college teams could be both families and lucrative business ventures. "You have a culture, you always want them to feel like they're a part of your family and will be part of your family," explained Duke University basketball coach Mike Krzyzewski in a 2007 speech describing his recruits. The coach was speaking to a group of business-men who paid $1,600 each to attend his annual leadership conference in Durham, North Carolina, which included the opportunity to attend a closed practice and watch Krzyzewski run his players through drills while providing the audience business and motivational tips. "It's like hiring," Krzyzewski told the crowd when describing his recruitment strategy. "I would never just hire people from a resume." Responded one IBM manager after the practice: "It was amazing how quickly the players changed their roles and got into whatever they were doing. That's very important in the business world."[2]

These connections between collegiate athletics and big business persist even as reports are beginning to question whether big-time sports actually bring in big-time money. According to a 1998 study by The Andrew W. Mellon Foundation, top-tier Division I programs spent an average of 38 million dollars per year, of which 45 percent went to football. At the University of Michigan, the school lost 2.8 million dollars on athletics, despite averaging 110,000 fans at each home football game. Revenue is failing to keep up with budgets, and ath-letic departments at all levels—from small liberal arts colleges to major pro-grams—are reporting more deficits.[3] Although diversity is rarely mentioned in contemporary discussions of revenue and general deemphasis on collegiate sport, race must factor into any future decisions regarding athletic programs, for if there is renewed backlash to college sport in the next twenty years the most significant impact will be its adverse affect on black enrollment. Thus, now more than ever Americans should reacquaint themselves with the history of black student athletes, especially the way in which they came to dominate American college football: a sport that represents the most popular, lucrative, and significant link between institutional education and athleticism in history.

Beginning in the late nineteenth century, African American students joined football teams at predominately white institutions in the North and Midwest. At times, their participation earned notable attention and challenged

Victorian notions of Anglo-Saxon manhood. Ivy Leaguers like William Henry Lewis and Paul Robeson parlayed gridiron achievement into influential positions as politicians and social activists. Others, like Fritz Pollard, continued to pursue football at the professional level, helping integrate the sport's first professional league in 1920, twenty-seven years before the restrictions on major league baseball fell. Yet most players, like George Flippin and Jack Trice, played in relative obscurity. Most important, the participation of a few dozen black athletes at predominately white schools before 1935 did not threaten the stability of intersectional contests between southern and northern schools. Integrated institutions, like those in the Ivy League, overwhelmingly abided by the "gentlemen's agreement," in which segregated schools agreed to play integrated opponents only if African American students were excluded from participating.

World War II, a watershed for civil rights in America, offered significant economic opportunities for many blacks and precipitated a renewed movement against southern Jim Crow; yet college sport had already presented a vision of unprecedented integration to its nationwide audience in the late 1930s. In particular, the immense popularity of black students at UCLA challenged the gentlemen's agreement in a new, more threatening way: by introducing the idea that entire teams consisting of black athletes could represent major white universities. African Americans nationwide embraced the Bruins as their own, even though the institution and surrounding neighborhoods were otherwise poor reflections of their own communities. Nevertheless, UCLA's rise to national prominence showed that black athletes, while providing a public face for white universities, successfully represented a form of integrated higher education that supposedly transcended mere tokenism. Moreover, African American collegians like Kenny Washington and Jackie Robinson were media darlings on the West Coast, and their stories provide evidence of an ongoing temporal and geographic shift in civil rights historiography. An examination of fan reaction to integrated education and the participation of black students in the West extends the narrative of African American civil rights beyond a Deep South/Progressive North binary, illuminating a more nuanced portrait of the black experience before World War II.

After the war, publicized disruptions over integration on the playing field—like the 1951 Johnny Bright incident and the 1956 Sugar Bowl—echoed the opening battles of the postwar civil rights movement in the Deep South. Yet in states like Missouri, Oklahoma, Iowa, and Nebraska, the entrenchment of intercollegiate athletics forced citizens to engage the movement's principles in regions where black boycotts and judicial challenges were rarer. While most fans in Oklahoma and Iowa reacted quietly to the formal desegregation of midwestern universities, Johnny Bright's assault generated intense public dialogue over sensitive issues, including individual rights, racism in the public sphere, and the physical intimidation of African Americans. These significant debates spoke to the very heart of the civil rights struggle, and, like the dramatic rise of black athletes at UCLA in the late 1930s, they too occurred in regions slighted by most narratives. Moreover, they reveal midwestern communities engaged in significant public discourse on civil rights five years before the Supreme Court's decision in *Brown*.

By the mid-1950s, critics at both ends of the political spectrum recognized that sports were meaningful, politicized activities that shaped regional identity—an idea some historians still hesitate to embrace. Governor Marvin Griffin's attempt to ban Georgia schools from participating in integrated contests offers an intriguing, rare example of the uncertainty surrounding the early days of "massive resistance" in the South. Six months after the Supreme Court ruled in *Brown v. the Board of Education* that school integration had to proceed "with all deliberate speed," Georgia citizens—from political leaders like Griffin and Herman Talmadge to rural readers of the *Columbus Ledger* and *Macon Telegraph*—analyzed the threat posed by Bobby Grier. Few other episodes triggered such criticism of Jim Crow politics from within the ranks of segregation's ardent supporters, and for many northern observers the reaction of Georgia's white collegians, who marched on the state capitol and governor's mansion, signaled the possibility that native Georgians might level significant criticism at the region's political leadership.

Meanwhile, integrated football in the 1950s offered black athletes like Grier an unparalleled, harrowing experience. As he traveled with his team throughout the decade, Grier was able to compare racial tension and public segregation up and down the country, from Pennsylvania and West Virginia, to Oklahoma and Louisiana—all before he even graduated from college. His numerous encounters with prejudice at the local level provide a model of complexity that all civil rights narratives should strive to achieve.

By 1970, the ultimate acceptance of black athletes on the playing field did not translate into equal and adequate opportunities for African American students at integrated colleges. Beginning in 1968, black athletes in the Western Athletic Conference—particularly at the University of Wyoming—altogether rejected the triumphant narrative of sport integration and articulated instead an alternative, unsettling vision. To them, America's infatuation with sport hindered blacks in higher education by limiting their options, perpetuating misunderstanding, stereotyping black masculinity, and reinforcing white domination in the form of all-powerful coaches and administrators. Indeed, on many integrated 1960s campuses the inherent dynamics of Jim Crow were only slightly altered, replaced by a more complex mixture of coddling and contempt. Even amid the decade's social turmoil, football rivaled other rituals that receive far more attention in both scholarly histories and popular memory. As a freshman at Wellesley College in 1968, Secretary of State Hillary Rodham Clinton never experimented with drugs, yet she often showed up at Harvard games with "a book in hand."[4]

Aside from Clinton, historians risk overemphasizing aspects of postwar youth culture if they fail to recognize how some young people posited radical change via cultural spectacles that usually represented All-American tradition-alism. Without necessarily embracing popular music, drugs, politics, or the antiwar movement, black athletes in the late 1960s nevertheless embodied the spirit of their times. Some, like Wyoming's Black 14, shaped the message of black power, mass protest, and youth rebellion to fit their own unique situations. Nevertheless, football fans in conservative states like Wyoming and Utah responded to their grievances within the broader context of the antiwar cru-sade, the burgeoning free speech movement, the growing youth counterculture, and their reaction to urban race riots. For these citizens, Huey Newton, Bobby Seale, or Harry Edwards were not the faces of black power; rather, students like Joe Williams—the senior from Texas who vented to his BSA friends about walk-ing through "a sea of whites" at UW—or Mel Hamilton, the Nebraska native who wanted to date a white girl in Laramie—embodied the black protest movement. Such encounters help complicate the very definition of black power on the nation's campuses, especially in conservative towns far removed from the cen-ters of student radicalism in the late 1960s and early 1970s.

Today, some of the very questions first raised by black athletes in 1968 remain unanswered, and schools can only address them by understanding the dual history of integrated college sport and its contemporary relationship with diversity in higher education. Has the growing presence and visibility of black athletes helped increase overall minority enrollment at America's top univer-sities? To what extent have schools linked athletic recruitment with racial diversity campaigns? For example, contemporary African American athletes at UCLA, which introduced Americans to a "black team" in 1939, continue to be invoked in broader debates over race and education. In 1996, the school's his-torical pride in accepting black athletes clashed with California's passage of Proposition 209, which eliminated the consideration of race and gender while preserving "heritage" (alumni) preferences in the admissions process at all University of California campuses. By 2006, opponents lamented that only 100 African Americans enrolled at UCLA—just 2 percent of the incoming class—yet many Americans paid little attention to the controversy. The fact that black players continued to dominate UCLA sports, their exploits splashed across the newspaper and television, undoubtedly impacted the reaction. For pessimists, UCLA's athletes simply provide a public façade of interracialism to shield the crisis of minority enrollment from public view.[5]

Yet now more than ever, black athletes today recognize that their repre-sentation in popular culture can also potentially translate into tangible political platforms. In 2007, several professionals who attended UCLA formed the "We Shall Not Be the Only Ones" campaign, designed to highlight the continued dis-crepancy between the level of African American participation in college sport and the decline in black students. Within weeks, the group—led by NBA basket-ball star and UCLA alumnus Baron Davis—managed to generate national cover-age and a meeting with the school's chancellor.[6] And problems like these are not exclusive to large research universities with top-tier, NCAA Division I athletic programs. Forty years after Joe Williams yearned for a stronger black community at the University of Wyoming, black athletes at institutions, both large and small, across the country still struggle with a lack of diversity outside the athletic department. During some periods, the number of black athletes continued to rise or hold steady even as black enrollment declined. From 1977 to 1984 the total number of African Americans attending college actually dropped from 1.1 million to 993,574, but the trend was largely invisible to fans of college sport.[7]

Today, athletes at many schools find themselves among the few African American students on campus, and often the disproportion of black males to black females remains as large a problem as overall minority enrollment. Many athletes also continue to report feeling simultaneously celebrated and misun-derstood. If anything, the story of how Williams moved from a small town in Texas to a large university in 1968—and ended up feeling more restricted and alienated than ever—complicates the popular, celebratory portraits of revolu-tionary college campuses in the late 1960s. This genuine struggle black athletes faced, even after their enrollment at sympathetic universities, provides a more nuanced and sobering portrait of desegregation.

These stories also help explicate the historical relationship between ama-teur black athletes and high-profile sporting celebrities—figures like Joe Louis and Muhammad Ali, whom historians have already incorporated into the civil rights narrative. At times, fans heaped enormous praise on successful collegians, yet they simultaneously expected black students to shoulder the heavy burden of responsibility that came with such opportunities. According to some critics, for the African American community to capitalize on their access to white teams, some student athletes not only had to overcome fierce prejudice but also con-struct positive public images. Historian Jules Tygiel characterized Robinson's 1947 debut in major league baseball as a "great experiment" in social integration. Likewise, in the case of collegians like UCLA's Kenny Washington, reaction to certain individual players generated national experiments that gauged the acceptance of blacks in higher education. Yet most African American athletes never received publicity that transcended their specific campus communities, in this way, the rise of intersectional competition and teams with fan bases that exceeded regional boundaries meant that intercollegiate athletics offered unique experiments in both national and local reaction to black students. Nonsport incidents like the 1962 James Meredith riots at the University of Mississippi could do the same, for by forcing the government to enforce federal law Meredith's supporters insisted that the integration of a regional university was a national question.

Yet such examples were all too rare outside the realm of sport. The most visible, popular, and consistent interactions between institutions of higher education were forged through athletics, and they still are today. With the ascendance of black athletes at schools around the country, sport defined integrated education for many Americans—certainly more than standard histories would lead us to believe. In the many months it took civil rights cases to wind their way through the courts, athletics offered sporting fans stark, daily reminders of the discrepancy between segregated and integrated American colleges, and these differences surfaced beyond the ratio of white students to black students. To follow intercollegiate competition, sporting fans also encountered sophisticated, diverse issues like educational policy, individual rights, and the relationship between public/private institutions and the state. Football fans in 1939 and 1955 found themselves explicating the power dynamics between state universities and local governments in Tennessee and Georgia. Those who followed the Johnny Bright controversy in 1951 grappled with the role of education policy in shaping regional identity—not to mention the issue of racial violence, so rarely discussed publicly in the South. Spectators of athletic unrest in the late 1960s used the incidents to articulate broader reaction to student protest, identity politics, and the first amendment.

In addition, athletes themselves responded differently to the growing presence of African Americans in sport. Players like Kenny Washington embraced the idea that their accomplishments held meaning beyond the game; they delivered speeches, joined campus organizations, and took on expanded roles with a maturity well beyond their years. Others like Johnny Bright and Bobby Grier were reluctant to embrace such positions, yet even in modest silence their commitment and desire to play without controversy still challenged black stereotypes. Unlike "lazy" or "radical" students intent on staking claims to freedom, black athletes appealed to many conservative Americans in the 1950s and 1960s because their strict work ethic and service to the university set them apart from the growing youth counterculture, even as their participation signaled that radical change was indeed taking place on the nation's campuses.

Amateur black athletes often found it difficult to address the growing public scrutiny surrounding their roles as spokespeople for an emerging generation of college-educated African Americans. Part of the challenge was in simultaneously handling the intense pressure that tied a school's athletic achievement to large economic payoffs; of course, there were the usual student tasks of finding a major, dating and socializing, studying for exams, making good grades, and trying to graduate. In essence, the story of integrating the country's most popular college sport reveals the significant differences between prominent African American political and cultural figures and the real experience of black student athletes in the civil rights era. Along with enriching the timeline of desegregation and the acceptance of black students in higher education, this gridiron story also illuminates the impact of athletic integration on American society at large, including individuals far removed from academic institutions. Now more than ever, college football's influence still shows an uncanny ability to reach beyond traditional sporting fans and student bodies. "It's the secret to . . . football," explained sixty-three-year-old Ronnie Thompson, one of the 66,233 who showed up for Virginia Tech's 2007 home opener in Blacksburg. "It could make us well."[8]

NOTES

PROLOGUE

1. "BCA Chief Building Case for Possible Violations of Federal Civil Rights Act," Associated Press, 18 December 2008; William C. Rhoden, "Dungy's New Path: Helping Create One for Black Coaches," *New York Times*, 18 February 2009. Rhoden often writes on the issue of black coaches as well as the relationship between sport history and contemporary black college athletes. See Rhoden, *Forty Million Dollar Slaves: The Rise, Fall, and Redemption of the Black Athlete* (New York: Crown Publishing, 2006).

2. Robert Sellers, "Black Student-Athletes: Reaping the Benefits or Recovering from the Exploitation," in *Racism in College Athletics: The African-American Athlete's Experience*, edited by Dana Brooks and Ronald Althouse (Morgantown, W.Va.: Fitness Information Technology, 1993), 144.

3. Bob Hohler, "Few Minorities Get the Reigns in College Football," *Boston Globe*, 21 September 2006; Richard Lapchick, "The 2008 Racial and Gender Report Card: College Sport," The Institute for Diversity and Ethics in Sport, 19 February 2009.

4. Murray Sperber, *Shake Down the Thunder: The Creation of Notre Dame Football* (Bloomington: Indiana University Press, 2002), 369–370; "In College Football, Notre Dame Looks Only to the Color of Money," *Journal of Blacks in Higher Education* 34 (Winter 2002): 47; Selena Roberts, "The Gamecocks Preach One Thing and Practice Another," *New York Times*, 24 November 2004, D1; Pete Thamel, "Lou Holtz Steps Down," *New York Times*, 23 November 2004, D7.

5. Joan Paul and Richard V. McGhee, "The Arrival and Ascendance of Black Athletes in the Southeastern Conference, 1966–1980," *Phylon* 45, no. 4 (1984): 284; William F. Reed, "Culture Shock in Dixieland," *Sports Illustrated*, 12 August 1991, 52.

6. George Sage, "Introduction," in Brooks and Althouse, *Racism in College Athletics*, 8; Lapchick, "The 2008 Racial and Gender Report Card."

7. Malcolm Moran, "In a Mystery, Holtz Quits Notre Dame," *New York Times*, 20 November 1996, B13; Jim Naughton, "Who Runs College Sports? A Million-Dollar Contract for a Football Coach in Florida Raises That Question," *Chronicle of Higher Education*, 22 November 1996.

CHAPTER 1   BEYOND JACKIE ROBINSON

Portions of this chapter appeared in "Beyond Jackie Robinson: Racial Integration in American College Football and New Directions in Sport History," *History Compass* 5, no. 2 (March 2007): 675–690.

1. "Roosevelt to Go to Boston," *New York Times*, 26 November 1898, 7; Evan J. Albright, "William Henry Lewis: Brief Life of a Football Pioneer," *Harvard Magazine*, December 2005, 44–45.

2. Alexander Weyand, *Football Immortals* (New York: Macmillan, 1962), 137–139; Donald Spivey, "The Black Athlete in Big-Time Intercollegiate Sports, 1941–1968," *Phylon* 44, no. 2 (1983): 117; Harold Wade, *Black Men of Amherst* (Amherst, Mass.: Amherst College Press, 1976), 14–21.

3. Wade, *Black Men of Amherst*, 15.

4. Theodore Roosevelt, *The Rough Riders* (New York: Collier, 1899).

5. "Harvard's Eleven to Return," *New York Times*, 24 September 1892, 5.

6. See Gail Bederman, *Manliness and Civilization* (Chicago: University of Chicago Press, 1995), and Michael Oriard, *Reading Football* (Chapel Hill: University of North Carolina Press, 1998).

7. John Hoberman, *Darwin's Athletes: How Sport has Damaged Black America and Preserved the Myth of Race* (New York: Houghton Mifflin, 1997); Othello Harris, "African-American Predominance in Collegiate Sport," in *Racism in College Athletics: The African-American Athlete's Experience*, edited by Dana Brooks and Ronald Althouse (Morgantown, W.Va.: Fitness Information Technology, 1999), 37–53; David K. Wiggins, "Great Speed but Little Stamina: The Historical Debate Over Black Athletic Superiority," in *The New American Sport History: Recent Approaches and Perspectives*, edited by S. W. Pope (Champaign: University of Illinois Press, 1997), 312–341.

8. John Behee, *Hail to the Victors* (Ann Arbor: University of Michigan Press, 1974), 32.

9. John Matthew Smith, "Breaking the Plane: Integration and Black Protest in Michigan State University Football during the 1960s," *Michigan Historical Review* 33, no. 2 (2007).

10. Albert Broussard, "George Albert Flippin and Race Relations in a Western Rural Community," *Midwest Review* 12 (1990): 1–15.

11. Michael Oriard, *King Football* (Chapel Hill: University of North Carolina Press, 2001), 285.

12. Oriard, *Reading Football*, 232.

13. Melvin R. Sylvester, "African Americans in the Sport Arena," Electronic Library of African American Studies, B. Davis Schwartz Memorial Library, C. W. Post Campus, Long Island University; *American National Biography*, edited by John Garraty and Mark Carnes (New York: Oxford University Press, 1999), vol. 1, 262; Carey Wintz and Paul Finkelman, eds., *Encyclopedia of the Harlem Renaissance* (London: Taylor and Francis, 2004), vol. 2, 996; Robert Peterson, *Pigskin: The Early Years of Pro Football* (New York: Oxford University Press, 1997), 178–179; "Football," *Time*, 11 November 1929.

14. "Negroes Riot at Football," *New York Times*, 25 November 1897, 1.

15. John Sayle Watterson, *College Football: History, Spectacle, Controversy* (Baltimore: Johns Hopkins University Press, 2000), 308–309. For a brief history of football at historically black colleges, see Michael Hurd, *Black College Football: One Hundred Years of History, Education, and Pride* (Virginia Beach, Va.: Donning Publishers, 1993).

16. George Sage, "Racial Inequality and Sport," in *Sport in Contemporary Society*, edited by D. Stanley Eitzen (London: Paradigm Publishers, 2005), 269.

17. Oriard, *King Football*, 299–313; Watterson, *College Football*, 308; George Sullivan, "Another Barrier That Fell 50 Years Ago Is Recalled," *New York Times*, 5 October 1997, SP15.

18. Woody Strode, *Goal Dust: An Autobiography* (Lanham, Md.: Madison Books, 1990), 29.

19. Nancy Serwint, "The Jack Trice Story: A Symbol of Sports Idealism Rediscovered," Proceedings of the North American Society of Sport History (NASSH) Conference, 26–29 May 1990, Banff, Alberta, Canada; Jack Trice Papers, Special Collections, Iowa State University Archives; John McCormick, "Once Upon a Time in Iowa," *Newsweek*, 17 September 1984, 11; Lou Ransom, "White University Rights 65-Year Wrong Done to Black Athlete," *Jet* (May 1988), 48–52.

20. Behee, *Hail to the Victors*; Harris, "African-American Predominance in Collegiate Sport," 54.

21. David Wiggins, "Prized Performers, But Frequently Overlooked Students," *Research Quarterly for Exercise and Sport* (June 1991): 168; John Hope Franklin, *From Slavery to Freedom: A History of African Americans* (New York: Alfred A. Knopf, 2000), 449.

22. Donald Spivey and Thomas Jones, "Intercollegiate Athletic Servitude: A Case Study of the Black Illini Student-Athletes, 1931–1967," *Social Science Quarterly* 55, no. 4 (March 1975): 943–944.

23. Elmer Mitchell, "Racial Traits in Athletics," *American Physical Education Review* 27 (1922): 151.

24. Ibid.

25. Ibid.

26. Alan Pollock, *Barnstorming to Heaven: Syd Pollock and His Great Black Teams* (Tuscaloosa: University of Alabama Press, 2006); Dan Burley, "Up Football's Glory Road," *New York Amsterdam News*, 9 December 1939, 18.

27. Henry Yu, "Tiger Woods at the Center of History: Looking Back at the Twentieth Century Through the Lenses of Race, Sports, and Mass Consumption," in *Sports Matters: Race, Recreation, and Culture*, edited by John Bloom and Michael Willard (New York: New York University Press, 2002), 322.

28. Ibid.

29. Russell Sullivan, *Rocky Marciano: The Rock of His Times* (Champaign: University of Illinois Press, 2002); Michael Isenberg, *John L. Sullivan and His America* (Champaign: University of Illinois Press, 1994).

30. Randy Roberts, *Papa Jack: Jack Johnson and the Era of White Hopes* (New York: Macmillan, 1983); Al-Tony Gilmore, *Bad Nigger! The National Impact of Jack Johnson* (Port Washington, N.Y.: Associated Faculty Press, 1975); Geoffrey C. Ward, *Unforgivable Blackness: The Rise and Fall of Jack Johnson* (New York: Alfred Knopf, 2004); Bederman, *Manliness*.

31. Bederman, *Manliness*, 8; Roberts, *Papa Jack*, 74; Gilmore, *Bad Nigger!*, 14.

32. Bederman, *Manliness*, 45.

33. Gerald Astor, ". . . And a Credit to His Race:" The Hard Life and Times of Joseph Louis Barrow, a.k.a. Joe Louis* (New York: Saturday Review Press, 1974).

34. *New York Amsterdam News*, 20 June 1936, 14.

35. Dominic J. Capeci, Jr., and Martha Wilkerson, "Multifarious Hero: Joe Louis, American Society and Race Relations during World Crisis, 1935–1945," *Journal of Sport History* 10 (Winter 1983): 5, 25.

36. Jeffrey T. Sammons, *Beyond the Ring: The Role of Boxing in American Society* (Chicago: University of Illinois Press, 1988).

37. Chris Mead, *Champion—Joe Louis, Black Hero in White America* (New York: Charles Scribner's Sons, 1985); Alexander Young, "Joe Louis, Symbol," Ph.D. diss., University of

Maryland, 1968; Thomas Hietala, *The Fight of the Century: Jack Johnson, Joe Louis, and the Struggle for Racial Equality* (London: M. E. Sharpe, 2002); Donald McRae, *Heroes Without A Country* (New York: HarperCollins, 2002); David Margolick, *Beyond Glory: Joe Louis vs. Max Schmeling and a World on the Brink* (New York: Alfred A. Knopf, 2005).

38. Lawrence Levine, *Black Culture, Black Consciousness* (College Park: University of Maryland Press, 1968), 126–130.

39. Steve Hannagan, "Black Gold," *Saturday Evening Post*, 20 June 1936, 76.

40. Ibid.; Capeci, "Multifarious Hero," 10; Young, *Joe Louis*, 96–99; "Title Talk Sidetracked," *Los Angeles Times*, 11 June 1936, A12.

41. Jules Tygiel, *Baseball's Great Experiment: Jackie Robinson and His Legacy* (New York: Oxford University Press, 1997); Maury Allen, "Pepper Street, Pasadena," in *The Jackie Robinson Reader*, edited by Jules Tygiel (New York: Penguin Books, 1997); Arnold Rampersad and Rachel Robinson, *Jackie Robinson: A Biography* (New York: Alfred Knopf Publishers, 1997).

42. Henry D. Fetter, "The Party Line and the Color Line: The American Communist Party, the Daily Worker and Jackie Robinson," *Journal of Sport History* 28, no. 3 (Fall 2001): 375–402.

43. Thomas Hauser, *Muhammad Ali: His Life and Times* (New York: Simon and Schuster, 1992).

44. Leon Gast, *When We Were Kings*, Polygram Video, 1996; Julio Rodriguez, "Documenting Myth: Racial Representation in Leon Gast's *When We Were Kings*," *Sports Matters*, 209.

45. Sammons, *Beyond the Ring*, 190–198.

46. Mike Marqusee, *Redemption Song: Muhammad Ali and the Spirit of the Sixties* (New York: Verso, 2005), 6.

47. Ibid., 2–3; Sammons, *Beyond the Ring*, 233.

48. Taylor Branch, *Parting the Waters: America in the King Years: 1954–63* (New York: Simon and Schuster, 1988), xii.

49. Ibid., xi.

50. Michael Eric Dyson, *I May Not Get There with You* (New York: Free Press, 2000); Aldon Morris, *The Origins of the Civil Rights Movement* (New York: Free Press, 1986).

51. Branch, *Parting the Waters*, 130.

52. David Garrow, ed., *The Montgomery Bus Boycott and the Women Who Started It: The Memoir of Jo Ann Gibson Robinson* (Knoxville: University of Tennessee Press, 1987), 43.

53. Brian Ward, *Just My Soul Responding: Rhythm and Blues, Black Consciousness, and Race Relations* (Berkeley: University of California Press, 1998).

54. Montye Fuse and Keith Miller, "Jazzing the Basepaths: Jackie Robinson and African American Aesthetics," *Sports Matters*, 119.

55. Bederman, *Manliness*; Roberts, *Papa Jack*; Ward, *Unforgivable Blackness*.

56. Paul Zimmerman, "Bruins, Troy Tie: SC, Vols in Bowl," *Los Angeles Times*, 10 December 1939, 1; "So. California Ties UCLA; Will Play Tennessee in Bowl," *New York Times*, 10 December 1939, 103.

57. Oriard, *King Football*, 10.

58. Oriard, "Muhammad Ali: The Hero in the Age of Mass Media," in *Muhammad Ali: The People's Champ*, edited by Elliott Gorn (Champaign: University of Illinois Press, 1995), 12.

59. Oriard, *King Football*, 9, 302, 316.

60. Ibid., 299–300; Watterson, *College Football*, 273–274.

61. Thomas Smith, "Outside the Pale: The Exclusion of Blacks from the National Football League, 1934–1946," *Journal of Sport History* 15, no. 3 (Winter 1988): 255–281.

62. Robert Dubay, "Politics, Pigmentation, and Pigskin: The Georgia Tech Sugar Bowl Controversy of 1955," *Atlanta History* 39 (Spring 1995): 21–35; Charles H. Martin, "Integrating New Year's Day: The Racial Politics of College Bowl Games in the American South," *Journal of Sport History* 24, no. 3 (Fall 1997): 358–377, and "Racial Change and Big Time College Football in Georgia," *Georgia Historical Quarterly* 80 (Fall 1996): 536–562; Watterson, *College Football*, 316–318; Oriard, *King Football*, 308–313.

63. Amy Bass, *Not the Triumph But the Struggle: The 1968 Olympics and the Making of the Black Athlete* (Minneapolis: University of Minnesota Press, 2002).

64. Harry Edwards, *The Revolt of the Black Athlete* (New York: Free Press, 1969); Arnold Hano, "The Black Rebel Who 'Whitelists' The Olympics," *New York Times*, 12 May 1968, SM32.

65. Beth Bailey, *Sex in the Heartland* (Cambridge, Mass.: Harvard University Press, 2002).

66. Anthony Ripley, "Negro Athletes Spark Uproar at University of Wyoming," *New York Times*, 1 November 1969, 15.

67. Watterson, *College Football*, 322–323, 347–348.

CHAPTER 2   "ON THE THRESHOLD OF BROAD AND
RICH FOOTBALL PASTURES"

Portions of this chapter appeared in "Sport History, Race, and the College Gridiron: A Southern California Turning Point," *Southern California Quarterly* 89, no. 2 (Summer 2007): 169–193, and "On the Threshold of Broad and Rich Football Pastures: Integrated College Football at UCLA, 1938–1941," in *Horsehide, Pigskin, Oval Tracts and Apple Pie: Essays on Sports and American Culture*, edited by Jim Vlasich (North Carolina: McFarland Press, 2005), 86–103.

1. Written by a UCLA student in 1925, "Hail Blue and Gold" served as the school's Alma Mater until students objected over the reference to "California of the south" in 1960; Clarence Wheeler, *Songs of UCLA* (Los Angeles: Bibo Music, 1930).

2. "Whatever Happened to Woody Strode?" *Ebony* (June 1982), 140–144.

3. Carol Harker Wilcox and Zach Schmidt, *Gridiron Glory: 100+ Years of Iowa Football* (Digital Exhibit), University of Iowa Alumni Association, www.iowalum.com/magazine/football_history

4. Woodrow Strode, *Goal Dust: An Autobiography* (New York: Madison Books, 1990), 26.

5. Ibid., 29.

6. Ibid., 26.

7. John Rothwell, *UCLA Magazine* (November 1939), 10.

8. *Southern Campus* 19 (1938): 215. Jerry Levie, "Ken over Grange!" *California Daily Bruin*, 23 October 1939, 3.

9. Rothwell, "Jack Robinson Registers in Extension," *California Daily Bruin*, 16 February 1939, 1.

10. Milt Cohen, "Robinson Sparkplug of Rally," *California Daily Bruin*, 9 October 1939, 1.

11. "Kenny Honored Over Air Friday," *California Daily Bruin*, 3 December 1939, 4.

12. *UCLA Magazine* (December 1940), 7.

13. James Goodman, *Stories of Scottsboro* (New York: Pantheon Books, 1994); Robin Kelley, *Hammer and Hoe: Alabama Communists During the Great Depression* (Chapel Hill: University of North Carolina Press, 1990); John Hope Franklin, *From Slavery to Freedom: A History of African Americans* (New York: Alfred A. Knopf, 2000), 342–356.

14. Benjamin Rader, *American Sports* (New York: Prentice Hall, 2004), 194–197.

15. Strode, *Goal Dust*, 21; Michael Denning, *The Cultural Front: The Laboring of American Culture in the Twentieth Century* (New York: Verso, 1997).

16. Brian Urquhart, *Ralph Bunche: An American Life* (New York: W. W. Norton, 1993).

17. Cohen, "Here's Our Angle," *California Daily Bruin*, 1 December 1939, 3.

18. Sam Sale, "Prejudice 'Rumored' to Have Played Major Role in Selections," *California Daily Bruin*, 5 March 1941, 3.

19. Strode, *Goal Dust*, 35.

20. "Minutes of the ASUCLA Board of Control, June 1935–June 1939," 3 March 1939, 84. "Minutes of the ASUCLA Board of Control, June 1940–June 1941," 8 August 1940, 82; "Whatever Happened to Woody Strode?" *Ebony* (June 1982), 144.

21. Arnold Rampersad and Rachel Robinson, *Jackie Robinson: A Biography* (New York: Alfred A. Knopf, 1997), 65.

22. *Pasadena Star-News*, 6 September 1939, cited in ibid., 65.

23. *Pasadena Star-News*, 18 October 18 1939, cited in ibid., 66.

24. B. J. Violet, "Teammates Recall Jackie Robinson's Legacy," *UCLA Today*.

25. Jackie Robinson to John Jackson (May 7, 1941), UCLA University Archives, Prints/Reference Collection Biographical Files, Series 745.

26. Jackie Robinson to John Jackson (November 6, 1941), UCLA University Archives, Prints/Reference Collection Biographical Files, Series 745.

27. Strode, *Goal Dust*, 64.

28. Ibid., 65.

29. "Prejudices Discussed," *California Daily Bruin*, 30 October 1939, 1.

30. William Forbes Oral History (300–341); UCLA Oral History Project, 68–69.

31. Josh Sides, *L.A. City Limits: African American Los Angeles from the Great Depression to the Present* (Berkeley: University of California Press, 2003), 2.

32. "Minutes of the ASUCLA Board of Control, June 1941–June 1942," 117, 121.

33. "Frogs Okay," *California Daily Bruin*, 29 September 1939, 7.

34. *Southern Campus* 22 (1941), 396.

35. "Stanford Scalps Bruins 12 Times," *The Goal Post*, 31 October 1942, 6.

36. Strode, *Goal Dust*, 64.

37. Paul Zimmerman, "Sport Post-Scripts," *Los Angeles Times*, 9 October 1939, A11.

38. Charles Paddock, "Spikes," *Pasadena Star-News*, 3 November 1939, 20.

39. Ibid.

40. Al Wolf, "Today's Game Full of Angels," *Los Angeles Times*, 9 December 1939, A9.

41. Paddock, "Spikes," *Pasadena Star-News*, 7 December 1939, 20.

42. "Pasadena Grid Player Arrested," *Los Angeles Times*, 7 September 1939, 14; "Negro Grid Star Forfeits Bond," *Los Angeles Times*, 19 October 1939, A12.

43. Rampersad and Robinson, *Jackie Robinson*, 64.

44. "Brother of Jack Robinson Beaten By Pasadena Police," *California Eagle*, 12 January 1939, 1.

45. "UCLA Defeats Huskies," *New York Times*, 8 October 1939, 90.

46. "Pass Traveled 62 Yards," *New York Times*, 6 December 1937, 20.

47. "Rally by UCLA Ties Oregon State," *New York Times*, 26 November 1939, 82.

48. Paddock, "Spikes," *Pasadena Star-News*, 6 November 1939, 14.

49. Allison Danzig, "Tennessee Hopes to Insure Rose Bowl Nomination by Beating Auburn Today," *New York Times*, 9 December 1939, 20.

50. Art Cohn, "Cohn-ing Tower," *Oakland Tribune*, 9 November 1939, D1. See Ralph Shaffer and Dan Arrighi, "Columnist Was Early, Angry Voice Against Sports Color Line," *Los Angeles Times* [Selected stories online], 22 March 2008, http://www.latimes.com/sports/la-spw-cohn22mar22,1,4704861,full.story.

51. Bob Foote, "Foote-Loose in Sports," *Pasadena Star-News*, 6 December 1939, 20.

52. Ibid.

53. Danzig, "Tennessee Hopes to Insure Rose Bowl Nomination by Beating Auburn Today," *New York Times*, 9 December 1939, 20.

54. Paddock, "Spikes," *Pasadena Star-News*, 6 November 1939, 14.

55. Ibid.

56. Ibid.

57. J. Cullen Fentress, "Down in Front," *California Eagle*, 9 November 1939, 3B.

58. Ibid.

59. Fentress, "Down in Front," *California Eagle*, 14 August 1939, 3B; "61 Huskies to Answer Grid Call at UCLA," *California Eagle*, 7 September 1939, 3B.

60. Dan Burley, "Up Football's Glory Road," *New York Amsterdam News*, 9 December 1939, 18.

61. "Lou Montgomery, Backfield Ace of Boston College, Isn't at All Upset over Being Benched Twice in Dixie Tilts," *New York Amsterdam News*, 11 November 1939, 18; Charles Martin, "Integrating New Year's Day: The Racial Politics of College Bowl Games in the American South," *Journal of Sport History* 24, no. 3 (Fall 1997): 362.

62. Neil Dodson, "Do Colored Athletes Help Cause of Jim Crow at Big White Universities?" *New York Amsterdam News*, 21 October 1939, 19.

63. Ibid.

64. Fay Young, "The Stuff IS Here," *Chicago Defender*, 16 December 1939, 26.

65. Fentress, "Down in Front," *California Eagle*, 16 November 1939, 2B.

66. *Daily Worker*, 21 December 1939, 8.

67. *California Eagle*, 31 December 1939, 8A.

68. "Chalks Up Another First," *New York Amsterdam News*, 7 December 1940. The article overlooked the case of William Henry Lewis at Harvard five decades earlier.

69. "UCLA Grid Stars and Coaches Entertained by Business Leaders," *California Eagle*, 16 November 1939, 2B.

70. Strode, *Goal Dust*, 62.

71. The 1942 ASUCLA Board of Control meeting minutes note that the "possibility of playing TCU in Forth Worth" was discussed with the "TCU grad manager." "Minutes of the ASUCLA Board of Control, June 1941–June 1942," 11 May 1942, 162.

72. Violet, "Teammates Recall Jackie Robinson's Legacy," *UCLA Today*.

73. Young, "The Stuff Is Here," *Chicago Defender*, 4 November 1939, 24.

74. Keith Guthrie, "Horned Frog Tracks," *The Skiff* (Texas Christian University), 6 October 1939, 3.

75. Ibid.

76. Danzig, "Tennessee Hopes to Insure Rose Bowl Nomination by Beating Auburn Today," *New York Times*, 9 December 1939, 20.

77. Bob Wilson, "Path to Rose Bowl Cleared for Vols," *Knoxville News-Sentinel*, 6 December 1939, 1.

78. Danzig, "Tennessee Hopes to Insure Rose Bowl."

79. "Stocking Fund Soars from Game Receipts," *Knoxville News-Sentinel*, 11 December 1939, 10.

80. "Next to Rose Bowl It's Empty Stocking Bowl in Importance," *Knoxville News-Sentinel*, 6 December 1939, 6.

81. Wilson, "Path to Rose Bowl Cleared."

82. Zimmerman, "Bruins, Troy Tie: SC, Vols in Bowl," *Los Angeles Times*, 10 December 1939, 1.

83. "So. California Ties UCLA; Will Play Tennessee in Bowl," *New York Times*, 10 December 1939, 103.

84. Ibid.

85. Zimmerman, "Bruins, Troy Tie."

86. Daniel, "And Rose Bowl Remains White as a New Lily," *New York Amsterdam News*, 16 December 1939.

87. Ibid.

88. "1939 UCLA 21st Annual Football Senior Banquet Program," (January 18, 1940), UCLA Special Collections #227, "Department of Intercollegiate Athletics (1921–1987)," Box 2.

89. Ibid.

CHAPTER 3   "A FIST THAT WAS VERY MUCH INTENTIONAL"

1. "Athlete Who Broke Color Barrier Dies," Associated Press, 13 May 2006.

2. John Hope Franklin, *From Slavery to Freedom: a History of African Americans* (New York: Alfred Knopf, 1988), 387.

3. Franklin, *From Slavery to Freedom*, 371, 388.

4. Gunnar Myrdal, *An American Dilemma: The Negro Problem and Modern Democracy* (New York: Harper, 1944), 1021–1023; reprinted in *Brown v. Board of Education: A Brief History with Documents*, edited by Waldo E. Martin, Jr. (New York: Bedford/St. Martin's, 1998), 103–107.

5. Martin Duberman, *Paul Robeson* (New York: Alfred A. Knopf, 1989), 203.

6. Ibid., 262.

7. Franklin, *From Slavery to Freedom*, 390–391.

8. Gerald Astor, *The Right to Fight: A History of African-Americans in the Military* (Norato, Calif.: Presidio Press, 1998), 4, 351.

9. Lizabeth Cohen, *A Consumer's Republic: The Politics of Mass Consumption in Postwar America* (New York: Alfred A. Knopf, 2003), 166.

10. Ibid.

11. *Congressional Record—Senate*, 29 June 1945, 6994–6998.

12. Duberman, *Paul Robeson*, 360; Al White, "Jackie Robinson Demanding $50,000 Salary for Work with Brooklyn Dodgers Next Year," *Black Dispatch*, 8 December 1951, 6; Ronald A. Smith, "The Paul Robeson-Jackie Robinson Saga and a Political Collision," *Journal of Sport History* 6, no. 2 (1979): 5–27.

13. "Richmond Thinks 'Jackie Robinson Story' Democratic," *Black Dispatch*, 12 August 1950, 7.

14. Gordon S. White, "Taking a Look Back at Drake," *New York Times*, 13 November 1985, B14.

15. Timothy Egan, *The Worst Hard Time: The Untold Story of those Who Survived the Great American Dust Bowl* (New York: Houghton Mifflin, 2006), 108.

16. Ibid., 108–109.

17. "I Told You So," *Black Dispatch*, 21 October 1951.

18. *Sipuel v. Oklahoma State Board of Regents*, 332 U.S. 631 (1948); Franklin, *From Slavery to Freedom*, 452.

19. George Lynn Cross, *Blacks in White Colleges: Oklahoma's Landmark Cases* (Norman: University of Oklahoma Press, 1975), 93–94.

20. Chief Justice Fred Vinson, Opinion of the Court in *McLaurin v. Oklahoma State Regents* (1950), reprinted in *Brown v. Board of Education*, 119; *McLaurin v. Oklahoma State Regents*, 339 U.S. 637 (1950).

21. *Sweatt v. Painter*, 339 U.S. 629 (1950); Robert Burk, "Symbolic Equality: The Eisenhower Administration and Black Civil Rights, 1953–1961," Ph.D. diss., University of Wisconsin–Madison, 1982, 192.

22. Cross, *Blacks in White Colleges*, 33.

23. Ibid., 71, 117.

24. *Redskin*, Oklahoma A&M College Yearbook, 1952.

25. See Jack Newcombe, *The Best of the Athletic Boys: The White Man's Impact on Jim Thorpe* (Garden City, N.Y.: Doubleday, 1975).

26. "Policy Is Due Soon," *Stillwater Gazette*, 3 June 1955, 1.

27. "Enroll at the A&M College," *Black Dispatch*, 10 September 1949, 4; "More than 350 Negro Teachers Attending Summer School at A&M College at Stillwater," *Black Dispatch*, 16 June 1951, 1.

28. Philip Rulon, *Oklahoma State University—Since 1890* (Stillwater: Oklahoma State University Press, 1975), 262, 278.

29. "Aggie in Ethiopia Faces Multitude of Problems," *Stillwater Gazette*, 5 June 1953, 7.

30. *Redskin*, Oklahoma A&M College Yearbook, 1952.

31. Cited in Rulon, *Oklahoma State University*, 280.

32. Doris Dellinger, *A History of the Oklahoma State University Intercollegiate Athletics* (Stillwater, Okla.: Stillwater Press, 1987), 172.

33. Ibid.

34. Dellinger, *Intercollegiate Athletics*, 175.

35. Leighton Housh, "Drake Quits Missouri Valley," *Des Moines Register*, 28 November 1951, 8; "Valley History," *Drake Times-Delphic*, 30 November 1951, 2.

36. John Sayle Watterson, *College Football: History, Spectacle, Controversy* (Baltimore: The Johns Hopkins University Press, 2000), 273.

37. Ibid., 274.

38. Volney Meece, "Cowboys Hammer Shockers, 43 to 0," *Daily Oklahoman*, 14 October 1951; Mike Blatz, "Dallas Braced for the Biggest Weekend of All," *Daily Oklahoman*, 13 October 1951.

39. Dellinger, *Intercollegiate Athletics*, 174–175.

40. "New Regime," *Oklahoma A&M College Magazine*, September 1950, 9; cited in Dellinger, *Intercollegiate Athletics*, 177.

41. "We Must Save Football, Pleads Stagg," *Des Moines Register*, 21 November 1951, 11.

42. Charles Martin, "Integrating New Year's Day: The Racial Politics of College Bowl Games in the American South," *Journal of Sport History* 24, no. 3 (Fall 1997): 362–363, 365.

43. Jaime Schultz, "Photography, Instant Memory and the Slugging of Johnny Bright," *Stadion* 32 (2006): 238; "Konstanty Named Athlete of Year," *New York Times*, 10 January 1951, 47.

44. Fay Young, "Bright Sets Record," *Chicago Defender*, 13 October 1951, 17.

45. Jack Kaley, "A History of Intercollegiate Football at Drake University," master's education thesis, Drake University, 1956, 189; "City Salutes Nation's Top Ground Gainer," *Drake Times-Delphic*, 12 October 1951, 1; Bob Dempsey, "John Adds 286 Yards As Team Wins 5 in Row," *Drake Times-Delphic*, 16 October 1951.

46. Blake Sebring, "Johnny Bright Could Do It All on the Field," *News-Sentinel* (Fort Wayne, Ind.), 30 December 1999, 1S.

47. Ibid.; Paul Morrison Oral History, Special Collections, Drake University Digital Archives.

48. Bill Connors, "Pokes Seeking First Victory in Four Tries," *Daily O'Collegian*, 13 October 1951, 6.

49. Cited in Adam Cohen, "The Color Line," *Oklahoma Today*, September–October 2001, 40.

50. "Bright a Marked Man on Saturday," *Stillwater News-Press*, 18 October 1951, 17.

51. "Sports by George," *Drake Times Delphic*, 19 October 1949, 5.

52. Bob Darcy, "Johnny Bright Comes to OAMC," *Daily O'Collegian*, 19 April 2002, 4A; Dave Hanson, "Bright Not Bitter: Blow Helped Clean Up Sports," *Des Moines Register*, 13 November 1980, 24.

53. Schultz, "Photography, Instant Memory and the Slugging of Johnny Bright," 239; Cyma Rubin, *Moment of Impact: Stories of the Pulitzer Prize Photographs*, Video Documentary (New York: A&E Television Networks, 1999).

54. Rubin, *Moment of Impact*.

55. "'Mr. Offense' to Lead Drake Invasion of Aggies Saturday," *Daily O'Collegian*, 16 October 1951, 4.

56. "Caught by the Camera," *Life*, 5 November 1951, 121.

57. "Charge Bright's Injury Was Intentional Blow," *Chicago Defender*, 27 October 1951, 16.

58. "Bright Injury 'Deliberate,' Players Say," *Des Moines Register*, 21 October 1951, 7.

59. Rubin, *Moment of Impact*.

60. Dave Hanson, "Bright Not Bitter," *Des Moines Tribune*, 13 November 1980, Special Collections, Drake University Digital Archives; Blair Kerkhoff, "Picture of Prejudice," *Kansas City Star*, 20 October 2001, Special Collections, Drake University Digital Archives.

61. "Mordecai Johnson Delivers Scathing Denunciation of Separate School System," *Black Dispatch*, 20 October 1951, 1; "Negroes Hold Up Plan to Break Segregation in City Schools," *Daily Oklahoman*, 19 October 1951, 7.

62. Cited in Darcy, "Johnny Bright Comes to OAMC," *Daily O'Collegian*, 19 April 2002, 4A.

63. Rubin, *Moment of Impact*.

64. Fordie Ross, "Broken Jaw Results from Pre-Meditated Assault," *Black Dispatch*, 27 October 1951, 2.

65. Jack Murphy, "Aggies Nudge Drake from Unbeaten List," *Daily Oklahoman*, 21 October 1951, B-1.

66. "Drake Players Say Aggies Deliberately Slugged Bright," *Stillwater News-Press*, 21 October 1951, 7.

67. Darcy, "Johnny Bright Comes to OAMC," *Daily O'Collegian*, 19 April 2002, 4A; "Ever See a Jaw Broken?" *Des Moines Register*, 21 October 1951, 1; "Bright's Jaw Still Leading Valley Talk," *Stillwater News-Press*, 23 October 1951, 8; "Bright Injury 'Deliberate,' Players Say," *Des Moines Register*, 21 October 1951, 1; Schultz, "Photography, Instant Memory and the Slugging of Johnny Bright," 240; "Students, Football Team Say Bright Affair Serious," *Drake Times-Delphic*, 23 October 1951, 1.

68. "Drake to Protest; Says Bets Made," *Stillwater News-Press*, 24 October 1951, 7.

69. Sec Taylor, "Chides Valley Boss on Not Seeing 'Play,'" *Des Moines Register*, 22 October 1951, 11.

70. "How Readers Reacted to Drake-A&M 'Johnny Bright Incident,'" *Des Moines Register*, 25 October 1951.

71. "Sluggings Aren't Accidents," *Life*, 5 November 1951, 124.

72. Schultz, "Photography, Instant Memory and the Slugging of Johnny Bright," 242.

73. Watterson, *College Football*, 64–66. See also Roosevelt's earlier writings, in which he weighed the benefits of football with the risks of provoking brutality in young people. Theodore Roosevelt, "Value of an Athletic Training," *Harper's Weekly*, 23 December 1893, 1236.

74. "Aggies Coach Calls Block Unintentional," *Los Angeles Times*, 23 October 1951, C3.

75. Brad Pye, "Pictures Reveal the Bright Truth," *California Eagle*, 25 October 1951.

76. "Drake and Johnny Bright," *Chicago Defender*, 8 December 1951, 10.

77. "Why Are They Afraid?" *Chicago Defender*, 10 November 1951, 10.

78. "Among 80 Letters Sent to John Bright," *Drake Times-Delphic*, 26 October 1951; "Letters Ask Detroit to 'Rough Up' Aggies," *New York Times*, 26 October 1951, 33.

79. "Jaw Closed Affair Here—Not at Drake," *Stillwater News-Press*, 24 October 1951.

80. Wally Wallis, "Illegal Blow KOs Bright—Whitworth," *Daily O'Collegian*, 23 October 1951, 13.

81. Fordie Ross, "Whitworth Admits Player Illegally Hit John Bright," *Black Dispatch*, 22 October 1951, 12.

82. "Aggie Cabinet Sends Regrets Over Incident," *Des Moines Register*, 27 October 1951, 9.

83. Norm Coder, "AGS: 'No Action Unless Protest Made,'" *Des Moines Register*, 23 October 1951, 13.

84. Rulon, *Oklahoma State University*, 292.

85. Cross, *Blacks in White Colleges*, 78.

86. "Too Quick-Fingered," *Stillwater News-Press*, 26 October 1951, 4.

87. John Cronley, "Once Over Lightly," *Daily Oklahoman*, 26 October 1951, 30.

88. "Shameful Stigma," *Daily Oklahoman*, 4 November 1951, 12.

89. Schultz, "Photography, Instant Memory and the Slugging of Johnny Bright," 240–241.

90. Henry Harmon Letter to Jack McClelland, 15 November 1951, Special Collections, Drake University Digital Archives.

91. Ibid.

92. "Valley Decides Against Action in Bright Case," *Daily Oklahoman*, 22 November 1951, 34.

93. "Drake Cancels," *Daily O'Collegian*, 28 November 1951, 6.

94. "Bradley, Following Drake's Suit, Quits Conference on Bright Issue," *New York Times*, 29 November 1951, 59.

95. "Wichita Stays in Valley, Regrets 2 Withdrawals," *Des Moines Register*, 30 November 1951, 13.

96. "Iron Jawed Loop," *Drake Times-Delphic*, 30 November 1951, 2.

97. Cronley, "Once Over Lightly," 16.

98. "Childish Temper Display," *Stillwater News-Press*, 2 December 1951, 20.

99. Lester Granger, "Battle Axe & Bread," *California Eagle*, 8 November 1951.

100. "Graduates Abhor Game Conduct," *Daily O'Collegian*, 23 October 1951, 2.

101. "Gridiron Reaction," *Daily Oklahoman*, 28 October 1951, 12.

102. "The Lesson of Johnny Bright," *Black Dispatch*, 3 November 1951, 4.

103. Cited in "Negro Paper Cites 10 on Rights Honor Roll," *New York Times*, 1 January 1952, 40.

104. Dellinger, *Intercollegiate Athletics*, 182.

105. Rulon, *Oklahoma State University*, 293.

106. Allison Danzig, "New N.C.A.A. Code Puts Teeth in Move to Correct Abuses," *New York Times*, 13 January 1952, S1.

107. Allison Danzig, "Ivy Agreement Is Strong Force in Battle against Abuses in College Sports," *New York Times*, 23 March 1954, 30; "How Racism Led to the Use of Face Guards on College Football Helmets," *Journal of Blacks in Higher Education* 49 (Fall 2005): 32.

108. Schultz, "Photography, Instant Memory and the Slugging of Johnny Bright," 247.

109. "Kazmaier Takes Heisman Trophy with Record Plurality of Votes," *New York Times*, 5 December 1951, 60; Sebring, "Johnny Bright Could Do It All," *News-Sentinel*, 30 December 1999, 1S.

110. Sec Taylor, "Are The Pros Cleaner?" *Des Moines Register*, 25 November 1951, 15; Cohen, "The Color Line," *Oklahoma Today* (September–October 2001), 40.

111. Martin, "Integrating New Year's Day," 367–368.

112. Rick Telander, "Big Hand for a Quiet Man," *Sports Illustrated*, 12 December 1988, 46–49; William Nack, "Barry Breaks Away," *Sports Illustrated*, 10 April 1989, 24–26, 31; "How Did I Get Through School When I Couldn't Read?" *Ebony* (October 1989), 102–106.

113. White, "Taking a Look Back at Drake," *New York Times*, 13 November 1985, B14; Brandon Cleaver, "Drake Football: Bulldogs' Win Gives Team Its Best Start Since 2000," *Des Moines Register*, 1 October 2006; Lisa Lacher, "Drake Names Field After Johnny Bright," Special Collections, Drake University Digital Archives.

CHAPTER 4   "WE PLAY ANYONE"

1. Jim Thomasson, "Governor's Mansion Stormed by Students," *New Orleans Times-Picayune*, 4 December 1955, 1; Dan Sweat, "Tech Students Jeer at Capitol, Mansion," *Atlanta Journal*, 3 December 1955, 1, 11; Bob Marbut, "Enraged Student Body Protests against Griffin's No-Bowl Demand," *Technique*, 6 December 1955, 1, 8; "Mercer Students

Hang Governor in Effigy," *Atlanta Constitution*, 4 December 1955, 1; "Tech Students Hang Griffin in Effigy," *New Orleans Times-Picayune*, 3 December 1955, 20; Remer Tyson, "University Students Hold Two Mass Demonstrations," *Red and Black*, 8 December 1955, 1, 5; "Tear Gas Breaks Up Riot of 1,000 Students at Athens," *Atlanta Journal*, 7 December 1955, 1, 14; Mike Edwards, "Tech, Georgia Taking Action in Raids," *Atlanta Journal*, 6 December 1955, 1, 17.

2. "Griffin 'Hung' at Oregon U.," *Pittsburgh Post-Gazette*, 5 December 1955, 9; "Tech Students Burn Effigy of Ga. Governor," *California Eagle*, 8 December 1955, 4.

3. "Ga. Tech Students Burn Governor in Effigy from Street Light Post," *New Orleans Times-Picayune*, 3 December 1955, 1.

4. Taylor Branch, *Parting the Waters: America in the King Years, 1954–63* (New York: Simon and Schuster, 1988), 112.

5. John Hope Franklin, *From Slavery to Freedom: A History of African Americans* (New York: Alfred A. Knopf, 2000), 463–466.

6. Patrick B. Miller, ed., *The Sporting World of the Modern South* (Champaign: University of Illinois Press, 2002), 3.

7. Andrew Doyle, "'Causes Won, Not Lost': College Football and the Modernization of the American South," *International Journal of the History of Sport* 11, no. 2 (August 1994): 231. See also Michael Oriard, *King Football* (Chapel Hill: University of North Carolina Press, 2001), 65–100; Robert Dubay, "Pigmentation and Pigskin: A Jones County Junior College Dilemma," *Journal of Mississippi History* 46 (February 1984): 43–50; Mike Butler, "Confederate Flags, Class Conflict, a Golden Egg, and Castrated Bulls: A Historical Examination of the Ole-Miss—Mississippi State Football Rivalry," *Journal of Mississippi History* 59, no. 2 (Summer 1997): 123–139; Andrew Doyle, "Turning the Tide: College Football and Southern Progressivism," in *Sporting World of the Modern South*, 101–123.

8. Andrew Doyle, "Bear Bryant: Symbol of an Embattled South," *Colby Quarterly* 32, no. 1 (March 1996): 77.

9. Willie Morris, *The Courting of Marcus Dupree* (Oxford: University of Mississippi Press, 1992), 47, 120. See also Allen Barra, *The Last Coach: A Life of Paul "Bear" Bryant* (New York: W. W. Norton, 2005); "The Bear in the Tower," *Newsweek*, 12 November 1979, 133.

10. Charles Wilson, "The Death of Bear Bryant," *South Atlantic Quarterly* 84 (1987): 282.

11. William F. Reed, "Archie and the War Between the States," *Sports Illustrated*, 12 October 1970, 14.

12. Earnest Reese and David Davidson, "Run for Respect: A Study of Black Football Players and the South," *Atlanta Journal* and *Atlanta Constitution*, 7 September 1986, A1.

13. Bob Grier, telephone interview, 1 June 2007 (Wexford, Pa.).

14. Robert Dubay, "Politics, Pigmentation, and Pigskin: The Georgia Tech Sugar Bowl Controversy of 1955," *Atlanta History* 39 (Spring 1995): 21–35.

15. Charles Martin, "Racial Change and Big Time College Football in Georgia," *Georgia Historical Quarterly* 80 (Fall 1996): 532–562. See also Martin, "Integrating New Year's Day: The Racial Politics of College Bowl Games in the American South," *Journal of Sport History* 24, no. 3 (Fall 1997): 358–377.

16. Grier, telephone interview.

17. Calvin Bergdall, "Oklahoma's Pounding Prentice," *Sport* 28 (November 1959): 34–35; James C. Hefley, "Prentice Gautt," in *Sports Alive!* (Grand Rapids, Mich.: Zondervan, 1966), 49–56; Gereon Zimmerman, "Prentice Gautt: Oklahoma's Quiet Powerhouse,"

Look, 13 October 1959, 51–54; Carol Burr, "Prentice Gautt: A Sooner's Story," *Sooner Magazine* (Spring 1987), 10–15.

18. Kevin Gaines, "The Historiography of the Struggle for Black Equality Since 1945," in *A Companion to Post-1945 America*, edited by Jean-Christophe Agnew and Roy Rosenzweig (Oxford: Blackwell Publishing, 2006), 222.

19. Glenda Gilmore, *Gender and Jim Crow* (Chapel Hill: University of North Carolina Press, 1996).

20. "90 Pct. of Negro Riders Ban Buses in Montgomery," *Atlanta Constitution*, 6 December 1955, 2.

21. "Buses Boycotted Over Race Issue," *New York Times*, 6 December 1955, 31; "Bus Boycott," *Pittsburgh Courier*, 17 December 1955, 1.

22. Grier, telephone interview.

23. Cited in Dubay, "Politics, Pigmentation, and Pigskin," 25.

24. "Racial Study Barred," *New York Times*, 1 November 1955, 21.

25. Charles Pou, "NAACP in Georgia Illegal, Fortson Says," *Atlanta Journal*, 1 December 1955, 1.

26. Charles Pou, "Ban Interracial Sports—Griffin," *Atlanta Journal*, 2 December 1955, 1; *Coleman v. Miller*, Appeal from the United States District Court for the Northern District of Georgia, No. 1:94-cv-1673-ODE (July 1997).

27. *Brown v. Board of Education*, 349 U.S. 294, 299, 75 S. Ct. 753, 756, 99 L. Ed. 1083 (1955); "Report of Governor Marvin Griffin to the People of Georgia," *Savannah Morning News*, 1 December 1955, 15.

28. "Report of Governor Marvin Griffin."

29. Katherine Barnwell, "Tech Computer Center Dedicated as 'Big Step,'" *Atlanta Constitution*, 3 December 1955, 3; "Look Who's 50!" *OIT Update*, Fall 2005 (Office of Information Technology, Georgia Tech University).

30. Martin, "Racial Change," 547, 551.

31. "Football for Fun," *Time*, 24 November 1952, 78; "The Happy Coach," *Time*, 12 November 1956, 83–84; Don Parker, "A Low Pressure Engineer," *Sports Illustrated*, 21 October 1957, 41. See also Doyle, "Bear Bryant," 79.

32. "Pitt Looked Real Tough—Dodd," *New Orleans Times-Picayune*, 26 November 1955, 33; "Shooting Victim Charges Force," *New Orleans Times-Picayune*, 27 November 1955, 1.

33. "Pitt Might Use Negro, Segregationists Protest," *Pittsburgh Post-Gazette*, 1 December 1955, 22; "Wrong Target," *Time*, 4 August 1958; Pou, "Ban Interracial Sports," *Atlanta Journal*, 2 December 1955, 1; "Most Regents Keep Silent on Bowl Ban," *Atlanta Journal*, 2 December 1955, 1.

34. "Text of Griffin Telegram," *Atlanta Journal*, 2 December 1955, 1.

35. Pou, "Ban Interracial Sports."

36. "Segregation Ban in Parks Decried," *New York Times*, 9 November 1955, 36.

37. "Report of Governor Marvin Griffin," *Savannah Morning News*, 1 December 1955, 15.

38. "A Chance to Play," *Time*, 21 November 1955; A. M. Rivera, "Six Arrested on Golf Course," *Pittsburgh Courier*, 17 December 1955, 13. See also Robert J. Robertson, *Fair Ways: How Six Black Golfers Won Civil Rights in Beaumont, Texas* (College Station: Texas A&M University Press, 2005).

39. Fred Digby, *The New Orleans Sugar Bowl Football Classic* (New Orleans: Franklin Printing, 1956), 11.

40. "Sugar Bowl Fever Mounts as Contingents Reach City," *New Orleans Times Picayune*, 30 December 1955, 1; Furman Bisher, "How I Love Tradition," *Atlanta Journal and Constitution*, 2 January 1956, 39.

41. "Atlantians to Back Their Tech Team at Big Bowl Game," *Atlanta Journal*, 30 December 1955, 18; "News for Bowl Visitors," *New Orleans Times-Picayune*, 1 January 1956, 1; "Longhorns Willing to Replace Georgia Tech," *Los Angeles Times*, 4 December 1955, 12.

42. Butch Curry, "Grier Ready for Sugar Bowl Game," *Pittsburgh Courier*, 31 December 1955, 24; "Georgia Students Protest," *New York Times*, 3 December 1955, 18.

43. Bill Keefe, "Viewing the News," *New Orleans Times-Picayune*, 2 December 1955, 32; 24 November 1955, 28; and 28 November 1955, 32; "Pittsburgh Officials in Town to Inspect Possible Training Sites," *New Orleans Times-Picayune*, 23 November 1955, 21.

44. Jeffrey T. Sammons, *Beyond the Ring: The Role of Boxing in American Society* (Champaign: University of Illinois Press, 1988), 108. See also Lane Demas, "The Brown Bomber's Dark Day: Louis-Schmeling I and America's Black Hero," *Journal of Sport History* 31 (Fall 2004): 259–260.

45. Roi Ottley, "Roi Ottley Says," *Chicago Defender*, 7 January 1956, 6.

46. "Action on NAACP Suit Considered," *New Orleans Times-Picayune*, 3 December 1955, 1; John Rousseau, "Jim-Crow Attempts in New Orleans Airport Charged," *Pittsburgh Courier*, 10 December 1955, 8.

47. Edward Murrain, "Sonny Side Up," *Chicago Defender*, 24 December 1955, 8. Grier, telephone interview.

48. Martin, "Integrating New Year's Day," 369.

49. "Local Officials Ignore Race Issue in Bowl Game," *Pittsburgh Courier*, 10 December 1955, 32.

50. Martin, "Integrating New Year's Day," 366–367.

51. "Racial Issue Prompts Move," *New Orleans Times Picayune*, 3 December 1955, 20; Mike Edwards, "Nationwide Messages Favor Tech Bowl Game with Pitt," *Atlanta Journal and Constitution*, 4 December 1955, 3G.

52. Tom Ross, "Georgia Views Varied on Tech in Sugar Bowl," *New Orleans Times-Picayune*, 6 December 1955, 29.

53. Jack Nelson, "Regents' Denial of Griffin Request on Athletics Is Predicted Today," *Atlanta Constitution*, 5 December 1955, 14.

54. "Georgia Tech Opens Sugar Drills Today," *New Orleans Times-Picayune*, 7 December 1955, 30.

55. "Local Officials Ignore Race Issue in Bowl Game"; Jimmy Brown, "Grier Plays Sugar Bowl, But Integration Will Be Partial," *Philadelphia Tribune*, 6 December 1955.

56. Jim Thomasson, "Governor's Mansion Stormed by Students," *New Orleans Times Picayune*, 4 December 1955, 1; "Wake Forest in Protest Riot," *Atlanta Journal*, 6 December 1955, 17; Robert Ratcliffe, "Behind the Headlines," *Pittsburgh Courier*, 17 December 1955, 13.

57. "Regents Sharply Divided on Griffin Athletic Bid," *Atlanta Constitution*, 5 December 1955, 14; Jim Thomasson, "Governor's Mansion Stormed by Students"; "Georgia Tech's Grid Future Hinges on Today's Conference," *New Orleans Times-Picayune*, 5 December 1955, 27; "Racial Issue Prompts Move."

58. "Georgia Tech Students Storm State Capitol in Sugar Bowl Row," *Philadelphia Inquirer*, 4 December 1955, 4.

59. Charles Pou, "Regents Give Full Okay to Tech-Pitt Bowl Game," *Atlanta Journal*, 5 December 1955, 1.

60. Tom Ross, "Georgia Views Varied on Tech in Sugar Bowl," *New Orleans Times-Picayune*, 6 December 1955, 29.

61. Dan Sweat, "Tech Students Jeer at Capitol, Mansion," *Atlanta Journal*, 3 December 1955, 1; "Regents Reject Move of Governor to Pull Tech Team from Bowl Game," *Savannah Morning News*, 5 December 1955, 1.

62. "Here's Full Text of Resolution Ok'd by Regents," *Atlanta Journal*, 5 December 1955, 1.

63. "Georgia Tech's Grid Future Hinges on Today's Conference"; Charles Pou, "Tech Students Stir Up Storm, Apologize to Pitt," *Atlanta Journal and Constitution*, 4 December 1955, 19.

64. M. L. St. John, "Regent Blasts Griffin on Tech-Pitt Game," *Atlanta Constitution*, 3 December 1955, 9; James Wynn, "Georgia Politics," *Red and Black*, 8 December 1955.

65. "Wake Up, Governor!" *Technique*, 6 December 1955, 8.

66. Marty Mule, *Sugar Bowl: The First Fifty Years* (Birmingham, Ala.: Oxmoor House, 1983), 102.

67. "Drinkard Out to Stop Funds If Tech Plays," *Atlanta Journal and Constitution*, 4 December 1955, 1.

68. Marvin Hill and Carl Kaufman, "Students View Drinkard Proposal," *Red and Black*, 8 December 1955, 13.

69. "Ridiculousness," *Red and Black*, 8 December 1955.

70. "Injecting Race Prejudice into a Football Game," *Philadelphia Inquirer*, 5 December 1955, 18.

71. "The Temper of the South," *Pittsburgh Courier*, 17 December 1955, 11.

72. "Here's How Ga. Tech Students Showed Wrath," *Afro-American*, 10 December 1955, 14.

73. "Teapot Tempest," *Chicago Defender*, 17 December 1955, 9; "Angry Students Burn Effigy of Georgia Govn'r," *California Eagle*, 8 December 1955, 1.

74. "Undue Political Interference," *Atlanta Daily World*, 4 December 1955, 4.

75. Marion Jackson, "Sports of the World," *Atlanta Daily World*, 7 December 1955, 5.

76. Robert Ratcliffe, "Behind the Headlines," *Pittsburgh Courier*, 10 December 1955, 9.

77. Benjamin Mays, "My View," *Pittsburgh Courier*, 31 December 1955, 8.

78. "Ave Commends Tech Students," *Columbus Ledger*, 7 December 1955, 1.

79. "ACLU Here Raps Griffin," *Pittsburgh Post-Gazette*, 5 December 1955, 9.

80. Vince Johnson, "Georgia Students Praised," *Pittsburgh Post-Gazette*, 8 December 1955.

81. "Employers' Hold on Labor Scored," *New York Times*, 4 December 1955, 86; "Largest Union Created As AFL and CIO Merged," *Savannah Morning News*, 4 December 1955, 1; "Damage Done in Tech Furor," *Columbus (Ga.) Ledger*, 6 December 1955, 4.

82. "Georgia Tech Students Riot to Save Sugar Bowl Game," *New York Times*, 4 December 1955, 1.

83. Reese and Davidson, "Run for Respect." See also John Vaught, *Rebel Coach: My Football Family* (Memphis: Memphis State University Press, 1971).

84. "On to New Orleans," *Pittsburgh Post-Gazette*, 16 December 1955, 12.

85. *Atlanta Journal*, 6 December 1955, 26; *Atlanta Constitution*, 6 December 1955, 4; *California Eagle*, 8 December 1955; *Red and Black*, 8 December 1955; *Pittsburgh Post-Gazette*, 5 December 1955, 12.

86. Cited in "Press Taunts Georgia Governor," *Afro-American*, 17 December 1955, 15.

87. "Common Sense Wins a Victory," *Atlanta Constitution*, 6 December 1955, 4; "Griffin's Teapot Tempest," *Atlanta Journal and Constitution*, 4 December 1955, 1; "Reader 'Humiliated' by Act of Governor," *Atlanta Journal*, 6 December 1955, 26.

88. Mike Edwards, "Nationwide Messages Favor Tech Bowl Game with Pitt," *Atlanta Journal and Constitution*, 4 December 1955, 30; "Regents Say Games Up to Coaches," *Atlanta Constitution*, 7 December 1955, 1; "Atlanta to Open Links," *New York Times*, 24 December 1955, 13.

89. "Georgia Deserves to Be Spared," *Atlanta Daily World*, 7 December 1955, 6; Robert Ratcliffe, "Behind the Headlines," *Pittsburgh Courier*, 17 December 1955, 13; "Tan Atlanta Is 'Amused,' Not 'Alarmed," *Afro-American*, 10 December 1955, 14.

90. "We Thank You, Governor," *Afro-American*, 17 December 1955, 4.

91. "Mixed Game Ban Upheld by Ga.," *Philadelphia Inquirer*, 6 December 1955, 38.

92. "Pittsburgh Test Oks for Jan. 2," *Philadelphia Inquirer*, 6 December 1955, 34; Charles Pou, "Leave Future Bowl Bids to Regents, Bloch Says," *Atlanta Journal*, 6 December 1955, 1.

93. "Regents' Policy Stand Draws Praise of Griffin," *Atlanta Journal*, 6 December 1955, 19.

94. "Griffin Claims 2 to 1 Favor Sports Stand," *Atlanta Journal*, 5 December 1955, 1; Tom Ross, "Decision to Allow Tech to Play in 'Sugar' Gets Mixed Reactions," *New Orleans Times-Picayune*, 6 December 1955, 28.

95. "Griffin Text on Action of Regents," *Atlanta Constitution*, 6 December 1955, 10.

96. "Governor Is Right, This Reader Avers," *Atlanta Journal*, 6 December 1955.

97. "Do Tech Student Mobs Disgrace Their School?" *Atlanta Constitution*, 10 December 1955.

98. Charles Pou, "Regents Give Full Okay to Tech-Pitt Bowl Game," *Atlanta Journal*, 5 December 1955, 1; "Letters to Editor," *Augusta Chronicle*, 6 December 1955, 6.

99. "Atlanta Newspapers Bring Disgrace to Journalistic Profession and Georgia" and "Regents Render Commendable Decision in Resolution," *Jackson Herald*, 8 December 1955, 2.

100. "Regents Ok Tech Play in Sugar Bowl," *Columbus (Ga.) Ledger*, 5 December 1955, 1.

101. Cited in "Tech to Keep Date in Sugar," *Columbus (Ga.) Ledger*, 1 December 1955, 48.

102. Johnny Hendrix, "A Tarnished Reputation," *Augusta Chronicle Herald*, 4 December 1955.

103. "State Is Split Widely on Issue," *Columbus (Ga.) Ledger*, 4 December 1955, 4.

104. Cited in "Tech," *Columbus (Ga.) Ledger*, 6 December 1955, 2.

105. Walter Bragg, "Georgia Viewed as Disgraced by Governor's Action," *Columbus (Ga.) Ledger*, 8 December 1955, 4.

106. Vincent Jones, "The Last Straw," *Jackson (Ga.) Progress Argus*, 8 December 1955.

107. "Straining at Gnats," *Augusta Chronicle*, 5 December 1955, 4.

108. Bill Allen, "Regent Head Declines to Make Issue Over Pitt Negro Player," *Atlanta Constitution*, 1 December 1955, 28; Ed Danforth, "Future Tech and Georgia Sports Programs Involved," *Atlanta Journal*, 2 December 1955, 1.

109. Furman Bisher, "What Makes a Panther Tick," *Atlanta Constitution*, 5 December 1955, 5.

110. "Grier Hard Running Back, Letter to Harvey Reveals," *Atlanta Daily World*, 6 December 1955, 7.

111. Bob Roesler, "Tom Jenkins Appears Lost to Pittsburgh for Sugar Bowl," *New Orleans Times-Picayune*, 30 December 1955; "Pro-Segregation Group Urges Tech Not to Play Panthers in Sugar Bowl," *Savannah Morning News*, 1 December 1955, 32.

112. "Georgia Tech Beats Pitt, 7–0, in Thrill-Packed Sugar Classic," *New Orleans Times-Picayune*, 3 January 1956, 1; Furman Bisher, "Tech Staves Off Pitt, 7–0, for Bruising Bowl Victory," *Atlanta Constitution*, 3 January 1956, 1, 8; Jack Gates, "Tech Out to Thwart Pitt Good Impression," *Columbus (Ga.) Ledger*, 2 January 1956, 15.

113. Reese and Davidson, "Run for Respect"; "The Big Play," *Atlanta Constitution*, 3 January 1956, 10; "Fay Says," *Chicago Defender*, 14 January 1956, 17; Grier, telephone interview.

114. Sterling Slappey, "Tech Has Old Score to Settle with Pitt Today," *New Orleans Times-Picayune*, 2 January 1956, 14; Bill Keefe, "Pitt Fumble Sets Up Tally," *New Orleans Times-Picayune*, 3 January 1956, 25; Ed Danforth, "An Ear to the Ground," *Atlanta Journal*, 3 January 1956, 14.

115. "Students Storm Georgia Capitol," *Philadelphia Inquirer*, 4 December 1955, 4-A; "Negro Glad Ga. Tech Gets Okay," *Pittsburgh Post-Gazette*, 6 December 1955, 23.

116. Mule, *Sugar Bowl*, 102.

117. Grier, telephone interview.

118. "Grier Is Popular with Teammates," *Pittsburgh Courier*, 10 December 1955, 1.

119. Buddy Diliberto, "Didn't Push Him, Says Bob Grier," *New Orleans Times-Picayune*, 3 January 1956, 26; "Pitt's Grier Likes Fans, Tech," *Atlanta Journal*, 3 January 1956, 14.

120. Pete Thamel, "For Black Star, Bittersweet Memories of Sugar Bowl," *New York Times*, 1 January 2006.

121. Ralph McGill, "Fine Grid Battle Dims Race Issue," *Atlanta Constitution*, 3 January 1956, 1; Marion Jackson, "Sports of the World," *Atlanta Daily World*, 3 January 1956, 5.

122. "Pitt Head Coach to Scout Vanderbilt Game Saturday," *New Orleans Times-Picayune*, 25 November 1955, 1; Furman Bisher, "As Tech's 7 Grew, So Did Bob Grier," *Atlanta Constitution*, 4 January 1956, 8.

123. "Football or Sociology?" *Augusta Chronicle*, 6 January 1956, 4A.

124. Johnny Hendrix, "Quietness and Jazz," *Augusta Chronicle*, 6 January 1956, 7B.

125. Lee Griggs, "Sugar Bowl," *Sports Illustrated*, 9 January 1956, 23.

126. "Pitt's Grier Likes Fans, Tech"; Furman Bisher, "Manage-aerial Genius," *Atlanta Constitution*, 3 January 1956, 8.

127. Gladwin Hill, "Racial Question at 'Bowl' Fades," *New York Times*, 1 January 1956, 42; Sterling Slappey, "Grier May Dance at Negro Party," *Columbus (Ga.) Ledger*, 1 January 1956, D1.

128. Paul Burton, "Grier Says 'Wrong Ruling' Won Game for Georgia Tech," *Atlanta Daily World*, 3 January 1956, 5.

129. Jackson, "Sports of the World."

130. Barry Abrams, "A Showdown in the Crescent City," *American Legacy* 14, no. 4 (Winter 2008): 19–23.

131. *Louisiana State Athletic Commission v. Dorsey*, 359 U.S. 533 (1959); Joan Paul and Richard V. McGhee, "The Arrival and Ascendance of Black Athletes in the Southeastern Conference, 1966–1980," *Phylon* 45, no. 4 (1984): 284; Mule, *Sugar Bowl*, 104.

132. Martin, "Racial Change and Big Time College Football," 552–560; "Integrating New Year's Day," 372; "Jones, Compton Battle in Jr. Rose Bowl Today," *Atlanta Constitution*, 10 December 1955, 5; Dubay, "Pigmentation and Pigskin," 43–50; Anthony Lewis, "Segregation Group Confers in Secret," *New York Times*, 30 December 1955, 1; "For Segregation," *New York Times*, 1 January 1956, E2.

133. "Georgia Governor Calls High Court 'Tyrannical,'" *New York Times*, 11 January 1956, 18.

134. Lula Garrett, "Ga. Tech Students' Uprising Indicates Hope," *Afro-American*, 7 January 1956, 6; Jackson, "Sports of the World."

135. "It Is the Right Thing to Do," *Tech Topics*, Georgia Tech Alumni Association, Fall 2001.

136. Reese and Davidson, "Run for Respect."

CHAPTER 5　"BEAT THE DEVIL OUT OF BYU"

1. William D. Carlson, "Four Seasons in Laramie (Adventures of a University President)," unpublished memoir, American Heritage Center, University of Wyoming, 22–1.

2. Ibid., 25–3.

3. Ibid.

4. Ibid.

5. K-2 Television News Transcript, 21 October 1969, Black Fourteen Collection (1969–1970), American Heritage Center, University of Wyoming (hereafter cited as Black Fourteen Collection).

6. John Hope Franklin, *From Slavery to Freedom: A History of African Americans* (New York: Alfred A. Knopf, 2000), 493, 558.

7. Benjamin Rader, *American Sports: From the Age of Folk Games to the Age of Televised Sports* (New York: Prentice-Hall, 2004), 244.

8. Jack Olsen, *The Black Athlete: A Shameful Story* (New York: Time-Life Books, 1968), 109.

9. Stu Camen, "Negroes Seem Unsatisfied Despite Bigger Rewards," *Provo Herald*, 2 January 1970; Donald Spivey, "Black Consciousness and Olympic Protest Movement, 1964–1980," in *Sport in America*, edited by Donald Spivey (London: Greenwood Press, 1985), 242; Thomas Smith, "Civil Rights on the Gridiron: The Kennedy Administration and the Desegregation of the Washington Redskins," *Journal of Sport History* 14, no. 2 (Summer 1987); Bill Russell, *Go Up for Glory* (New York: Coward-McCann, 1966); Jack Olsen, "Part 2: Pride and Prejudice," *Sports Illustrated*, 8 July 1968, 31.

10. Harry Edwards, *The Revolt of the Black Athlete* (New York: Free Press, 1969). See also Edwards, "Sport Within the Veil: The Triumphs, Tragedies and Challenges of Afro-American Involvement," *Annals of the American Academy of Political and Social Science* 445 (September 1979): 116–128.

11. Arnold Hano, "The Black Athlete Who 'Whitelists' the Olympics," *New York Times*, 12 May 1968, SM32; Jack Olsen, "Part 1: The Cruel Deception," *Sports Illustrated*, 1 July 1968, 15.

12. Hano, "The Black Athlete," *New York Times*, 12 May 1968, SM32.

13. Ibid.

14. Spivey, "Black Consciousness and Olympic Protest," 239.

15. Amy Bass, *Not the Triumph But the Struggle: The 1968 Olympics and the Making of the Black Athlete* (Minneapolis: University of Minnesota Press, 2002), xvii.

16. Olsen, "Cruel Deception," 17; Jack Olsen, "Part 4: In the Back of the Bus," *Sports Illustrated*, 22 July 1968, 79; Hano, "The Black Rebel."

17. Bass, *Not the Triumph*, xx.

18. Rader, *American Sports*, 324.

19. Beth Bailey, *Sex in the Heartland* (Cambridge, Mass.: Harvard University Press, 2002).

20. NCAA-TV revenues went from just over two million dollars in 1959 to twelve million by 1970. See John Watterson, *College Football: History, Spectacle, Controversy* (Baltimore, Md.: Johns Hopkins University Press, 2000), 287.

21. Ibid., 301.

22. "End of the Dream," *Time*, 24 May 1963; Charles Martin, "Integrating New Year's Day: The Racial Politics of College Bowl Games in the American South," *Journal of Sport History* 24, no. 3 (Fall 1997): 364–365.

23. "In Black and White," *Sports Illustrated*, 19 February 1968, 10; Franklin, *From Slavery to Freedom*, 449.

24. Steve Murdock, "Steve's Soliloquy," *Riverton Ranger*, 22 October 1969.

25. Wallace Turner, "LDS Letter Reaffirms Position on Negroes," *New York Times*, 9 January 1970.

26. "14 Black Athletes at Wyoming Are Suspended," Black Fourteen Collection; Robert Lipsyte, "The Dissenter Joins Four Horsemen of College Football Apocalypse," *Baltimore Sun*, 18 November 1969.

27. For a statistical analysis of "stacking," see Gregg Jones, "Racial Discrimination in College Football," *Social Science Quarterly* 68, no. 1 (1987): 70–83.

28. Susan Rayl, "Who Killed Willie Muldrew?" Proceedings of the North American Society of Sport History (NASSH) Conference, 24–25 May 2001, University of Western Ontario.

29. David Wiggins, "'The Future of College Athletics Is at Stake:' Black Athletes and Racial Turmoil on Three Predominantly White University Campuses, 1968–1972," *Journal of Sport History* 15, no. 3 (Winter 1988): 304–333.

30. Watterson, *College Football*, 321, 324–325; Clifford A. Bullock, "Fired by Conscience," in *Readings in Wyoming History*, edited by Philip Roberts (Laramie, Wy.: Skyline West Press, 2000), 185; John Long, "Four Black Washington Gridders Suspended," *Laramie Daily Boomerang*, 1 November 1969, 14; Olsen, "Pride and Prejudice," 25; "Negro Tryouts Tonight: Pom-Pon Plans Set," *Lawrence (Kan.) Journal-World*, 10 May 1968; Wiggins, "The Future of College Athletics is at Stake," 306; Martin, "Integrating New Year's Day," 373.

31. Olsen, "Part 3: In an Alien World," *Sports Illustrated*, 15 July 1968, 41–43.

32. "Black Hired Hands," *Nation*, 5 August 1968, 68; Olsen, "Cruel Deception," 27.

33. "The Negro Question," *Time*, 18 October 1963.

34. Bullock, "Fired by Conscience," 85; Gary James Bergera and Ronald Priddis, *Brigham Young University: A House of Faith* (Salt Lake City, Utah: Signature Books, 1985), 298.

35. "WAC Council Reaches No Conclusion Tuesday," *Laramie Daily Boomerang*, 5 November 1969, 9.

36. "What Is the Cougar Club?" Cougar Club Historical Files, Brigham Young University Archives (hereafter cited as BYU Archives).

37. Olsen, "Cruel Deception," 27; "WAC Grid Attendance Nears Million Mark," *Provo Herald*, 4 January 1970.

38. "Lloyd Eaton Looks For 100th Win Today" and "A Different View of Stadium," *Laramie Daily Boomerang*, 4 October 1969, 1, 4; Pete Fetsco, "After Rough Sledding, Cowboys Snow Miners," *Laramie Daily Boomerang*, 12 October 1969, 12; Joe Carnicelli, "Pokes Now Ranked 12th," *Laramie Daily Boomerang*, 14 October 1969, 8; "Annual Resident Population for Wyoming and Counties: 1970 to 1980," Wyoming Department of Administration and Information, Division of Economic Analysis, 20 April 2002.

39. "Brigham Young versus Wyoming," Game Program, College of Physical Education Files, Brigham Young University Archives.

40. "Five Black Players Charge White Athletes Are Favored," *Laramie Daily Boomerang*, 22 October 1969, 3; "Biographical Data," Black Fourteen Collection; Michael

McElreath, *The Black 14* [VHS recording] (Laramie: University of Wyoming, 1997); Bullock, "Fired by Conscience," 187.

41. McElreath, *The Black 14*.

42. "Biographical Data," Black Fourteen Collection.

43. Audio Recording; "Black Fourteen Meeting," *Free Lunch*, 17 December 1969, 3, Black Fourteen Collection.

44. "Jerry Rubin Appearance Is Protested," *Denver Post*, 22 December 1969, 17; "'Chicago 8' Defendant to Speak in January," *Branding Iron*, 19 December 1969, 1; "Wyoming Welcomes Rubin," *Free Lunch*, 13–19 January 1970, 2., Black Fourteen Collection ; Demonstrations Are Set At Casper and Laramie," *Laramie Daily Boomerang*, 15 October 1969, 10.

45. Watterson, *College Football*, 322; "It's Time to Take a Stand," *Laramie Daily Boomerang*, 12 October 1969, 4; Pete Fetsco, "Negro Athletes Out for Failure to Abide by Athletic Department Rules," *Laramie Daily Boomerang*, 19 October 1969, 1.

46. Philip White, author interview, 25 August 2006 (Laramie, Wy.).

47. "Wonderful Whiteoming," *Free Lunch*, 4 December 1969, 4, Black Fourteen Collection.

48. "What Did Happen at the University of Wyoming?" *Powell Tribune*, 28 October 1969.

49. Carlson, "Four Seasons in Laramie," 25–2.

50. "Minutes of the Western Athletic Conference Athletic Directors' Section Meeting," College of Physical Education Files, BYU Archives.

51. McElreath, *The Black 14*.

52. Watterson, *College Football*, 323.

53. "Racial Unrest—Wyoming," *ABC Evening News*, 24 October 1969. Located in the Vanderbilt Television News Archive, Vanderbilt University (hereafter cited as Vanderbilt TV News Archive).

54. James E. Barrett, *"Williams v. Eaton*: A Personal Recollection," in *Readings in Wyoming History*, 197.

55. Pat Putnam, "No Defeats, Loads of Trouble," *Sports Illustrated*, 3 November 1969, 26.

56. McElreath, *The Black 14*.

57. Putnam, "No Defeats," 27; McElreath, *The Black 14*.

58. Carlson, "Four Seasons in Laramie," 25–3.

59. Miscellaneous Notes, Black Fourteen Collection; McElreath, *The Black 14*.

60. Barrett, *"Williams v. Eaton*," 198.

61. Carlson, "Four Seasons in Laramie," 25–3.

62. BSA Flier, 18 October 1969, Black Fourteen Collection.

63. *Branding Iron*, 22 October 1969; White, interview.

64. Pete Fetsco, "Negro Athletes Out for Failure to Abide by Athletic Department Rules," *Laramie Daily Boomerang*, 19 October 1969, 1; McElreath, *The Black 14*; White, interview.

65. "Brigham Young versus Wyoming," Game Program, College of Physical Education Files, BYU Archives; Camen, "Negroes Seem Unsatisfied Despite Bigger Rewards," *Provo Herald*, 2 January 1970.

66. Jordan Bonfante, "OJ," *Life*, 27 October 1967, 74B.

67. Frank Deford, "Ready If You Are, O.J.," *Sports Illustrated*, 14 July 1969, 16.

68. O.J. Simpson (with Pete Axthelm), *O.J.: The Education of a Rich Rookie* (New York: Macmillan, 1970), 9, 12.

69. "Racial Unrest—Wyoming."

70. Putnam, "No Defeats," 27.

71. "Racial Unrest—Wyoming"; "Black Protest—University of Wyoming," *NBC Evening News*, 22 October 1969; Vanderbilt TV News Archive.

72. Carolyn Pratt, "Football Rule Modified Some," *Laramie Daily Boomerang*, 24 October 1969, 1; *Tinker v. Des Moines* 393 U.S. 503 (1969).

73. "Eaton Backed Solidly in Football Crisis," *Star Valley Independent*, 23 October 1969; "Eaton to Continue As Cowboy Coach," *Daily Times*, 21 October 1969, 1.

74. "Eaton to Continue As Cowboy Coach."

75. Bruce Bennett, "Executive Sports Editor," *Duluth News-Tribune*, 31 October 1969.

76. "Black Protest—University of Wyoming"; William Ashworth, "Inside Story of Fired Black Athletes," *Jet*, 13 November 1969, 62.

77. Betty Rider Bass, "Editor's Corner," *Douglas Budget*, 30 October 1969.

78. "They Will Be Heard," *Laramie Daily Boomerang*, 21 October 1969, 4.

79. "Emotion, Not Logic, Prevailing in Laramie," *Denver Post*, news clipping, Black Fourteen Collection.

80. Charles Chamberlain, "Carter Fined $1,000 After Speaking on Bear Situation," *Evanston Times*, 16 December 1969.

81. Olsen, "Part 4: In the Back of the Bus," 41.

82. Reprinted in Roger Stanton, "Blacks Ill-Advised, Says Football Writer," *Laramie Daily Boomerang*, 22 November 1969, 9.

83. Putnam, "No Defeats," 27.

84. Ibid.; "Alumni Association Adds Support to Eaton, Trustees in Grid Ruling," *Laramie Daily Boomerang*, 22 October 1969, 1; Larry Birleffi, "Larry Birleffi on Sports," *Laramie Daily Boomerang*, 22 October 1969, 8.

85. "Time for Strong Leadership," news clipping and letter to Irene Schubert, Riverton, Wyoming, 2 October 1969; Black Fourteen Collection.

86. Carlson, "Four Seasons in Laramie," 25–4; "UW Black Chancellor Says Negroes Want Citizens Rights," *Daily Times*, 21 October 1969, 6; McElreath, *The Black 14*; "Black Rally to Precede Cowboy Tilt," *Provo Herald*, 5 February 1970.

87. McElreath, *The Black 14*.

88. "WAIIA with Eaton," *Torrington Telegram*, 30 October 1969.

89. "Black Athlete Incident Panther Sponsored?" *Laramie Daily Boomerang*, 18 December 1969, 12.

90. Letter to Irene Schubert, Cheyenne, Wyoming, 29 January 1970, Black Fourteen Collection; Carlson, "Four Seasons in Laramie," 25–3.

91. Watterson, *College Football*, 324; "Quoth the Craven: Nevermore," *Free Lunch*, 20 November 1969, 2, Black Fourteen Collection; "Arts, Science College Condemns Eaton," *Northern Wyoming News*, 31 October 1969.

92. "Claims Support Grows for Black UW Football Players," *Northern Wyoming Daily News*, 21 October 1969.

93. "Quoth the Craven: Nevermore" and "Athletic Department? Answers Lent's Reply," *Free Lunch*, 20 November 1969, 2, 6, Black Fourteen Collection.

94. "Football Team Dilemma Puts Wyoming Unity to Big Test," *Daily Times*, 28 October 1969; "Students March In Support of Black Athletes," *Laramie Daily Boomerang*, 24 October 1969, 3.

95. "Negro Cage Players Show Up for Practice," *Daily Times*, 21 October 1969; Bullock, "Fired by Conscience," 184; "Three Negro Tracksters Quit Wyoming Squad," 30 October 1969 and "White Wyoming Track Star Quits," 10 December 1969, news clippings; BSA meeting notes, 27 October 1969, Black Fourteen Collection.

96. Photograph, Black Fourteen Collection.

97. Ashworth, "Inside Story of Fired Black Athletes," 68; White, interview.

98. Putnam, "No Defeats, Loads of Trouble," 27; "BSA Suit Set to Seek $1 Million," *Laramie Daily Boomerang*, 25 October 1969, 3.

99. Ashworth, "Inside Story of Fired Black Athletes," 67; "Three Picket Eaton," *Riverton Ranger*, 27 October 1969.

100. Willie Black, "Too Busy Thinking about My Survival," *Free Lunch*, 4 December 1959, 7, Black Fourteen Collection; "New Newspaper Appears at WU," *Denver Post*, 25 November 1969, 3; Carol Hopkins, "Farmer Speaks on Black Dissent," *Branding Iron*, 19 December 1969; Richard McCall, "Black Americans Seek Self-Identity," *Laramie Daily Boomerang*, 19 December 1969, 8.

101. *Revelations*, #10, 3 November 1969, Black Fourteen Collection.

102. "Eaton Has Big Support From University Students," *Laramie Daily Boomerang*, 25 October 1969, 3; "Football Team Dilemma Puts Wyoming Unity to Big Test," *Daily Times*, 28 October 1969.

103. Internal Memo, Black Fourteen Collection.

104. "Casper Trial Is Postponed Due to Adverse Black Image," *Laramie Daily Boomerang*, 14 November 1969, 1.

105. Putnam, "No Defeats, Loads of Trouble," 27; "Quarterback Club Raises Fund for UW Athletics," *Daily Times*, 23 October 1969; "Football Team Dilemma Puts Wyoming Unity to Big Test," *Daily Times*, 28 October 1969.

106. Memo, Black Fourteen Collection.

107. Letter to Schubert, 29 January 1970, Black Fourteen Collection.

108. "Basin Residents Show Support for Coach Eaton," *Basin Republican Rustler*, 23 October 1969; "Chamber Backs Eaton's Action," *Northern Wyoming Daily News*, 21 October 1969; "Football Team Dilemma Puts Wyoming Unity to Big Test," *Daily Times*, 28 October 1969; "Annual Resident Population for Wyoming Counties and Municipalities," Wyoming Department of Administration and Information, Division of Economic Analysis, 20 April 2002; "Davis Agrees with UW Coach," *News-Record*, 23 October 1969; "Rotary Club Resolution Approves Eaton's Actions," *Daily Times*, 22 October 1969.

109. "Congratulations Coach" and "People Aren't Equal," *Laramie Daily Boomerang*, 22 October 1969, 9.

110. Larry Jarrett, "QBC Banquet Roars with Success," *Laramie Daily Boomerang*, Black Fourteen Collection.

111. "Our Opinion," *Sheridan Press*, 23 October 1969; "An Unfortunate Incident," *Star Valley Independent*, 23 October 1969; "On Our Quiet Town," *Independent-Record*, 30 October 1969.

112. "The Rules for Everyone or a Few?" *Laramie Daily Boomerang*, 19 October 1969, 4; "Civil Rights on the Playing Field," *Denver Post*, 9 November 1969.

113. "Eaton to Continue As Cowboy Coach."

114. Robert Lipsyte, "The Dissenter Joins Four Horsemen of College Football Apocalypse," *Baltimore Sun*, 18 November 1969.

115. Jim Graham, "Eaton Took Right Stand," *Denver Post*, 22 October 1969.

116. "Blacks Say 'WAC No Place for Us,'" *Powell Tribune*, 14 November 1969; "WAC Suspends Meet When 50 Black Students Show Up," news clipping, Black Fourteen Collection; "WAC Session Disrupted by Black Students," *Laramie Daily Boomerang*, 6 November 1969, 12.

117. "Utah State Blacks May Protest BYU," *Riverton Ranger*, 5 November 1969; "Blacks Get UNM Support," *Free Lunch*, 16 December 1969, 5, Black Fourteen Collection; "Arizona Faculty to Discuss Riot" and "Student Senate Calls for Resignation of U. of A. President," *Salt Lake Tribune*, 13 January 1970; William Mefford, "Protesters Attempt to Disrupt Game," *Provo Herald*, 9 January 1970; "Protesters Will Be Disciplined," *Provo Herald*, 21 January 1970; "Huskies to Seek Review of Relations with BYU," *Salt Lake Tribune*, 4 February 1970.

118. "San Jose Will Play—With Armbands," *Northern Wyoming Daily News*, 23 October 1969, 3; "Wilkinson Airs Race Policy," College of Physical Education Files, BYU Archives; "President Denies BYU Has Racist Policies," *Laramie Daily Boomerang*, 26 November 1969, 2.

119. "WAC Council Reaches No Conclusion Tuesday," *Laramie Daily Boomerang*, 5 November 1969, 9; "Stanford Officials Reveal Refusal to Schedule BYU," *Laramie Daily Boomerang*, 13 November 1969, 10; Lester Kinsolving, "Stanford Seen Inconsistent on LDS Status," *Deseret News*, 28 December 1969, 42; William F. Reed, "The Other Side of 'The Y,'" *Sports Illustrated*, 6 January 1970, 38–39. See also O. Kendall White and Daryl White, "Abandoning an Unpopular Policy: An Analysis of the Decision Granting the Mormon Priesthood to Blacks," *Sociological Analysis* 41, no. 3 (Autumn 1980): 231–245.

120. "U. Professor Criticizes Stanford, Y. on Issue," *Salt Lake Tribune*, 8 January 1970; "Another Garbage Dump," *Salt Lake Tribune*, 5 January 1970.

121. Max Rafferty, "'Coalition' Interferes with LDS Religious Rights," *Salt Lake Tribune*, 14 December 1969, 18A; Joe Watts, "Protest Gets Out of Hand after Concessions Made to Militants," *Provo Herald*, 6 February 1970; Wallace Turner, "LDS Letter Reaffirms Position on Negroes," *Salt Lake Tribune*, 9 January 1970; "Policy Statement of Presidency," *Deseret News*, 10 January 1970; "Right to Protest Mormon Policy," *Denver Post*, 12 January 1970, 16.

122. "UW Blacks Claim: 'Prevented Unconstitutionally from Playing,'" *Powell Tribune*, 14 November 1969; "Black Hearings Begin; Kerr Will Rule Within One Week," *Laramie Daily Boomerang*, 11 November 1969, 1; Court Transcript, Black Fourteen Collection. 123. "Black Athletes to Appeal Judgment," *Riverton Ranger*, 18 November 1969.

124. McElreath, *The Black 14*; "Biographical Data," Black Fourteen Collection.

125. Rick Reilly, "Eaton Has No Regrets, Says He'd Do It Again," *Denver Post*, 9 May 1982, 7; Bob Hammond, "Lloyd Eaton Dies in Idaho," *Laramie Daily Boomerang*, 16 March 2007.

126. Lyndon W. Cook, *The Revelations of the Prophet Joseph Smith* (Salt Lake City: Deseret Book Company, 1983); Kenneth Briggs, "Mormon Church Strikes Down Ban against Blacks in Priesthood," *New York Times*, 10 June 1978, 47; "Brigham Young University and the Racial Doctrines of the Mormon Church," *The Journal of Blacks in Higher Education* 20 (Summer 1998): 22–23.

EPILOGUE

1. "Tears, Then Cheers at Virginia Tech Opener," Associated Press, 1 September 2007.

2. "Business Leaders Pay $800,000 to See Coach K," Associated Press, 17 October 2006.

3. James L. Shulman and William G. Bowen, *The Game of Life* (Princeton, N.J.: Princeton University Press, 2001).

4. Mark Leibovich, "In Turmoil of '68, Clinton Found a New Voice," *New York Times*, 5 September 2007.

5. Carmina Ocampo, "Prop 209: Ten Long Years," *Nation*, 11 December 2006.

6. J. A. Adande, "Davis Acts to Spark African American Growth at UCLA," *Los Angeles Times*, 29 March 2007, D1.

7. John Hope Franklin, *From Slavery to Freedom: A History of African Americans* (New York: Alfred A. Knopf, 2000), 449.

8. "Tears, Then Cheers at Virginia Tech Opener."

SELECTED BIBLIOGRAPHY

ARCHIVES

1955 Sugar Bowl Vertical File, Georgia Institute of Technology Archives.

Administrative Files, Department of Athletics, UCLA Archives.

Associated Students of UCLA, Board of Directors Files, UCLA Archives.

Black Fourteen Collection (1969–1970), American Heritage Center, University of Wyoming.

Carl Simmons Oral History, LDS African American Oral History Collection, Brigham Young University Archives.

College of Physical Education Files, Brigham Young University Archives.

Congressional Record, United States Congress.

Cougar Club Historical Files, Brigham Young University Archives.

Dorothy Peel Papers, UCLA Archives.

Edward Dickson Papers, UCLA Special Collections.

Gehrig Leonard Harris Oral History, LDS African American Oral History Collection, Brigham Young University Archives.

Irene Tresun Alumna Files, UCLA Archives.

Jackie Robinson Biographical File, UCLA Archives.

Jack Trice Papers, Special Collections, Iowa State University Archives

John Jackson Papers, UCLA Archives.

Johnny Bright Digital Archives, Special Collections, Drake University Archives.

Paul Morrison Oral History, Special Collections, Drake University.

Rodney Lester Oral History, UCLA Oral History Project.

Supreme Court Justice Hugo LaFayette Black Papers, Manuscript Division, Library of Congress, Washington, D.C.

Vanderbilt Television News Archive, Vanderbilt University.

William D. Carlson Presidential Papers, American Heritage Center, University of Wyoming.

William Forbes Oral History, UCLA Oral History Project.

PUBLISHED SOURCES

Albright, Evan. "William Henry Lewis: Brief Life of a Football Pioneer: 1868–1949." *Harvard Magazine* 108, no.2 (November-December 2005): 43–44.

Allen, Maury. *Jackie Robinson: A Life Remembered.* New York: Franklin Watts, 1987.

Astor, Gerald. "...And a Credit to His Race": The Hard Life and Times of Joseph Louis Barrow.* New York: Saturday Review Press, 1974.

Bailey, Beth. *Sex in the Heartland.* Cambridge, Mass.: Harvard University Press, 2002.

Barra, Allen. *The Last Coach: A Life of Paul "Bear" Bryant.* New York: W. W. Norton, 2005.

Barrett, James E. "*Williams v. Eaton*: A Personal Recollection." In *Readings in Wyoming History*, edited by Philip Roberts. Laramie, Wy.: Skyline West Press, 2000.

Bass, Amy. *Not the Triumph But the Struggle: The 1968 Olympics and the Making of the Black Athlete*. Minneapolis: University of Minnesota Press, 2002.

———. "Whose Broad Stripes and Bright Stars? Race, Nation, and Power at the 1968 Mexico City Olympics." In *Sports Matters: Race, Recreation, and Culture*, edited by John Bloom and Michael Willard, 185–209. New York: New York University Press, 2002.

Bederman, Gail. *Manliness and Civilization*. Chicago: University of Chicago Press, 1995.

Behee, John. *Hail to the Victors*. Ann Arbor: University of Michigan Press, 1974.

"Black Teams, White Coaches," *Journal of Blacks in Higher Education* 49 (Autumn 2005): 32.

Bloom, John, and Michael Willard, eds. *Sports Matters: Race, Recreation, and Culture*. New York: New York University Press, 2002.

Branch, Taylor. *At Canaan's Edge: America in the King Years, 1965–68*. New York: Simon and Schuster, 2006.

———. *Parting the Waters: America in the King Years, 1954–63*. New York: Simon and Schuster, 1988.

———. *Pillar of Fire: America in the King Years, 1963–65*. New York: Simon and Schuster, 1998.

"Brigham Young University and the Racial Doctrines of the Mormon Church." *Journal of Blacks in Higher Education* 20 (Summer 1998): 22–23.

Brooks, Dana, and Ronald Althouse, eds. *Racism in College Athletics: The African-American Athlete's Experience*. Morgantown, W.Va.: Fitness Information Technology, 1993.

Broussard, Albert. "George Albert Flippin and Race Relations in a Western Rural Community." *Midwest Review* 12 (1990): 1–15.

Bullock, Clifford. "Fired By Conscience: The Black 14 Incident at the University of Wyoming and Black Protest in the Western Athletic Conference, 1968–1970." In *Readings in Wyoming History*, edited by Philip Roberts. Laramie, Wy.: Skyline West Press, 2000.

Burr, Carol. "Prentice Gautt: A Sooner's Story." *Sooner Magazine* (Spring 1987): 10–15.

Butler, Mike. "Confederate Flags, Class Conflict, a Golden Egg, and Castrated Bulls: A Historical Examination of the Ole-Miss–Mississippi State Football Rivalry." *Journal of Mississippi History* 59, no.2 (Summer 1997): 123–139.

Capeci, Dominic, and Wilkerson, Martha. "Multifarious Hero: Joe Louis, American Society, and Race Relations during World Crisis, 1935–1945." *Journal of Sport History* 10 (Winter 1983): 5–25.

Cohen, Lizabeth. *A Consumer's Republic: The Politics of Mass Consumption in Postwar America*. New York: Alfred A. Knopf, 2003.

Cross, George. *Blacks in White Colleges: Oklahoma's Landmark Cases*. Norman: University of Oklahoma Press, 1975.

Demas, Lane. "The Brown Bomber's Dark Day: Louis–Schmeling I and America's Black Hero." *Journal of Sport History* 31 (Fall 2004): 253–271.

Dellinger, Doris. *A History of the Oklahoma State University Intercollegiate Athletics*. Stillwater: Oklahoma State University Press, 1987.

Denning, Michael. *The Cultural Front: The Laboring of American Culture in the Twentieth Century*. New York: Verso, 1997.

Diggins, John Patrick. *The Proud Decades: America in War and Peace, 1941–1960*. New York: W. W. Norton, 1988.

Dittmer, John. *Local People: The Struggle for Civil Rights in Mississippi*. Chicago: University of Illinois Press, 1994.

Doyle, Andrew. "Bear Bryant: Symbol of an Embattled South." *Colby Quarterly* 32, no. 1 (March 1996): 72–86.

———. "Causes Won, Not Lost: College Football and the Modernization of the American South." *International Journal of the History of Sport* 11 (August 1994): 231–251.

Doyle, William. *An American Insurrection: The Battle of Oxford, Mississippi, 1962.* New York: Doubleday, 2001.

Dubay, Robert. "Pigmentation and Pigskin: A Jones County Junior College Dilemma." *Journal of Mississippi History* 46 (February 1984): 43–50.

———. "Politics, Pigmentation, and Pigskin: The Georgia Tech Sugar Bowl Controversy of 1955." *Atlanta History* 39 (Spring 1995): 21–35.

Duberman, Martin. *Paul Robeson.* New York: Alfred Knopf, 1989.

Dyson, Michael Eric. *I May Not Get There with You.* New York: Free Press, 2000.

Edmonds, Anthony. *Joe Louis.* Grand Rapids, Mich.: William B. Eerdmans, 1973.

Edwards, Harry. *The Revolt of the Black Athlete.* New York: Free Press, 1969.

Eitzen, D. Stanley. *Sport in Contemporary Society.* London: Paradigm Publishers, 2005.

Falkner, David. *Great Time Coming: The Life of Jackie Robinson from Baseball to Birmingham.* New York: Simon and Schuster, 1995.

Franklin, John Hope. *From Slavery to Freedom: A History of African Americans.* New York: Alfred A. Knopf, 2000.

Fuse, Montye, and Miller, Keith. "Jazzing the Basepaths: Jackie Robinson and African American Aesthetics." In *Sports Matters: Race, Recreation, and Culture,* edited by John Bloom and Michael Willard. New York: New York University Press, 2002.

Garrow, David, ed. *The Montgomery Bus Boycott and the Women Who Started It: The Memoir of Jo Ann Gibson Robinson.* Knoxville: University of Tennessee Press, 1987.

Gems, Gerald. *For Pride, Profit, and Patriarchy: Football and the Incorporation of American Cultural Values.* London: Scarecrow Press, 2000.

Gilmore, Al-Tony. *Bad Nigger!: The National Impact of Jack Johnson.* Port Washington, N.Y.: Associated Faculty Press, 1975.

Gilmore, Glenda. *Gender and Jim Crow.* Chapel Hill: University of North Carolina Press, 1996.

Goodman, James. *Stories of Scottsboro.* New York: Pantheon Books, 1994.

Gorn, Elliott, ed. *Muhammad Ali: The People's Champ.* Champaign: University of Illinois Press, 1998.

Hauser, Thomas. *Muhammad Ali: His Life and Times.* New York: Simon and Schuster, 1992.

Hietala, Thomas R. *The Fight of the Century: Jack Johnson, Joe Louis, and the Struggle for Racial Equality.* London: M. E. Sharpe, 2002.

Hoberman, John. *Darwin's Athletes: How Sport has Damaged Black America and Preserved the Myth of Race.* New York: Houghton Mifflin, 1997.

Hurd, Michael. *Black College Football: One Hundred Years of History, Education, and Pride.* Virginia Beach, Va.: Donning Publishers, 1993.

Isenberg, Michael. *John L. Sullivan and His America.* Champaign: University of Illinois Press, 1994.

Jones, Gregg. "Racial Discrimination in College Football." *Social Science Quarterly* 68, no. 1 (1987): 70–83.

Kopecky, Pauline. *A History of Equal Opportunity at Oklahoma State University.* Stillwater: Oklahoma State University Press, 1990.

Levine, Lawrence. *Black Culture, Black Consciousness.* New York: Oxford University Press, 1977.

Louis, Joe. *The Joe Louis Story.* New York: Grosset and Dunlap, 1953.

———. *Joe Louis: My Life.* New York: Harcourt Brace Jovanovich, 1978.

Marcello, Ronald. "The Integration of Intercollegiate Athletics in Texas: North Texas State College as a Test Case, 1956." *Journal of Sport History* 14, no. 3 (Winter 1987): 286–316.

Margolick, David. *Beyond Glory: Joe Louis versus Max Schmeling and a World on the Brink.* New York: Alfred A. Knopf, 2005.

Marqusee, Mike. *Redemption Song: Muhammad Ali and the Spirit of the Sixties.* New York: Verso, 2005.

Martin, Charles H. "Integrating New Year's Day: The Racial Politics of College Bowl Games in the American South," *Journal of Sport History* 24, no. 3 (Fall 1997): 358–377.

———. "Racial Change and Big Time College Football in Georgia." *Georgia Historical Quarterly* 80 (Fall 1996): 532–562.

Martin, Waldo. *Brown v. Board of Education: A Brief History with Documents.* New York: Bedford/St. Martin's, 1998.

McRae, Donald. *Heroes without A Country: America's Betrayal of Joe Louis and Jesse Owens.* New York: HarperCollins, 2002.

Mead, Chris. *Champion—Joe Louis, Black Hero in White America.* New York: Charles Scribner's Sons, 1985.

Miller, Patrick, ed. *The Sporting World of the Modern South.* Chicago: University of Illinois Press, 2002.

Morris, Aldon. *The Origins of the Civil Rights Movement.* New York: Free Press, 1986.

Morris, Willie. *The Courting of Marcus Dupree.* Oxford: University of Mississippi Press, 1992.

Olsen, Jack. *The Black Athlete: A Shameful Story.* New York: Time-Life Books, 1968.

———. "Part 4: In the Back of the Bus," *Sports Illustrated,* 22 July 1968, 38–41.

———. "Part 3: In an Alien World," *Sports Illustrated,* 15 July 1968, 28–43.

———. "Part 2: Pride and Prejudice," *Sports Illustrated,* 8 July 1968, 18–31.

———. "Part 1: Cruel Deception," *Sports Illustrated,* 1 July 1968, 12–27.

Oriard, Michael. *King Football.* Chapel Hill: University of North Carolina Press, 2001.

———. *Reading Football.* Chapel Hill: University of North Carolina Press, 1998.

Paul, Joan, and McGhee, Richard V. "The Arrival and Ascendance of Black Athletes in the Southeastern Conference, 1966–1980." *Phylon* 45, no. 4 (1984): 284–297.

Pennington, Richard. *Breaking the Ice: The Racial Integration of Southwest Conference Football.* London: McFarland Press, 1987.

Peterson, Robert. *Pigskin: The Early Years of Pro Football.* New York: Oxford University Press, 1997.

Pope, S. W., ed. *The New American Sport History: Recent Approaches and Perspectives.* Chicago: University of Illinois Press, 1997.

Putney, Clifford. *Muscular Christianity.* Cambridge, Mass.: Harvard University Press, 2001.

Rader, Benjamin. *American Sports: From the Age of Folk Games to the Age of Televised Sports.* New York: Prentice-Hall, 2004.

Rampersad, Arnold, and Rachel Robinson. *Jackie Robinson: A Biography.* New York: Alfred A. Knopf, 1997.

Rhoden, William C. *Forty Million Dollar Slaves: The Rise, Fall, and Redemption of the Black Athlete.* New York: Crown Publishing, 2006.

Roberts, Randy. *Papa Jack: Jack Johnson and the Era of White Hopes.* New York: Macmillan, 1983.

Robinson, Jackie. *I Never Had It Made: An Autobiography.* Hopewell, N.J.: Ecco Press, 1995.

Ross, Charles, ed. *Race and Sport: The Struggle for Equality on and off the Field.* Oxford: University Press of Mississippi, 2004.

Rulon, Philip. *Oklahoma State University—Since 1890.* Stillwater: Oklahoma State University Press, 1975.

Sammons, Jeffrey T. *Beyond the Ring: The Role of Boxing in American Society.* Chicago: University of Illinois Press, 1988.

Schultz, Jaime. "Photography, Instant Memory and the Slugging of Johnny Bright." *Stadion* 32 (2006): 233–254.

Shulman, James L., and William G. Bowen. *The Game of Life*. Princeton, N.J.: Princeton University Press, 2001.

Sides, Josh. *L.A. City Limits: African American Los Angeles from the Great Depression to the Present*. Berkeley: University of California Press, 2003.

Simpson, O. J. (with Pete Axthelm). *O.J.: The Education of a Rich Rookie*. New York: Macmillan, 1970.

Smith, John Matthew. "Breaking the Plane: Integration and Black Protest in Michigan State University Football during the 1960s." *Michigan Historical Review* 33, no. 2 (2007): 101–130.

Smith, Ronald A. "The Paul Robeson-Jackie Robinson Saga and a Political Collision." *Journal of Sport History* 6, no. 2 (1979): 5–27.

Smith, Thomas. "Civil Rights on the Gridiron: The Kennedy Administration and the Desegregation of the Washington Redskins." *Journal of Sport History* 14, no. 2 (Summer 1987).

———. "Outside the Pale: The Exclusion of Blacks from the National Football League, 1934–1946." *Journal of Sport History* 15, no. 3 (Winter 1988).

Sperber, Murray. *Shake Down the Thunder: The Creation of Notre Dame Football*. Bloomington: Indiana University Press, 2002.

Spivey, Donald. "The Black Athlete in Big-Time Intercollegiate Sports, 1941–1968." *Phylon* 44, no. 2 (1983): 116–125.

———. "Black Consciousness and Olympic Protest Movement, 1964–1980." In *Sport in America*, edited by Donald Spivey, 239–262. London: Greenwood Press, 1985.

———. "'End Jim Crow in Sports': The Protest at New York University, 1940–1941." *Journal of Sport History* 15, no. 3 (Winter 1988): 255–281.

———. "Intercollegiate Athletic Servitude: A Case Study of the Black Illini Student-Athletes, 1931–1967." *Social Science Quarterly* 55, no. 4 (March 1975).

———. *Sport in America*. London: Greenwood Press, 1985.

Strode, Woody. *Goal Dust: An Autobiography*. Lanham, Md.: Madison Books, 1990.

Sullivan, Russell. *Rocky Marciano: The Rock of His Times*. Champaign: University of Illinois Press, 2002.

Tygiel, Jules. *Baseball's Great Experiment: Jackie Robinson and His Legacy*. New York: Oxford University Press, 1997.

Urquhart, Brian. *Ralph Bunche: An American Life*. New York: W. W. Norton, 1993.

Van Leuven, Hendrik. *Touchdown UCLA: The Complete Account of Bruin Football*. Tomball, Tex.: Strode Publishers, 1982.

Wade, Harold. *Black Men of Amherst*. Amherst, Mass.: Amherst College Press, 1976.

Ward, Geoffrey C. *Unforgivable Blackness: The Rise and Fall of Jack Johnson*. New York: Alfred A. Knopf, 2004.

Watterson, John Sayle. *College Football: History, Spectacle, Controversy*. Baltimore: Johns Hopkins University Press, 2000.

Wiggins, David K. "Great Speed but Little Stamina: The Historical Debate Over Black Athletic Superiority." In *The New American Sport History: Recent Approaches and Perspectives*, edited by S. W. Pope, 312–341. Champaign: University of Illinois Press, 1997.

———. "'The Future of College Athletics Is at Stake:' Black Athletes and Racial Turmoil on Three Predominantly White University Campuses, 1968–1972." *Journal of Sport History* 15, no. 3 (Winter 1988): 304–333.

Wiggins, David K. "Prized Performers, But Frequently Overlooked Students: The Involvement of Black Athletes in Intercollegiate Sports on Predominately White University Campuses, 1890–1972." *Research Quarterly for Exercise and Sport* 62 (June 1991): 164–177.

———. "The Year of Awakening: Black Athletes, Racial Unrest, and the Civil Rights Movement of 1968." In *Glory Bound: Black Athletes in a White America.* Syracuse, N.Y.: Syracuse University Press, 1997.

Wilson, Charles. "The Death of Bear Bryant." *South Atlantic Quarterly* 84 (1987): 282–295.

Yu, Henry. "Tiger Woods at the Center of History: Looking Back at the Twentieth Century Through the Lenses of Race, Sports, and Mass Consumption." In *Sports Matters: Race, Recreation, and Culture*, edited by John Bloom and Michael Willard, 320–355. New York: New York University Press, 2002.

INDEX

Abdul-Jabbar, Kareem, 105
academics, 2, 106, 113–114, 120
Agnew, Spiro, 122
Alcindor, Lew (later Kareem Abdul-Jabbar), 105, 107
Alexander, Archie, 7
Ali, Muhammad, 12, 17–18, 107
All-Americans. *See* College Football All-America Team
amateurism, 6, 12, 20, 26–27, 43, 118–122, 125, 131, 134–135
American Civil Liberties Union (ACLU), 91
American Dilemma, An (Myrdal), 50
American Federation of Labor (AFL), 75, 91
American Football League (AFL), 48, 99
American Indians, 7, 35–36, 54–55
Amherst College, 5
Amos 'n' Andy (radio program), 32
Anderson, Charlie, 40
Anderson, Marian, 50
Atlanta Stadium, 94
Atlanta University, 92–93
Atlantic Coast Conference (ACC), 70
Arizona State University, 113
armed forces, integration of, 50. *See also* Vietnam War
Arnold, Robert, 87
Associated Students of UCLA (ASUCLA), 34–35
athletics, deemphasis on, 32, 57, 67–69
Auburn University, 3, 36, 38, 40, 44
authenticity, 19–20

Barrett, James E., 131
Bartlett, Ray, 29, 34, 46
baseball, 6, 11, 16–17, 29, 49, 94, 106
basketball, 3, 8, 29, 33–34, 65, 112, 124, 130, 135
Beamon, Bob, 112, 122
Beardley, William, 64
Bennett, Henry, 55, 65–66
Big Eight Conference, 23, 52, 56–57, 59, 70
Big Nine Conference. *See* Big Ten Conference
Big Seven Conference. *See* Big Eight Conference
Big Ten Conference, 7, 49, 52, 57, 78, 108
Bishop College, 131
Black, Julian, 15

Blackburn, Jack, 15
Black Coaches and Administrators (BCA), 1
black colleges, 8–10, 51
Black Muslims, 104. *See also* Nation of Islam (NOI)
Black Panther Party, 25–26, 104, 122–123, 133
Black Power salute. *See* Olympic games
Black Student Alliance (BSA), 26, 102, 110, 114–116, 122, 125, 129, 138
Black Student Organization (BSO), 111
"Bleeding Kansas," 23, 66
Bloch, Charles, 88, 93
Bobby Dodd Stadium (Georgia Tech University), 100–101
Bobby Jones Municipal Golf Course (Atlanta), 83–84
Bodenhamer, W. T., 82
Boston College, 40, 47, 85
Boston University, 40
boxing, 6, 12–18, 107–108
Bradley, Harold, 7
Bradley, Tom, 35, 42
Bradley University, 56, 67
Brigham Young University, 26, 103, 110–133
Bright, Johnny, 23–24, 58–71, 93, 136, 140
Brooklyn Dodgers, 29, 51
Brotherhood of Sleeping Car Porters, 33. *See also* railroad porters
Brown, Jim, 78, 109
Brown University, 7–8
Brown v. Board of Education, 19, 24–25, 54, 60, 77–78, 80–83, 85, 90, 100, 137
Brundage, Avery, 107
Bryant, Paul ("Bear"), 69, 75–76, 82, 129
Buffalo Bills, 118
Bullock, Matthew, 7
Bunche, Ralph, 33
Burns, Tommy, 12
bus boycott. *See* Montgomery bus boycott
Butler, Sol, 7

California Proposition 209, 138–139
Camp, Walter, 6
campus life, 105–106, 108–109, 111, 114, 138. *See also* dating; housing; teammates
Canadian Football League (CFL), 24, 70
Carlisle Indian Industrial School, 7
Carlos, John, 107, 131

Carlson, William, 102–104, 115–120, 123–124, 131
Carnera, Primo, 14, 39
Caroline, James (J.C.), 78
Carr, Arthur, 7
Carter, Hodding, 97
Carter, Virgil, 121
Chadwell, George, 7
Chambers, A. B., 58
cheerleaders, 111
Chicago Bears, 131
Chicago Seven, 103
Church of Jesus Christ of Latter Day Saints (LDS), 110–133
citizens' councils, 78–81, 82–84, 86, 88, 95, 100
Civilian Conservation Corps (CCC), 31
Civil Rights Act of 1964, 104, 109–110
Clemson University, 38, 40
Cleveland Browns, 78
Clinton, Hillary Rodham, 137
coaches, 41–42, 57, 75–76, 82, 105–106, 114, 116–117, 131–132; African American, 1–3, 71, 111
Coleman, Dick, 111
College Football All-America Team, 8, 30–31, 33, 41, 78
College Football Hall of Fame, 48
College of the Pacific, 86
Colorado State University, 113, 130
Communist Party, 16, 32–33, 41
Compton College, 100
Confederate flag, 76, 111, 118
Congress of Industrial Organizations (CIO), 75, 91
Congress of Racial Equality (CORE), 125
Cooke, Sam, 19
Cornell University, 114
Cotton Bowl, 40, 57, 78, 82, 86, 109
Cross, George Lynn, 53–54, 56, 65
Cunningham, Sam, 76

Dallas Cowboys, 131
Daniels, Roger, 116
Dartmouth College, 7
Daughters of the American Revolution (DAR), 50
dating, 30, 33, 99, 112, 114. See also campus life; housing; women
Davis, Baron, 139
Davis, Ernie, 109
Democratic National Convention of 1968, 75
Dexter Avenue Baptist Church (Montgomery, Ala.), 74
Dillard University, 99
Dixiecrats, 53
Dodd, Bobby, 82–83, 88, 95, 100–101, 127
Dorsey v. Louisiana State Athletic Commission, 100
Double Victory ("Double V") campaign, 14, 22
Drake Stadium, 58–59. See also Johnny Bright Field
Drake University, 21, 23–24, 56, 58–71

Drinkard, John, 89–90
Du Bois, W.E.B., 5, 13, 50
Dubuque College, 7
Duke University, 29, 38, 70, 135

Eagleson, Preston, 7
East Carolina University, 134
Eastland, James, 51
East-West Shrine game, 41
Eaton, Lloyd, 103, 105–106, 113–133
Edmonds, Wayne, 3
Edwards, Harry, 25, 106–108, 110, 117–118, 122, 129, 138; Revolt of the Black Athlete, 106
Emory University, 72–73
enrollment, African American, 9–10, 100, 109–110, 112, 133, 135, 138–139
Epps, Bobby, 96
Evers, Medgar, 104
Executive Order 8802 (1941), 31

Fair Employment Practices Committee (FEPC), 31
Farmer, James, 125
Farragut Hotel (Knoxville, Tenn.), 46
Faubus, Orval, 78
Federal Housing Administration (FHA), 74
Federal Writers' Project (FWP), 32
Flippin, George A., 7, 136
Florida Agricultural and Mechanical (A&M) University, 8
Foreman, George, 17, 107–108
Fortson, Ben, 80
Frazier, Joe, 17
freedom rides, 104–105

Garvey, Marcus, 13
Gast, Leon, 17
Gator Bowl, 57
Gautt, Prentice, 78
gentlemen's agreement, 21–22, 28, 38, 40, 47, 81–82, 93, 136
Georgia Institute of Technology. See Georgia Tech University
Georgia Tech University, 21, 24–25, 72–73, 76–77, 79–101
GI Bill, 51
Gifford, Frank, 70
Gipp, George, 20
golf, 83–84, 92
Goodman, Andrew, 104
Gordon, John, 87
Grambling University, 8, 116
Grange, Red, 20, 31
Grier, Bobby, 74, 77–80, 85–87, 93, 95–101, 137, 140
Grier, Roosevelt, 78
Griffin, John, 114
Griffin, Marvin, 21, 24–25, 72–77, 79–101, 137

Hamilton, Mel, 114, 116, 123, 138
Hamilton, Tom, 20
Hampton University, 8
Hannah, John, 57
Harmon, Henry, 67

Harriman, Averell, 91
Harris, Roy, 83, 86–88
Harrison, Edwin, 100
Hartsfield, William, 72, 83–84, 92
Harvard University, 5, 7–8, 32, 134, 137
Hathaway, Stanley, 117–118, 120, 122
Hayden, Tom, 115
Hayes, Woody, 78
Heisman Trophy, 58, 70, 78, 109, 118
Hill, Ron, 114
Hoffman, Abbie, 115
Hoggard, Dennis, 57, 109
Hollywood Bears, 48
Holmes, Hamilton M., 84
Holt Street Baptist Church (Montgomery, Ala.), 80
Holtz, Lou, 2–3
Horrell, Edwin C. ("Babe"), 31, 34, 39, 127
House Un-American Activities Committee (HUAC), 51
housing, 59, 98–99. See also campus life
Howard University, 8, 60
Huntley, Chet, 120
Hysaw, Willie, 116–118, 123

Iba, Henry, 56, 65
in loco parentis, 3, 122
Indiana University, 7, 58, 70, 108, 111
International Labor Defense (ILD), 32
International Olympic Committee (IOC), 107
Interstate Commerce Commission (ICC), 85
Iowa State Teachers College (Northern Iowa University), 58
Iowa State University, 8, 111
Ivy Agreement, 69
Ivy League, 5, 32, 52, 59, 69

Jackie Robinson Story, The (film), 49, 51
Jackson, Levi, 59
Jackson, W.T.S., 5
Japanese internment, 35
Jewett, George, 7
Jim Thorpe: All-American (film), 55
Johnny Bright Field (Drake University), 71
Johnson, Jack, 12–15, 20, 22
Johnson, Lyndon, 75
Johnson, Mordecai, 60–61
Jones, Howard, 30, 37
Junior Rose Bowl, 100
Justice, Charlie, 58

Kansas City Monarchs, 16, 19
Kansas State University, 49, 51
Keith, Floyd, 1
Kemp, Ray, 7
Kennedy, Robert, 91
Kennon, Robert, 86
Kerr, Ewing T., 131
Kimball, Spencer W., 133
King, Martin Luther Jr., 18–19, 74, 91, 104–105, 107
Kipke, Harry, 20
Knoxville, Tenn., 44–46
Krzyzewski, Mike, 135

Lancaster, Burt, 55
Langston University, 55
Lansdell, Grenville, 46
Lee, Howard J., 7
Lewis, William Henry, 5–8, 12, 20, 42, 136
Lewis, Woodley, 57
Lillard, Joe, 7
Little, Malcolm. See Malcolm X
Little Rock Nine, 66, 78
Lombardi, Vince, 121
Long, Huey, 75
Los Angeles, 33, 35–37, 43
Los Angeles Rams, 48, 78
Louis, Joe, 6, 12–16, 20, 22, 24, 27, 32, 39, 41–43, 85
Louisiana Legislative Act 579, 100
Louisiana State University, 3, 11
loyalty oath, 90, 111

MacArthur, Douglas, 50
Macon, Eddie, 86
Malcolm X, 17, 104–105
Manley, Dexter, 71
manliness, 13
Mann Act, 13
March on Washington, 29, 47, 50
Marciano, Rocky, 12
Marshall, Robert, 8
Marshall, Thurgood, 53
Matson, Ollie, 78
Mays, Benjamin, 91
Mays, Willie, 107
McElhenney, Hugh, 70
McGee, Tony, 114, 131
McLaurin v. Oklahoma State Regents, 53–54, 60, 66, 69
McMullen, Joe, 110
Melton, Quimby, 87
Memorial Coliseum (Los Angeles), 28, 31, 43, 46
Mercer University, 72
Meredith, James, 2, 25, 91, 139
Meyer, Leo ("Dutch"), 43–44
Michelosen, Johnny, 96, 98
Michigan State University, 7, 57, 111
Mississippi State University, 3
Missouri Valley Conference (MVC), 23, 52, 56–60, 62, 65–67
Mitchell, Elmer D., 10–11
Mitchell, John, 75–76
Moissant International Airport (New Orleans), 85
Montgomery, Lou, 40, 47, 85
Montgomery bus boycott, 29, 74, 77, 79–80
Moore, Ivie, 114
Morehouse College, 91
Morgan State University, 116
Mormon church. See Church of Jesus Christ of Latter Day Saints (LDS)
Morrison, Edward, 7
Moss, C. L., 87
Muhammad, Elijah, 104–105
Murray, Johnston, 52–53
Murray, William ("Alfalfa Bill"), 52–53

music, 19, 94, 108
Myers, David, 7
My Lai, 103
Myrdal, Gunnar, *An American Dilemma*, 50

Namath, Joe, 121
Nation of Islam (NOI), 17–18. *See also* Black Muslims
National Association for the Advancement of Colored People (NAACP), 19, 31, 37, 53–55, 60, 80, 82, 104–105
National Basketball Association (NBA), 105
National Civil Rights Museum, 19
National Football League (NFL): black players in, 105, 121; and Johnny Bright, 70; and Kenny Washington, 41; in New Orleans, 99–100; postwar integration, 24, 29, 48, 78, 96; prewar integration, 8; and University of Wyoming "Black 14," 131
Native Americans. *See* American Indians
Negro League baseball, 6, 11, 16
New Deal, 31
New England Patriots, 131
New Orleans, 84–87
New Orleans Mid-Winter Sports Association, 84, 100
"New" South, 81
Newton, Huey, 138
New York Giants, 78, 96
New York University, 7
Neyland, Bob ("Major"), 38, 44, 46–47, 82
nicknames, 35
Nixon, E. D., 80
Northwestern University, 7, 40
Notre Dame University, 2–3, 10, 29–30, 58, 82, 109

Oberlin College, 7
officials, game. *See* referees
Ohio State University, 7, 9, 40, 78
Oklahoma, black residents, 53–55
Oklahoma Agricultural and Mechanical (A&M) College. *See* Oklahoma State University
Oklahoma State University, 21, 23–24, 52, 54–71, 78
Olsen, Jack, 105–106, 112, 121
Olympic games, 9, 18, 39, 106–108, 112, 129, 131
Orange Bowl, 57, 70, 82
Oregon State University, 37, 111
Owens, Jesse, 9, 32, 39, 42, 107, 129

Pacific-10 (Pac Ten) Conference. *See* Pacific Coast Conference (PCC)
Pacific Coast Conference (PCC), 36–37, 39
Pacific Coast Pro Football League, 48
Parks, Rosa, 19, 79
Pasadena City College, 29
Patterson, Fred, 7
Pennsylvania State University, 57, 70, 78, 109
Philadelphia Eagles, 70
Pierce, Chet, 8, 134
Pitzer, Kenneth, 130

Pollard, Fritz, 8, 136
press box, 86
Price, Clarence ("Nibs"), 34
Princeton University, 2, 32, 97, 111
professional football, 7. *See also* American Football League (AFL); Canadian Football League (CFL); National Football League (NFL)
Pulitzer Prize, 70
Purdue University, 58

quarterbacks, African American, 111

race, theories of, 11–14
race riots. *See* urban riots
radio, 2, 29, 31–32
Rafferty, Max, 130
railroad porters, 33, 43–44
Randolph, A. Philip, 33, 47, 50, 75
Reagan, Ronald, 29, 106, 110
recruitment, 102–103, 112
referees, 66–67, 97
regionalism, 32, 139–140
Reserve Officers' Training Corps (ROTC), 77
resistance, massive, 81, 137
restrictive covenants, 74
Reuther, Walter, 91
Rice, David, 88, 91, 95
Rickey, Branch, 16
Robeson, Paul, 8, 43, 50–51, 136
Robinson, Edgar, 37
Robinson, Harold, 49
Robinson, Jackie: aesthetic style and authenticity, 19–20; with Brooklyn Dodgers, 51; importance to scholars, 12, 27, 139; integrating Major League Baseball, 6, 16–17, 24; letter to Harold Robinson, 49; reaction to Georgia Tech and 1956 Sugar Bowl, 91; support for Harry Edwards, 107; at UCLA, 22, 28–31, 33–38, 46, 136
Robinson, John, 59, 61–63, 70
Romney, George, 112
Roosevelt, Eleanor, 50
Roosevelt, Franklin Delano, 31–32, 35, 47, 50
Roosevelt, Theodore, 2, 5–8, 24, 64
Rose Bowl, 8, 10, 29, 32, 36–39, 44, 46–49, 57, 78, 82. *See also* Junior Rose Bowl
"Rough Riders," 5
Roxborough, John, 15
Rozelle, Pete, 99–100
Rubin, Jerry, 115
rugby, 6
Russell, Bill, 105; *Go Up for Glory*, 105
Rutgers University, 2, 8, 50

safety, 69, 93
Sanders, Barry, 70
San Francisco Clippers, 48
San Jose State College (SJSC). *See* San Jose State University
San Jose State University, 25, 106–107, 110–111, 116, 119, 122
Santa Clara University, 37
Schmeling, Max, 14–15, 39

Schwerner, Michael, 104
Scottsboro trial, 15, 32
Seale, Bobby, 104–105, 138
Selassie, Haile, 55
sex. *See* campus life; dating; housing; women
Shelburne, John A., 7
Shields-Watkins Stadium (University of Tennessee), 44
Shippley, Hugh, 7
Show Boat (film), 50
Simmons, Bill, 100
Simmons, Ozzie, 29
Simpson, Orenthal James (O.J.), 118–119, 134–135; *O.J.: The Education of a Rich Rookie*, 118–119
Sipuel v. Oklahoma State Regents, 53, 60
sit-ins, 104–105
Slater, Fred ("Duke"), 7
Smith, Clyde, 58
Smith, Gideon, 7
Smith, Jimmy, 40
Smith, M.M. ("Muggsy"), 87
Smith, Tommie, 107, 131
Smith, Wilbanks, 61, 65
Social Darwinism, 13
social functions. *See* campus life; dating; housing; teammates
South, importance of college football in, 75–77, 95–96
Southeastern Conference (SEC), 3
Southern Methodist University, 43
Spanish-American War, 5
spectators, 86–87, 93–94, 98, 108, 113, 118, 125, 134
Spooner, John, 87
sportsmanship, 64–65, 68–69
sportswriters, importance of, 14, 16, 21
"stacking," of teams, 111, 162n27
Stagg, Amos Alonzo, 57
Stanford University, 35–36, 130
St. Charles Hotel (New Orleans), 85, 99
St. Louis University, 56
"strenuous life," 6
Strode, Woodrow ("Woody"), 28–30, 33–36, 38, 43, 45–46, 48
Students for a Democratic Society (SDS), 108
Sugar Bowl: 1941 game, 40, 47; 1956 game, 21, 24–25, 73–74, 76–77, 79–101, 136; 1968 game, 102, 113; 1972 game, 111; and the University of Georgia, 57
Sullivan, John L., 12
Sun Bowl, 86, 113
Sweatt v. Painter, 54, 60
swimming, 37
Syracuse University, 7, 78, 109, 111

Taft, William Howard, 5
Taliaferro, George, 70
Talmadge, Herman, 80, 82–83, 137
Taylor, Brice, 8, 30
teammates: African American, 59–60; white, 34–35, 60, 97–98. *See also* campus life; housing

television, 2, 4, 6, 52, 56–57, 60, 108, 119–120
Texas A&M University, 43
Texas Christian University, 31, 43–44
Texas College of Mines and Metallurgy. *See* University of Texas at El Paso (UTEP)
Texas Western College. *See* University of Texas at El Paso (UTEP)
Thomas, Charles, 40
Thorpe, Jim, 7, 54–55
Till, Emmett, 100
Tinker v. Des Moines, 120
Townsend, Willard, 75
track and field, 9–10, 29, 37, 60, 111–112, 124
Trice, Jack, 8–9, 136
Trigg, Joseph, 7
Triplett, Wallace, 57, 70, 109
Truman, Harry, 55
Tufts University, 7
Tulane University, 84, 86, 99
Tunnel, Emlen, 78
Turner, James, 7

Ultang, Donald, 59, 61–63, 70
unions, 33, 75
United Service Organizations (USO), 48
United States Naval Academy, 86
University of Alabama, 3, 23, 29, 69, 75–76
University of Arizona, 113, 130
University of California, Berkeley, 34, 36, 106, 111
University of California, Los Angeles (UCLA), 20–22, 28–48, 105, 136, 138–139
University of Chicago, 122
University of Detroit, 56, 58, 65
University of Florida, 3, 40
University of Georgia, 3, 11, 23, 57, 72, 84, 89–91, 94, 100–101
University of Houston, 56
University of Illinois, 10, 78
University of Iowa, 2, 7, 29, 78
University of Kansas, 23, 111
University of Kentucky, 3, 112
University of Maryland, 108
University of Michigan, 7–8, 81, 135
University of Minnesota, 8
University of Mississippi, 2–3, 11, 25, 76, 81, 86, 91, 109, 139
University of Missouri, 7, 70
University of Montana, 36
University of Nebraska, 7, 23, 70
University of New Mexico, 113, 129–130
University of North Carolina, 58
University of Oklahoma (OU), 40, 52–53, 55–58, 61, 69–71, 77–78, 111
University of Oregon, 7, 36, 57, 73
University of Pennsylvania, 5
University of Pittsburgh, 24, 73–74, 77–78, 82, 85–89, 95–101
University of San Francisco, 78
University of Southern California (USC), 8, 28–31, 36–39, 44, 46–48, 76, 118
University of Tennessee, 3, 29, 36, 38–40, 44–47

University of Texas, 54, 57, 84–86
University of Texas at El Paso (UTEP), 86, 111–113
University of Toledo, 78
University of Tulsa, 56, 67
University of Utah, 113
University of Virginia, 8, 134
University of Washington, 31, 111, 130
University of Wyoming, 21, 25–26, 102–133, 137–138
urbanization, 16, 74, 104–105
urban riots, 105, 119, 123, 138
Utah State University, 129

Vanderbilt University, 3
Van Leer, Blake, 88, 92
Vaught, John, 91
Vietnam War, 17, 105, 107–108; 1969 moratorium, 103, 115, 120, 122
Vinson, Fred, 54
Virginia Tech University, 134, 141

Wake Forest University, 87
Walker, Herschel, 101
Wallace, George, 76, 126
War Memorial Stadium (University of Wyoming), 113–114, 118, 126
Warner, Glen ("Pop"), 7
Washington, Alton, 7
Washington, Booker T., 13
Washington, Kenneth ("Kenny"), 28–29, 31, 33–38, 41–43, 46–48, 136, 139–140
Washington, Richard, 3

Washington, William, 7
Washington, D.C., postwar integration, 75
Washington Redskins, 131
Washington State University, 37
Watkins, Robert, 78
Watterman, Bill, 131
Wellesley College, 137
Wells, Ida B., 13
Western Athletic Conference (WAC), 108, 111, 113, 115–116, 129–130, 137
When We Were Kings (documentary film), 17
While Thousands Cheer (film), 48
White, Walter, 31
Whitworth, J. B., 57–60, 65–66, 68–69
Wichita University, 56–57, 59, 67
Wilkinson, Ernest, 130
Willham, Oliver, 65
Williams, Jaye, 7
Williams, Joe, 102–106, 110, 113, 116–117, 126, 131, 138
Williams, Ted, 116
Williams College, 7
Williams v. Eaton, 131
women, 84, 94, 111, 125, 139. See also campus life; cheerleaders; dating
Woods, Earl, 49
Woods, Tiger, 11–12, 49
Works Progress Administration (WPA), 31
wrestling, 130
Wynne, Johnny, 29

Yale University, 5–6, 32, 59
Young, Claude ("Buddy"), 78

ABOUT THE AUTHOR

LANE DEMAS is an assistant professor of U.S. history at Central Michigan University, where he teaches courses in African American history and sport history. *Integrating the Gridiron* stems from a longstanding interest in issues of race, ethnicity, and sport. He has previously written on heavyweight boxer Joe Louis and Greek-American immigration, publishing in the *Journal of Sport History, History Compass, Southern California Quarterly*, and the *Journal of Modern Hellenism*.